Bantam/Britannica Books

**Unique, authoritative guides
to acquiring human knowledge**

What motivates people and nations? What
makes things work? What laws and history lie
behind the strivings and conflicts of
contemporary man?

One of mankind's greatest natural endowments
is the urge to learn. Bantam/Britannica books
were created to help make that goal a reality.
Distilled and edited from the vast Britannica
files, these compact introductory volumes offer
uniquely accessible summaries of human
knowledge. Oceanography, politics, natural
disasters, world events—just about everything
that the inquisitive person wants to know about
is fully explained and explored.

BANTAM/BRITANNICA BOOKS

The Ocean
Mankind's Last Frontier

**Prepared by
the Editors of
Encyclopaedia
Britannica**

THE OCEAN: MANKIND'S LAST FRONTIER
Bantam edition/November 1978

Bantam Books are published by Bantam Books, Inc. Its trademark, consisting of the
words "Bantam Books" and the portrayal of a bantam, is registered in the United
States Patent Office and in other countries. Marca Registrada. Bantam Books, Inc.,
666 Fifth Avenue, New York, New York 10019.

Printed in the United States of America

Foreword:
Knowledge for Today's World

One of mankind's greatest natural endowments is the urge to learn. Whether we call it knowledge-seeking, intellectual curiosity, or plain nosiness, most people feel a need to get behind the newspaper page or the TV newscast and seek out the background events: What motivates people and nations? What makes things work? How is science explained? What laws and history lie behind the strivings and conflicts of contemporary man? Yet the very richness of information that bombards us daily often makes it hard to acquire such knowledge, given with authority, about the forces and factors influencing our lives.

The editors at Britannica have spent a great deal of time, over the years, pondering this problem. Their ultimate answer, the 15th Edition of the *Encyclopaedia Britannica*, has been lauded not merely as a vast, comprehensive collection of information but also as a unique, informed summary of human knowledge in an orderly and innovative form. Besides this work, they have also thought to produce a series of compact introductory volumes providing essential information about a wide variety of peoples and problems, cultures, crafts, and disciplines. Hence the birth of these Bantam/Britannica books.

The Bantam/Britannica books, prepared under the guidance of the Britannica's Board of Editors, have been distilled and edited from the vast repository of information in the Britannica archives. The editors have also used the mine of material in the 14th Edition, a great work in its own right, which is no longer being published because much of its material did not fit the design imposed by the 15th. In addition to these sources, current Britannica files and reports—including those for annual yearbooks and for publications in other languages—were made available for this new series.

All of the Bantam/Britannica books are prepared by Britannica editors in our Chicago headquarters with the assistance of specialized subject editors for some volumes. The Bantam/Britannica books cover the widest possible range of topics. They are current and contemporary as well as cultural and historical. They are designed to provide *knowledge for today*—for students anxious to grasp the essentials of a subject, for concerned citizens who want to know more about how their world works, for the intellectually curious who like good reading in concise form. They are a stepping-stone to the thirty-volume *Encyclopaedia Britannica*, not a substitute for it. That is why references to the 15th Edition, also known as *Britannica 3* because of its three distinct parts, are included in the bibliographies. While additional research is always recommended, these books are complete unto themselves. Just about everything that the inquisitive person needs to catch up on a subject is contained within their pages. They make good companions, as well as good teachers. Read them.

The Editors,
Encyclopaedia Britannica

Contents

Introduction:
Exploring the Ocean Frontier

In all of the satellite photographs taken of the Earth, the predominant feature has been the blue of the world's oceans. This has confirmed what geographers have long known— that the Earth is a water planet, and that its 330 million cubic miles of water cover 70.8% of its surface. Despite the fact that almost three-quarters of the Earth's surface is water, scientists have only begun to comprehend the seas, and the countries of the world have only begun to develop the ocean's potential to serve mankind.

Since the middle of the nineteenth century, scientists have rigorously analyzed the motions and the contents of the sea. They have probed the energy generated by its tides, waves, and surges, and they have mapped its great horizontal surface, submarine currents, and powerful, upthrusting vertical currents near the continents. Oceanographers have charted the bottom topography of the seabed with its shallow continental shelves, slopes, and submarine canyons that plunge abruptly to almost seven miles below sea level—much farther below the surface than Mount Everest is above it. These charts describe broad sweeping abyssal plains, freckled with volcanic mountains called *seamounts* and flat-topped mountains called *guyots*. They have been used to pinpoint pockets of oil and gas locked in the seabed and mineral-rich, potato-shaped manganese nodules resting on the ocean floor.

Biologists, working with oceanographers, have counted tens of thousands of different species of animal and plant life inhabiting the oceans, from microscopic bacteria and minuscule plankton to 100-ton whales—life that swims, drifts, or rides piggyback as parasites. Swirling interactions have been found at the boundaries of the sea, between sea and coast, between sea and seabed, and between sea and atmosphere. Meteorologists have studied the interaction between ocean and atmosphere where energy and matter are exchanged to generate our global weather and ocean water evaporates to become the source of rain, snow, and polar ice caps.

Since the early 1960s, man's relationship with the sea has undergone spectacular changes. The importance of the ocean as an aid in meeting the pressing needs of society has been realized by governments as well as scientists. Along with rapid progress in technology, the concerned interest of individual countries in shaping policies and developing institutions has facilitated cooperative approaches to international problem-solving. The concept of oceanography as a pure science has become archaic. The application of oceanographic discoveries affects more than the scientist and the university professor. It also affects the engineer, industrialist, fisherman, vacationer, government official, and diplomat.

The Coastal Zone

Man's exploitation of the sea has been most extensive where land and sea meet—in the coastal zone. Most of the world's population has settled within a short distance of the sea or along navigable rivers leading to the sea. In the United States, for example, 75% of the population lives in states bordering on a 17,000-mile coastline, and 45% of its urban population lives directly on the coast. Because the bulk cargoes of ore, fuel, and chemicals—which underpin a technological society—are transported easily by sea, the majority of the country's heavy industry has always been attracted to the coastal zone. The industrial concentration generates further commercial markets and labor pools, so that by the year 2000 most of the megalopolises, the super cities, will no doubt be packed along the coastal zone.

Long before they were utilized by man the coastal zone's estuaries, lagoons, wetlands, and beaches were sanctuaries for waterfowl, nurseries for coastal fisheries, and habitats of a rich variety of plants and animals. The coastal ecology is fragile and perishable, however, and some of the most fearsome ravages of nature visit there each year, eroding beaches and filling channels.

Much more damaging have been the vast quantities of municipal and industrial wastes, the chemicals—pesticides and fertilizers—and the hot waters poured into the convenient sink of the sea, polluting the brackish waters, the freshwater streams, and the swamplands. These wastes, upsetting nature's balance, kill many forms of animal life. In some instances marine organisms concentrate these pollutants and pass them on through the food chain.

In the mid-1960s a new peril emerged: the threat of massive oil pollution from wrecked tankers such as the *Torrey Canyon*, which ran aground off England in 1967, and the

Ocean Eagle, which broke up off Puerto Rico in 1968, and from runaway underwater oil wells such as those that fouled the Santa Barbara Channel, Calif., in 1969. Even greater hazards could result from the 300,000-ton supertankers and the increased amount of offshore deep-sea drilling.

In February 1973 the U.S. National Oceanic and Atmospheric Administration (NOAA) reported that 700,000 square miles of ocean along the eastern coast of the United States and in the Caribbean were far more polluted than had been previously thought. Tests made by scientists on three survey ships during the summer of 1972 had revealed heavy concentrations of oil, tar, and bits of plastic. More than half the samples of plankton taken in the survey had shown evidence of oil contamination.

Simply stated, there is an increasing pressure for more intense and more variegated use of a scarce, perishable resource. Solutions must be found that will provide for the many diverse and often conflicting coastal demands, public and private, while still preserving the ocean environment so that it will continue to yield long-term social and economic benefits.

Some technologies that have brought about this ecological imbalance have also been employed to combat it. Chemical compounds, for example, have been manufactured that will disperse oil slicks without doing additional harm to the sea and shore life. A new branch of biological engineering has emerged that studies the feasibility of stabilizing beaches with grass, moving river-spawning fish over dams, exploiting offshore platforms as fish havens, and employing estuaries for intensive mariculture.

Man is utilizing science and engineering to assist him in defining the ecological balance; in describing the natural forces at work and predicting the consequences of man's activities; in managing the ocean resources; in controlling water quality, inhibiting beach erosion, fostering construction of offshore airports, nuclear power plants, or supertanker terminals; and in sculpturing the coastline so as to enhance the Earth's natural endowment.

Food for a Growing Population

Since World War II the world seafood catch has grown at a faster rate than agricultural production. With advances in marine research, it has been possible to predict the distribution and abundance of fishery stocks and provide a sound basis for fish harvests of optimum yield consistent with resource-conservation policy.

Marine technology has advanced the art of fish finding and harvesting so that the greater numbers of rare as well as common species can be caught more efficiently. It is expected that men will eventually look to agriculture to cultivate, augment, herd, and select fish. Raised in suitable estuaries, artificially cultured fish could yield more protein per acre than beef cattle or grain.

Almost every study of human nutrition has concluded that the scale, severity, and duration of the world's food problems are massive—so great in fact that only a long-range, innovative effort unprecedented in human history can master them. Food from the sea offers a partial answer; fish are 15% protein and contain a favorable amino acid balance necessary for the human diet. Modern engineering has made possible the production of fish protein concentrate (FPC)—a pure, tasteless, odorless, and relatively imperishable powder made from whole fish that can be added to other foods as a dietary supplement.

Energy and Minerals for an Industrialized Society

After World War II, industrialists began to turn to the sea for energy, principally from petroleum and gas. During the 1960s fuel was produced from about 6,000 offshore wells on the continental shelf of the United States and eight other countries. In 1968 offshore petroleum production accounted for 16% of the world output and was expected to rise to 30 or 40% by the year 2000. Gas, too, was extracted from seabed reserves, but it supplied only a small amount of the world's total gas production.

Virtually all existing offshore wells have been drilled into the continental shelf (the submerged coastal terrace extending an average of 50 miles seaward). The world's continental shelves comprise an area equal to one-quarter of the continents; in such countries as Canada and Indonesia the contiguous shelf almost doubles the land area. Few of these expansive undersea extensions of the continents have been surveyed, but the increasing demand for shelf resources has precluded any further delay.

The world's demand for minerals has also increased rapidly and is expected to double by 1980. The ocean holds and hides an abundance of minerals: placer deposits of gold; ilmenite and diamonds; shallow-water commercial concentrations of sand, gravel, oyster shells, and lime mud; deep-ocean nodules containing cobalt, nickel, copper, manganese, and other metals; phosphorite; metalliferous muds rich in copper and zinc; and other minerals. The demand for these natural resources will necessarily mount as world markets grow and improved technology makes marine sources competitive with terrestrial ones.

Technological Development

In the past, man's innate curiosity about the world around him has been the strongest motivation for his study of the ocean. In order to satisfy the increasing demands for more productive use of the ocean, however, he needs a great deal more knowledge about the marine environment. Obtaining that knowledge is the task of the oceanographer and marine scientist.

Oceanography (or, as some prefer, oceanology) is not a single science but a composite of many basic sciences applied to the marine environment—biology, geology, chemistry, physics, and mathematics. Synthesizing these specialized branches of knowledge is the domain of descriptive oceanography, and complementing them are all the fields of engineering—civil, mechanical, electrical, and metallurgical.

The science of oceanography is slightly more than one hundred years old. Since 1872, when H.M.S. *Challenger* weighed anchor and set off on its round-the-world cruise, the ocean sciences have yielded some remarkable discoveries. Since World War II, especially, oceanographers have learned much about the topography of the ocean floor.

They have found that land and seabed rocks are distinctly different and that the continents' granitic base is lighter and thicker than the seabed's basaltic crust. They have discovered evidence of a ridge-rift system through all ocean basins that has led to a new concept of seafloor spreading, which may hold the key to the origin and development of ocean basins and continents and may help to unravel the riddle of the Earth's structural history. They have unveiled vast, unsuspected subsurface countercurrents, as big and powerful as the Gulf Stream, flowing underneath the known surface currents. And they have also brought up samples of the curious and rich mineral nodules that rest in vast quantities on the deep-ocean floor.

Once the ocean basins seemed stable and permanent features of the Earth, but it is now known that they are continuously changing in size and configuration at rates that are almost directly observable. Seafloor spreading from the midoceanic ridges carries the entire mass of suboceanic sediments, together with everything living on them, on a giant conveyor belt that spreads out from the middle ridge, apparently to plunge into the relatively small and localized oceanic deeps.

There is good reason to believe that the ocean basins have been growing steadily since their beginnings. The ecosystem consequences of the concept of young and dynamic ocean basins have not been fully examined, but it is likely that they will influence knowledge about the geochemistry of the oceans and possibly the age, origin, and distribution of the ocean biota as well.

The ocean is the primary source of much of the world's weather and the source of most of the moisture upon which life depends. With a better understanding of the relationships of the total land-air-sea environment, oceanographers, working with meteorologists, will be better able to predict, influence, and perhaps control weather phenomena—a matter of major importance to everyone.

Since the early days of the space age, scientists have had the advantage of observations from spacecraft that have enabled them to ascertain and study sea temperatures, currents, wave conditions, and underwater conditions in clear, shallow coastal areas. Unmanned buoys, which were to be established in a worldwide network, would provide periodic data transmissions about sea conditions, below the surface and above, via satellite to central data banks.

Sonar has been used to locate and judge the quantity of fish populations. Underwater television has made possible reconnaissance at almost any depth; wreckage of the U.S.S. *Scorpion* was sighted in more than 10,000 feet of water. Geological cores have been taken of sediments at depths of many thousands of feet.

Records for deep-sea drilling have been set by the *Glomar Challenger*, a vessel equipped to use the most advanced technology, which is capable of drilling in 20,000 feet of water and bringing back core samples from as much as 2,500 feet below the ocean floor. The ship was one of the first nonmilitary vessels to use a new navigation satellite for precise positioning to within 200 yards.

As is true in all sciences, discoveries raise more questions than they answer. Unlocking the secret of the oceans with conventional ships and instruments would be an overwhelming task, involving hundreds of ships for decades. With advancing ocean technology, however, tasks once considered unaccomplishable in the ocean's demanding and corrosive environment have begun to yield to human initiative and skill. With the aid of modern technology, man has learned more about the oceans since 1940 than he had in the preceding two thousand years.

Man in the Sea

Nowhere is the new ocean technology more dramatic in its extension of the scientist's ability to observe than in the development of an effective way to put man himself in the sea—either in deep-diving research submersibles or with a self-contained underwater breathing apparatus (scuba) strapped to his back. More than any other single tool, the deep submersible has added a new dimension to man's quest to use the sea.

The first such vehicle, a bathyscaphe, was built in 1948 under the direction of Swiss scientist-engineer Auguste Piccard. This device was an underwater blimp that gained its vertical mobility by means of a large gasoline-filled buoyancy tank. The second bathyscaphe, *Trieste*, skippered by Piccard's son Jacques and U.S. Navy Lieutenant Don Walsh, although cumbersome and without much horizontal mobility, made a record-breaking descent of 35,800 feet into the Mariana Trench in 1960.

The second generation of such vehicles were designed as true submarines that gained depth capabilities by using high-strength materials in the pressure hull. *Aluminaut*, the first such design, was distinctive because of its 15,000-foot capability—fully twenty times that of the true submarines then operating. In 1969 the U.S. Navy's five-man nuclear research vessel NR-1 joined this underwater fleet. The NR-1 was distinctive because of its nuclear power plant, which was a marked advance over the range-limiting battery power of its deep-diving precursors.

The U.S. Navy's Man-in-the-Sea project, France's Pre-Continent operations, and the Ketzeh operation by the Soviet Union have sought to develop new equipment to enable man to live and work under water—eventually at a depth of 1,000 feet. In a series of U.S. Navy Sealab experiments, aquanauts have lived in habitats on the ocean floor at depths of 200 feet for several weeks.

International Cooperation

Approximately 100 countries front on the sea. As they expand their activities in the oceans with new technology for exploitation, the likelihood of conflict increases. Some countries have already asserted jurisdiction hundreds of miles seaward, thus diminishing the traditional freedom of the seas. Long-range fishing fleets of certain countries have threatened coastal fisheries historically essential to others, and the possibility for stationing weapons of mass destruction on the sea floor has raised the specter of an arms race in the oceans.

Because the seas are so vast and generally beyond national sovereignty, international cooperation has been widespread in oceanography for many years. The International Geophysical Year (1957–59) was a healthy stimulus to cooperative efforts begun earlier, particularly because an international exchange of data from scientific investigations was encouraged.

Since then, much successful international collaborative planning has been undertaken, including the International Indian Ocean Expedition (1962–65), the International Cooperative Investigation of the Tropical Atlantic (1963), and the Cooperative Study of the Kuroshio Current (1965–69). In addition, international fisheries commissions have been empowered to study, conserve, and regulate regional fisheries.

In recognition of the rapidly growing significance of ocean resources and the increasing importance of an understanding of ocean processes, U.S. President Lyndon B. Johnson proposed in 1968 that the countries of the world join together in a concerted, long-term cooperative program of ocean exploration. He proposed an initial ten-year period of expanded collaborative effort to be designated the International Decade of Ocean Exploration (IDOE).

The decade of the 1970s was conceived to be a period of intensified collaborative planning, development of national capabilities, and execution of worldwide programs of oceanic research and resource exploration. A broad program of ocean exploration is now being carried out through a cooperative effort by thirty countries. A major accomplishment has been the measurement of pollutants in the deep ocean.

Most countries, however, give most of their financial support to programs close to their own shores, such as exploration of the continental shelf and of their coastal fishery stocks. Even though countries are moving farther out to sea every year, much of the world's ocean exploration activity will probably continue to be this type of coastal activity.

In response to the manifest need for control over the exploitation of the ocean's resources, the United Nations Law of the Sea Conference was convened in 1958 and continued to meet at intervals during the 1960s and 1970s. Agreement was reached in such areas as territoriality, transit rights, pollution control, and research, but as of 1977 a virtual deadlock had been reached in the critical issue of undersea mining.

As man looks to his future relationship with the sea, it is evident that the years since World War II have been a turning point. As man moves across the continental shelf and reaches toward the ocean floor, complex new questions will arise of how best to mobilize the existing resources to meet the expanding needs. While the task is formidable, its accomplishment promises to inspire and reward those who accept the challenge to probe the secrets of the sea.

I. DISCOVERY OF THE OCEAN

*Although man traces his evolutionary ancestry
to the sea, he is a terrestrial creature who discovered the world ocean only in comparatively
recent times. To the ancients, the sea that lay
beyond the horizon was unknown, the stuff of
myths and legends—a great "river of ocean"
that flowed through a dark and mysterious
land.*

*Yet, long before the first navigator set his
course to carry him beyond the sight of land,
the power and mystery of the ocean had a pro-
found effect on the human imagination. As in
the book of Genesis, creation myths of many
peoples describe the formation of land out of
the primeval ocean. In the literature and art of
both the Eastern and Western worlds the ocean
continues to serve as a symbol of the awesome
power of nature.*

*One of the most far-reaching ideas of the
Great Age of Discovery was the recognition
that all the seas and oceans are interconnected
and that there is only one world ocean. This
discovery was as important as the discovery of
the New World in forming modern man's conception of the planet on which he lives.*

1.
The Ocean and Man's Imagination

When British naturalist Charles Darwin expounded his theory of evolution (1859), one of its most thought-provoking implications was the idea of a common ancestor of all living things, including, of course, man. The mysterious common ancestor probably started life in the oceans about three billion years ago. Unfortunately, no fossil records can be found until much, much later, because those tiny, boneless organisms died and dissolved in the moving water. Yet a record of sorts remains of man's evolutionary roots in the ocean. The word *ocean* itself gives a clue as to how intimately the ocean was associated with the beginnings of the human race. *Ocean* came into English from the French *océan*, which was ultimately derived from the Greek *okeanós*, the great river or outer sea that encompassed the ancient world of Eurasia and Africa. Beyond this "river of ocean," to the west, were a land where the sun never shone, a country of dreams, and an entrance to the underworld.

The Ocean in Mythology

In the ancient Greek poet Hesiod's *Theogony* ("the origin of the gods") the ocean was personified as Oceanus, the son of Uranus (sky, or heaven) and Gaia (earth), the husband of Tethys (a titaness), and the father of three thousand stream spirits and four thousand ocean nymphs. It should not surprise us, then, that the mythologies of ancient peoples, both East and West, particularly those living on islands and seacoasts, should be peopled with sea gods and sea goddesses and preserve accounts of the creation of the world from a primeval ocean. It is as if the evolutionary experience had imprinted the image of the ocean in the depths of man's consciousness.

Even today the most widely recognized sea god is the trident-bearing Greek Poseidon (the Roman Neptune). Traditionally, Poseidon was a son of Cronos, an ancient chief god, and Rhea, a fertility goddess. He was also brother of Zeus, the sky and weather god, and of Hades, the god of the underworld. When the three brothers deposed their father, the kingdom of the sea fell by lot to Poseidon, whom the Greek writer Homer represented as dwelling in a place in the depths of the Aegean Sea.

Poseidon's trident, which he used to raise storms, may have originally been a humble fish-spear. In any case, when Poseidon is represented in Greek art he is shown not only with his trident but also with a dolphin and a tunnyfish (or tuna).

The goddess of the sea was Amphitrite, Poseidon's wife and one of the fifty daughters (the Nereids) of Nereus, nicknamed "Old Man of the Sea," and Doris, the daughter of Oceanus. Poseidon chose Amphitrite from among her sisters as the Nereids danced on the isle of Naxos. Refusing his offer of marriage, she fled to Atlas, from whom she was retrieved by a dolphin sent by Poseidon. Amphitrite then became Poseidon's wife. (He rewarded the dolphin by making it a constellation.)

Although Aphrodite (the Roman Venus) is generally identified as the goddess of sexual passion and beauty, she was in fact widely worshiped as a goddess of the sea and seafaring. Because the Greek word *aphros* means "foam," the legend arose that Aphrodite was born from the white foam produced by the severed genitals of Uranus after his son Cronos threw them into the sea.

Atlantis and Other Lost Islands

Somewhere in the dim border between legend and protogeography lies the Greek legend of the lost island or continent of Atlantis. In the fourth century B.C. the philosopher Plato in the *Timaeus* described how Egyptian priests, in conversation with Solon, represented the island as a country larger than Asia Minor with the ancient Libya situated just beyond the Pillars of Hercules. Beyond it lay an archipelago of lesser islands. Atlantis had, the legend went, been a powerful kingdom nine thousand years before the birth of Solon, and its armies had overrun the Mediterranean lands. Finally the sea overwhelmed Atlantis, and shoals marked the spot. In the *Critias* Plato adds a history of the ideal commonwealth of Atlantis.

It is impossible to decide how far this legend is of Plato's invention and how far it is based on facts of which no record now remains. Medieval writers, receiving the tale from Arabian geographers, believed it true along with traditions of other islands in the western sea: the Greek Isles of the Blest, or Fortunate Islands; the Welsh Avalon; the Portuguese Antilia, or Island of Seven Cities; and Saint Brendan's Island, the subject of many sagas in many languages. All except Avalon were marked on maps of the fourteenth and fifteenth centuries and formed the objects of many voyages.

Somewhat similar legends are those of the island of the Phaeacians in the Greek writer Homer's *Odyssey*; the island of Brazil; the sunken land of Lyonnesse off the Cornish coast; the lost Breton city of Is; and the French Isle Verte and Portuguese Ilha Verde—or "Green Island." The last appears in many folk tales from Gibraltar to the Hebrides and until 1853 was marked on English navigational charts (44°18' N, 26°10' W).

A Far Eastern Creation Myth

Wherever primitive man lived beside the ocean, drew fish from its depths, and suffered from its storms, the ocean loomed large in the myths he made to explain the beginnings of things. As it was with the Greeks, so it was with the Japanese.

The creation of the Japanese islands is described in the story of the brother-sister pair Izanagi and Izanami, who, standing on the Floating Bridge of Heaven, stirred the chaotic primeval brine with a heavenly spear until the liquid curdled and thickened. When they drew up the spear, the drops of brine falling back into the ocean formed an island they called Onogoro. The two divinities descended to the island, and from their union were created numerous islands and deities.

Izanagi's son, Susanowo, who was born from his nose, was the storm god and ruled the Sea Plain. Susanowo's violent and outrageous behavior earned him the sobriquet of the Impetuous Male. He was an incorrigible delinquent, running amok through the rice fields and defiling the living quarters of his sister, the goddess of the sun. In Susanowo are personified the more terrifying and destructive aspects of the ocean.

The Ocean in the Old Testament

"In the beginning God created the heaven and the earth. And the earth was without form, and void; and darkness was upon the face of the deep." So begins the Judeo-Christian myth of creation that continues in the first chapter of Genesis to describe the creation of the continents and the oceans and the "great whales" and other creatures that live therein.

One of the best-remembered and most dramatic Old Testa-

Izanagi and Izanami by Kobayashi Eitoku

ment stories of man and the ocean is of course the story of Jonah. The biblical account tells of a great storm striking the ship on which Jonah, a recalcitrant prophet, has taken passage. While Jonah sleeps in the ship's hold the crew decide by lot that he is the cause of the storm and cast him overboard into the sea, where he is swallowed by "a great fish." While in the belly of the fish, Jonah prays, declaring his repentance, "And the Lord spoke unto the fish, and it vomited out Jonah upon the dry land." Much energy and emotion has been spent arguing the literal possibility of this great sea story. It is most certainly allegorical. (The German-born psychoanalyst and social philosopher Erich Fromm interprets the story as a dream sequence in which a number of improbable events are tied together by Jonah's need for security.)

The poet who wrote Psalm 104 expressed man's sense of wonder when contemplating the immensity of the ocean:

> O Lord, how manifold are thy works! in wisdom hast thou made them all: the earth is full of thy riches. So is this great and wide sea, wherein are things creeping innumerable, both small and great beasts. There go the ships: there is that leviathan, whom thou hast made to play therein. These wait all upon thee; that thou mayest give them their meat in due season.

The Ocean in Literature

The beginnings of Western fictional literature are found in the *Iliad* and *Odyssey* of Homer, the (traditionally) blind poet who sang of the "wine-dark sea." The *Odyssey* can be read as a sea story whose central theme is the wanderings of Odysseus (Ulysses) from Troy back home to Ithaca, his itinerary consisting of a ten-year journey among real or mythical islands and seacoasts of the Mediterranean. The extent to which the *Odyssey* can be read as history and Odysseus's stopping places identified with real locations is a fascinating subject for speculation. Scylla and Charybdis, for example, are represented as two immortal and irresistible monsters who beset the narrow waters traversed by Odysseus in his wanderings. They have been localized in the Strait of Messina, Scylla being on the Italian shore and Charybdis on the Sicilian. Scholars have noted that Homer's stories of Odysseus's piracy and raids are typical of the great raids on Egypt in 1192 and 1187 B.C.

From the beginnings of English literature in the folk epics of an island people, the sea and seafarers have had a prominent place among English-speaking peoples. It is no accident that in the fourteenth century the poet Geoffrey Chaucer included among the Canterbury pilgrims a Shipman, or sailor. The Shipman, who is thought to be based on a real person, is a piratical but experienced sea captain,

> *Hardy, and wise in all things undertaken,*
> *By many a tempest had his beard been shaken.*
> *He knew well all the havens, as they were,*
> *From Gottland to the Cape of Finisterre,*
> *And every creek in Britanny and Spain;*
> *His vessel had been christened* Madeleine.

William Shakespeare, like Chaucer, was a landsman whose great plays work themselves out on *terra firma*. Yet, in the first scene of *The Tempest* (1611–12), his boatswain radiates authority as he encourages his fainthearted crew to try to save the ship:

> *Down with the topmast! Yare! Lower, lower! Bring her*
> *to try with the main-course!*

For all of Shakespeare's land battles there is but one sea fight, the disastrous—to Antony and Cleopatra—naval component of the battle of Actium:

> *She once being loofed,*
> *The noble ruin of her magic, Antony,*
> *Claps on his sea-wing, and (like a doting mallard)*
> *Leaving the fight in heighth, flies after her.*

Another great British dramatist who rarely left the land was George Bernard Shaw. One of Shaw's most vivid creations, however, was the ancient but still fiery Captain Shotover (*Heartbreak House*, 1920) who declaimed:

> *At sea nothing happens to the sea. Nothing happens to*
> *the sky. The sun comes up from the east and goes down*
> *to the west. The moon grows from a sickle to an arc*
> *lamp, and comes later and later until she is lost in the*
> *light as other things are lost in the darkness. After the*

> *typhoon, the flying-fish glitter in the sunshine like*
> *birds. It's amazing how they get along, all things con-*
> *sidered. Nothing happens, except something not worth*
> *mentioning. . . . Nothing but the smash of the drunken*
> *skipper's ship on the rocks, the splintering of her rotten*
> *timbers, the tearing of her rusty plates, the drowning of*
> *the crew like rats in a trap.*

Certainly the best known (and most frequently misquoted) sea poem in the English language is Samuel Taylor Coleridge's *The Rime of the Ancient Mariner* (1798). Much more than a tale of the sea, it is an allegory of man's moral and religious nature. The main narrative tells how a sailor who has committed a crime against the life principle by killing an albatross suffers from torments, physical and mental, in which the nature of his crime is made known to him. By killing the bird that hovered near the ship, the mariner has destroyed one of the links that bind all living creatures together in joyful communion. His own consciousness is affected: the sun, previously seen as glorious, is now a bloody sun, and the energies of the deep are seen as corrupt.

> *The very deep did rot; O Christ!*
> *That ever this should be!*
> *Yea, slimy things did crawl with legs*
> *Upon the slimy sea.*

Of all the literary works that make use of the ocean and of seafaring characters, however, none has fixed itself more thoroughly in the consciousness of the English-speaking world than Herman Melville's *Moby Dick* (1851). Melville—a penniless young New Yorker—had learned the life of a whaler by signing on before the mast on two whaling voyages to the South Pacific. Profoundly struck by his experiences, his imagination was unloosed to create the epic and mythic story of Captain Ahab's vengeful and disastrous search for the white whale, who represents for him all the evil in the world.

Far from being a simple sea story, *Moby Dick* is an allegory of man's place in the cosmic order. The ocean is not merely the locale of the great chase but also takes on a personality of its own. Melville concluded the climactic scene in which the white whale destroys the whale ship *Pequod* with "Now small fowls flew screaming over the yet yawning gulf; a sullen white surf beat against its steep sides; then all collapsed, and the great shroud of the sea rolled on as it rolled five thousand years ago."

Melville's only rival as a novelist of the sea is Joseph Conrad, the Polish-English author of such books as *Lord Jim* (1900) and *Typhoon* (1903). Like Melville, Conrad wrote about the moral issues confronting the individual faced with nature's invariable unconcern, most often the unconcern of the sea, which Conrad had sailed as an officer in the British merchant sevice. The most durable of Conrad's tormented heroes is probably Lord Jim, the young English mate of the unseaworthy steamer *Patna*, who, although to all appearances manly and resolute, inexplicably deserts his sinking ship, abandoning 800 Muslim pilgrims to death. The novel is not only a vivid reconstruction of shipboard and longshore life in Southeast Asia in the late 1800s but—more important —it is also one of literature's most penetrating explorations of the perplexing, ambiguous problem of lost honor and guilt, expiation and heroism.

The continued popularity of the ocean as a stage on which human dramas are played is attested to by such twentieth-century works as H. M. Tomlinson's *The Sea and the Jungle*, Nicholas Monsarrat's *The Cruel Sea*, C. S. Forester's vigorous chronicles of Horatio Hornblower, and the novel, play, and film versions of Herman Wouk's *The Caine Mutiny*.

The Ocean in Art

As was the case with literature, one can only sample a few items from the vast museum that could be devoted to works of art concerned with man's relationship to the ocean. Winslow Homer, one of the greatest nineteenth-century American painters, made the sea the dominant theme of his work. In the summer of 1883 Homer saw a demonstration in Atlantic City, N.J., of the use of a breeches buoy for rescue from the sea. In the following year he painted his large, impressive, and immediately popular painting, *The Life Line*, one of several he did on the rescue theme, depicting the dramatic transfer of an unconscious female from a wrecked ship to shore. During the next few years Homer's interest shifted from the edge of the sea to the sea itself. He painted heroic men in the act of pitting their strength, intelligence, and experience against the mighty sea. In the most impressive of these works, *Fog Warning* (1885), night is falling, fog is rolling in, and a lone fisherman in a dory calculates the distance and the time remaining for him to get back to his ship.

In England, J. M. W. Turner, perhaps the greatest land-scapist of the nineteenth century, excelled in marine paint-ing, even surpassing the seventeenth-century Dutch marine painters with their busy, vigorous canvases of fat-bellied merchantmen and fishing sloops scudding through choppy seas. Among Turner's noted sea paintings are *The Shipwreck* (1805), *Wreck of a Transport Ship* (1810), *The Slave Ship* (1840), and *Peace: Burial at Sea* (1841–42). His work is char-acterized by its forcefulness and high-keyed color.

The Japanese woodblock printmaker Hokusai has, since the later nineteenth century, impressed Western artists, crit-ics, and art lovers more than any other single Asian artist. What may well be the greatest fine print any artist has ever made is his *The Breaking Wave off Kanagawa*—commonly referred to simply as "The Wave." (From *Thirty-Six Views of Mt. Fuji*, 1826–33.) Though physically hardly larger than a page of typing paper, "The Wave" encompasses a world filled with beauty and terror as two boatloads of fishermen crouch in the sterns of their sampans in anticipation of the impact of the great wave. The wave rises like a mountain, but it is no inanimate thing. Instead, the spray at the breaking edge is represented as a hundred eager hands that reach out to grasp the boats lying in the trough. Snow-clad Mount Fuji stands serene in the distance; by comparison, the breaking wave is immense. For the fishermen, the wave is, for a long instant, the entire world.

Fog Warning by Winslow Homer

The Slave Ship by J.M.W. Turner

The Breaking Wave off Kanagawa by Hokusai Katsushika

2.
Seafarers and Discoverers

The period from the earliest recorded history to the beginnings of the fifteenth century saw knowledge of the world widen from a river valley surrounded by mountains or desert (the views of Babylonia and Egypt) to a Mediterranean world with hinterlands extending from the Sahara to the Gobi deserts and from the Atlantic to the Indian oceans (the views of Greece and Rome). Later, knowledge expanded again to include the far northern lands beyond the Baltic and another and dazzling civilization in the Far East. The explorations that eventually proved the existence of a single world ocean called for imagination and nerve far beyond the ordinary. Whatever the motives of these explorers of the ocean (some were idealistic but others piratical or simply greedy), their names form a roll of honor in the precarious enterprise of extending man's knowledge of his world: the Greek Pytheas, the Norsemen Othar of Helgeland and Eric the Red, the Portuguese Bartolomeu Dias de Novais and Vasco da Gama, the Italians Christopher Columbus and John Cabot (Giovanni Caboto), the Spaniards Vasco Nuñez de Balboa, Juan Díaz de Solís, Ferdinand Magellan, and Juan Sebastian del Cano, and the Englishmen Martin Frobisher, John Davis, and Francis Drake.

Egyptians and Phoenicians

The Egyptians had explored and conquered large tracts of land before the fourteenth century B.C., both southward up the Nile River and northeastward to the borders of Assyria, but the first seagoing explorers seem to have been the Phoenicians, who made Sidon a commercial port as early as 1400 B.C. and later raised Tyre to equal fame. The merchant adventurers of Tyre and Sidon explored the whole coast of the Mediterranean, founding the colony of Carthage before 800 B.C. They and other colonizers on the shores of the Iberian peninsula sailed northward along the Atlantic coast, probably trading with Cornwall in the British Islands for tin, and to the south, going far along the west coast of Africa. With the support of Egypt they traded also on the Red Sea, reaching lands yielding gold and ivory, probably on the coast of Africa or Arabia.

It is probable the Phoenicians also reached India from the Red Sea. Herodotus heard in Egypt that in the days of King Necho (600 B.C.) a Phoenician fleet, sent from the Red Sea southward along the African coast, had returned to Egypt by the Pillars of Hercules (the Strait of Gibraltar).

Greeks

The maritime trade of the Greek city-states and their colonies became more important than that of the Phoenicians soon after the fifth century B.C. Greek ships sailed beyond the Mediterranean, opening up the Black Sea on the east and the borders of the Atlantic Ocean on the west. Massilia (Marseilles) was a colony of Greeks from Phocaea, and from there a voyage of great importance was made by Pytheas in about 330 B.C. Pytheas was probably the first navigator to fix the position of the lands he reached by crude astronomical obser-

The world as it was known to Greek geographers of the fifth century B.C. was surrounded by the *okeanos* (oceanus) or great river.

vations, and he seems to have been a keen observer of places and people.

Pytheas coasted the Bay of Biscay and the east of Britain as far as Orkney, where he heard a report of Thule, a more northern land, and a confused hint of the Arctic region. On a later voyage he coasted along the east side of the North Sea and probably entered the Baltic.

During the same years the conquests of Alexander the Great opened to the Greek world a knowledge of the continent of Asia; General Nearchus conducted a fleet from the mouth of the Indus to the Persian Gulf. In the following centuries the Ptolemies, Greek kings of Egypt, encouraged exploration, and in about 115 B.C. Eudoxus of Cyzicus explored the Arabian Sea under their auspices. He planned to circumnavigate Africa but could not get support for so daring a project.

Romans and Arabs

The rise and extension of the Roman Empire called for scouting expeditions largely on land. In about A.D. 79, however, Hippalus learned from the Arabs of the regular changes of the monsoons and made these winds serve him as the means of establishing a trade route between the Red Sea and India across the open ocean, whereas earlier navigators had had to hug the coast. Trade along this route continued to develop, and a century later Pausanias makes it appear that direct communication had even been opened up with China.

After the fall of the Roman Empire and the incursion of barbarians from the north a wave of Arab domination surged over the Asiatic and African provinces and swept far into the southern peninsulas of Europe. The geographical learning of the Greeks and Romans passed to the Arabs and was forgotten in Christian Europe, where the conception of the globe degenerated to that of a flat disk with Jerusalem at the center. The Arabs trading with India, China, and the east coast of Africa had acquired a sound knowledge of the Indian Ocean before the year 1000.

Norsemen

Meanwhile the Norsemen from the fjords of Scandinavia were harrying the coasts of northern Europe and even making their way into the Mediterranean. Othar of Helgeland discovered the North Cape and, rounding it, proceeded as far as the White Sea in the middle of the ninth century. Later he visited the court of Alfred the Great, the English king who first reduced to writing the discoveries of the earliest polar exploration and introduced to literature the midnight sun of the Arctic summer. Late in the ninth century Iceland was colonized from Norway, and in 982 Eric the Red, sailing westward, discovered Greenland. Soon afterward his son Leif Ericson, sailing to the southwest, came on a new land, which he named Vinland, and he was thus the first European to reach America.

Portuguese

Long voyages out of sight of land began in the fifteenth century after the use of the magnetic compass had become general. As early as the thirteenth century, charts had been prepared to guide navigators from port to port; they were quite accurate with regard to the Mediterranean coasts. Latitude could be measured with fair accuracy by the use of the astrolabe, though the measurement of longitude remained a matter of guesswork. Portuguese captains were preeminent in making long voyages into the open ocean under these conditions.

A large amount of geographical data was collected in Portugal by Prince Henry the Navigator, and the earliest great voyages were undertaken under his auspices. The first objective of the Portuguese was the exploration of the African coast with the hope that eventually a way would be found to reach India by sea.

The Azores, 800 miles out in the open Atlantic, were rediscovered and settled in 1432, while successive expeditions stimulated by Prince Henry crept by degrees along the Sahara coast to the fertile lands beyond. In 1462, after Henry's death, the Portuguese reached Sierra Leone and a few years later explored the whole Guinea coast.

Additional discoveries followed rapidly. In 1481 the equator was crossed; in 1482 Diogo Cam passed the mouth of the Congo; and in 1488 Bartolomeu Dias, by a splendid effort, fetched a wide sweep far out of sight of land and reached Mossel Bay. In returning he saw the southern part of Africa and according to one tradition named it the Cape of Storms. The king of Portugal, seeing the wealth of the Indies within his grasp, changed the name to the Cape of Good Hope. Vasco da Gama realized that hope in 1498 by sailing around the cape to the Arab port of Mombasa, from where, with the aid of local pilots, he reached India and fulfilled the dream of ages. Luis Vaz de Camões, who himself made the voyage a half century later, celebrated the achievement in his epic poem, *Os Lusíadas*.

Italians

Two Italians in the service of foreign powers were among the greatest explorers of the ocean. Christopher Columbus, a native of Genoa who had much experience of navigating the Atlantic and who had sailed to Iceland, became possessed with the idea of reaching the east coast of Asia by sailing westward. He spent many years trying to find a patron, and in 1492 he had almost persuaded the king of England and the king of Spain to embark on the enterprise. The king of England hesitated the longer, and Columbus with Spanish ships made an easy passage from the Azores to the islands that he named the West Indies. After other voyages to the West Indies, Columbus died in 1506 in the belief that he had reached the islands off the coast of Asia.

The merchants of Bristol, England, had often sent their ships on several weeks' sail to the westward into the Atlantic in search of legendary islands. In 1497 the Venetian sea captain John Cabot, no doubt inspired by the success of Columbus, persevered until he found the coasts of Labrador and Newfoundland and, though the quest was not then pursued, pegged out a claim to England's oldest colony.

Spanish

The Spanish companions of Columbus continued to cruise among the West Indies and quickly traced out the shores of the Spanish Main to the south and the limits of the Caribbean Sea to the west and north. In 1513 Vasco Nuñez de Balboa caught the first glimpse of an inaccessible ocean to the west from "a peak in Darien" and recognized that Asia was still far off.

Other Spanish captains discovered the mouth of the Amazon River and the coast of Brazil and, realizing that America was a solid obstacle between Europe and Asia, pushed forward to discover a passage to the south. In 1516 Juan Díaz de Solís reached the Río de la Plata, which seemed to offer a way through. Four years later Ferdinand Magellan showed that it was only an estuary and, proceeding southward, found and passed through the tortuous strait that now bears his name, so piercing the barrier of America.

Persevering in the face of every difficulty that could befall

On Sept. 25, 1513, the Spanish conquistador and explorer Vasco Nuñez de Balboa became the first European to view the vast Pacific.

an explorer, Magellan pushed on across the incredible breadth of the Pacific Ocean. Although he met his death in the Philippines in 1521, his ship, the *Vittoria,* under Juan Sebastian del Cano, returned to Spain with a handful of survivors in 1522 by the Cape of Good Hope after completing the first circumnavigation of the globe.

French, English, and Dutch

The sixteenth century saw the maritime power of the Portuguese and Spanish challenged by the enterprise of France, England, and the Netherlands, whose sailors disregarded papal bulls assigning spheres of exploration and private agreements between Spain and Portugal. These other Europeans established their claims to shares in the new world and in the sea routes to the east.

French fishermen following in the track of Cabot early began to frequent the Grand Banks of Newfoundland, and the king of France in 1525 sent out Giovanni da Verrazano, a Florentine, who explored the coast of North America between the lands discovered by Cabot in the north and by the Spaniards in the south. He found no way through. Ten years later a French expedition under Jacques Cartier set out to search the Gulf of Saint Lawrence for a way to the far east. In his second voyage of 1535 Cartier ascended the Saint Lawrence to the present site of Montreal and, although only the name of Lachine Rapids remains of this attempt to reach China, spent two years in the effort to start the French colony of Canada.

Queen Elizabeth I saw a wave of enthusiasm for discovery sweep over England—rousing sailors, soldiers, merchants, parsons, philosophers, poets, and politicians to vie with each other in promoting expeditions overseas for the glory of their country and their own fame and profit. The gallants of the court were ever ready to command the expeditions for which shrewd city merchants found the means, while quiet scholars such as Richard Hakluyt promoted the work by recording the great deeds of earlier as well as contemporary adventurers. Hakluyt's *The Principall Navigations* (1589) is to this day delightful reading and, supplemented by *Hakluytus Posthumus or Purchas His Pilgrimes* (1625), forms the only record of many great expeditions.

In England as elsewhere at first the object was to find a westward route to the far east. Richard Chancellor tried for a northeast passage in 1553, and though he got no further than the White Sea he went on by land to Moscow and opened up direct trade between England and Russia. In 1576 Martin Frobisher made a spirited attempt to find a northwest passage to China and reached the coast of Labrador at its northern extremity. John Davis, one of the greatest Arctic explorers of all time, took up the quest in 1585, and in successive years he navigated the broad strait that bears his name to 72° N, finding open sea to the northward and hope of an ultimate passage westward.

Francis Drake, setting out to trace a route from the other direction, made the second circumnavigation of the world in 1577–80. He passed the Strait of Magellan, after which he was blown southward to 56° S, and satisfied himself that the Atlantic and Pacific oceans met south of Tierra del Fuego. Drake proceeded northward and explored the Pacific coast of North America to 48° in vain search of a passage to the east. Eventually he returned by the Philippines and the Cape of Good Hope. Thomas Cavendish repeated the voyage in 1586–88, adding to the confidence with which long voyages were undertaken.

Walter Raleigh, Humphrey Gilbert, and many more took part in exploring the North American Atlantic coast, and in 1600 Queen Elizabeth granted a charter to the East India Company, which initiated direct trade with India and prepared the way for the British Empire to the east. Spanish exploration from the Pacific ports of Spain's American possessions was renewed, partly no doubt in order to anticipate British discoveries. The Dutch made many attempts to find a northern passage to China in the last decade of the sixteenth century. Willem Barents, after discovering Spitsbergen, was icebound on the north coast of Novaya Zemlya, and after wintering there made a heroic journey by boat along the coast. He died, but his crew returned safely in 1597.

In the seventeenth century the search for a northern passage to the far east still went on. The work of Davis was followed by that of Henry Hudson, who in 1607 reached a latitude of 81° N in the Spitsbergen region; in 1610 he discovered the inland sea now known as Hudson Bay. William Baffin came later, reaching about 77° 45' N in 1616 and naming Smith Sound to the north of the great bay called after him at the end of Davis Strait.

The great period of Dutch voyages began with the formation of the Dutch East India Company in 1602, though Dutch merchant adventurers, sailing by the Cape of Good Hope, had been active on the coast of Japan by 1600 and soon after were successful rivals to the Portuguese already established in India and the Malay Archipelago.

Antonio van Diemen, governor of the Netherlands East Indies, resolved in 1642 to explore the coast of the continent of Australia and sent Abel Janszoon Tasman to carry out the task. Tasman's voyage was the greatest contribution to exploration since Magellan's feat. Tasman sailed westward across the Indian Ocean to Mauritius, then in a great sweep southward and eastward he came on high land that he named Van Diemen, though it was later changed to Tasmania. Sailing farther east he came on the west coast of New Zealand. He sailed on to the Fiji Islands and returned along the north coast of New Britain and New Guinea to Batavia (Djakarta).

The Voyages of Captain Cook

A new era of exploration, which raised British maritime enterprise to a unique place in the eyes of the world, was introduced with the three great voyages of James Cook. The first of these voyages, from 1768 to 1771, was undertaken in part to observe the transit of Venus of 1769 from a suitable place in the Pacific. This mission was carried out, but much more was accomplished: many island groups in the Pacific were discovered, New Zealand was identified as being separate from the Antarctic, and much of the east coast of Australia was surveyed with amazing accuracy.

It was on Cook's second voyage of 1772 to 1775 that the chronometer was first used, which for the first time permitted the accurate determination of longitude. Cook sailed far to the south of the Antarctic circle and proved beyond doubt that habitable land did not exist to the south of the known continents. Perhaps the greatest result of this voyage, however, was the proof that scurvy was preventable by proper diet.

The third voyage, begun in 1776, had the objective of seeking a northern passage from the Pacific to the Atlantic. Cook surveyed the northern part of the Pacific coast of North America and, after passing through the Bering Strait, pushed northward to 70° N, where he was stopped by ice. In these voyages Cook not only had sailed completely around the world but had covered more than 140° of latitude. On retiring to Hawaii for the winter Cook was killed by natives in 1779.

The eighteenth century saw the completion of the great task of outlining the continental shores. Even those of the

Arctic Ocean had been traced out by such Russian travelers as Vitus Bering (by birth a Dane), Semen Deshnev, and Simeon Chelyuskin, whose name remains on the most northerly cape of the old world. The great voyages of exploration that followed in the nineteenth and twentieth centuries were directed toward the interiors of the continents and the ice-bound polar regions.

Far Eastern and Pacific Navigators

For Europeans and Arabs, the exploration of the world ocean radiated outward from the Mediterranean. It was of course quite otherwise for the peoples of Asia.

The Chinese junk is a superb sailing vessel that has been called the ultimate in aerodynamic efficiency. Nobody knows how long junks have sailed the Far Eastern seas, but they were making prosperous voyages to India in the ninth century and for a time controlled the Indian Ocean. Through the Middle Ages Chinese merchantmen sailed regularly to Indonesia, Ceylon, India, the east coast of Africa, and even to Aden (Yemen).

The Chinese invented the lodestone compass long before the eleventh century, but by 1085 they were using the floating needle, or magnetic compass which was described by

Junks have plied Far Eastern trade routes since ancient times. Characteristic features are the high stern and lugsails with several battens extending across their whole width.

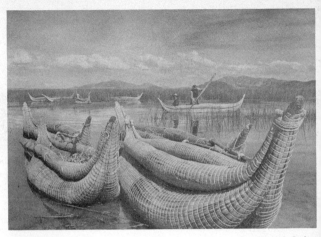

Rafts made of balsa, somewhat like the canoes used on Peru's Lake Titicaca, could have been the first vessels to cross the Pacific.

Shen Kua in his book of that year. The dry compass (with pivoting needle) was also devised in China, during the thirteenth century, but was not in general use until it was reintroduced in the sixteenth century by the Portuguese and Dutch.

Some of the greatest explorations of all time, however, were carried out in prehistoric times without benefit of the compass or other instruments of navigation by the people known as Polynesians. The origins of the Polynesian peoples are still under debate, a vigorous minority advocating a South American origin. In 1947 the Norwegian ethnologist Thor Heyerdahl demonstrated that balsa rafts such as were employed by the Inca Indians of Peru could have reached the Polynesian Islands. Most of the evidence arguing such a connection, however, does not bear careful scrutiny, and a general belief that the Polynesian migration began in southeast Asia is in the majority. In any case, the voyages that made landfalls on tiny islands and atolls throughout the vast reaches of the Pacific represented some of the most remarkable feats of navigation ever carried out.

The Polynesians' twin-hulled sailing vessels, their genius for organizing and equipping settlement expeditions, and their skill in guiding themselves across the open ocean by means of the stars, winds, and ocean currents enabled them to settle the whole of Polynesia in a relatively short time, once the movement had begun. Radiocarbon dates obtained on charcoal from fireplaces have determined that Viti Levu, the main island in the Fijian group, was inhabited by 1200 B.C., the Marquesas Islands by 124 B.C., Easter Island by about A.D. 600, and Hawaii and New Zealand by about A.D. 750.

The watercraft used by the ancient migrants were probably crude rafts or coracles; but, however simple, those that developed and were used thousands of years later to explore and settle the far reaches of Micronesia and Polynesia were impressive indeed. These were great double-hulled craft capable of a voyage of a month or longer, carrying a hundred or more voyagers and their provisions, as well as domesticated animals and plants for propagation in a new homeland. Perhaps most remarkable of all was the accuracy of their navigation, performed without compass or sextant but with charts consisting of sticks tied together in a pattern in which the intersections represented islands.

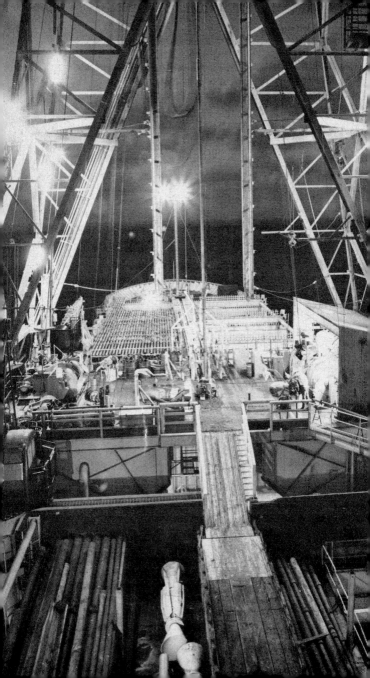

II. STUDY OF THE OCEAN

The practical value of ocean exploration has long been established by those countries that exploit the ocean's natural resources, transport goods and people across its surface, or maintain national security by controlling its shipping lanes. Ocean-exploration achievements in the 1970s were strongly dependent on new technologies and included a submerged circumnavigation of the world; transits beneath the North Pole and the Arctic ice cap; discovery of major new features of the seafloor, including a 40,000-mile-long mountain-range system under the Atlantic, Indian, and Pacific oceans; observations of major ocean-current systems; and evidence of major historical changes in the sea and the basins that contain them.

All of these accomplishments can be traced to new instruments and vehicles with capabilities not available to earlier investigators. Sixty ships from forty countries were combined during the International Geophysical Year (IGY) in 1957–58 and demonstrated the feasibility of carrying out oceanographic studies on a massive scale.

3.
Oceanography and Oceanographers

Modern oceanography began in the mid-1800s when Matthew Fontaine Maury, an American naval officer, assembled and analyzed the qualitative observations and simple measurements of waves, winds, and currents gathered routinely by nineteenth-century mariners. He spent a lifetime compiling charts of major currents, prevailing winds, and storm tracks. Marine biology exploration got its initial impetus at about the same time. The Englishman Edward Forbes was one of the first to make combined use of the related sciences now called oceanography. Using a naturalist's dredge, he discovered that ocean-bottom geology and marine life were closely related. His dredging revealed that the features of the ocean floor were as varied and complex as those of the land masses, or continents. He noted that the chemistry and physics of the sea influenced the type and quantity of animals and plants in a given locality. Forbes thereby introduced a fundamental interdisciplinary approach to oceanography.

The Challenger Expedition

The general lack of knowledge of the deep sea and the practical need for the successful laying of expensive transoceanic cables led a British professor, William B. Carpenter, to initiate the greatest oceanographic project of the nineteenth century, one that marked the beginning of oceanography as an integrated science. A committee established by the Royal Society in London wrote out a comprehensive deep-sea exploration program, and the British Admiralty made H.M.S. *Challenger* available for a four-year around-the-world expedition.

Oceanographers, until recent years, have had to make do with ships and platforms constructed originally for purposes other than ocean research. The *Challenger* was such a vessel, but it was also one of the most substantial of its time. A fully rigged corvette of 2,306 tons with auxiliary steam power, the ship compared favorably with modern vessels in oceanographic service. The crew and scientists on the *Challenger*'s around-the-globe trip logged 68,890 nautical miles through all the major oceans and gathered data and samples from waters of all depths and at almost all latitudes. From December 7, 1872, to May 26, 1876, such a wealth of information was amassed that twenty years were required for the compilation of the resulting fifty thick volumes.

The success of the *Challenger* led to a series of other national oceanographic expeditions during the rest of the century. Notable among these were the expeditions of the U.S. marine zoologist Alexander Agassiz and of Prince Albert of Monaco, who sent his own fleet of yachts on voyages for deep-sea research.

Twentieth-Century Oceanography

By the beginning of the twentieth century, oceanography was firmly established but primarily within institutions devoted to the biological sciences. By the 1930s small seashore laboratories were established by virtually every European country.

The practical value of oceanographical techniques was demonstrated during World War II. Acoustical devices, for example, were successfully employed in locating submarines. They were also used for wave forecasting and reconnoitering beaches in advance of landings. During the immediate postwar period, theoretical studies enabled oceanographers to translate water-temperature and salinity data into water-flow data (speed and direction), thereby providing subsurface water movement tracking. The currents could not be observed directly, however, until the 1950s, when improved technology appeared in two forms: a special marker buoy to identify deepwater currents and a modern echo sounder to provide a continuous silhouette of the sea floor over which a ship is passing.

The echo sounder, however, would at times show a seafloor depth of a few hundred feet when the true bottom was actually several thousand feet below. No physical explanation seemed plausible for this newly discovered phenomenon until a zoologist surmised that the echoes might come from vast populations of marine organisms—a hypothesis now universally accepted. Evidence indicating the specific organisms causing the echoes had to await development of deep-submersible technology, but in the 1960s the deep-diving bathyscaphe *Trieste* and the submersible *Alvin* viewed and photographed large concentrations of these organisms.

The national oceanographic program in most countries is a combined effort by government laboratories and academic institutions, with the government providing most of the funds and general coordination. Private enterprise, particularly in the petroleum industry, has become a significant participant in oceanographic exploration. Marine fisheries have been closely allied to oceanography for many decades, and the industry depends upon biological oceanographers for information about the marine environment.

The principal international oceanographic organization is the Intergovernmental Oceanographic Commission (IOC) of the United Nations Educational, Scientific, and Cultural Organization (UNESCO), which was founded in 1961. UNESCO also operates an Office of Oceanography that provides staff support. Other important international undertakings in oceanography have included the International Council of Scientific Unions, the International Geophysical Year (1957–58), the Barbados Oceanographic and Meteorological Experiment (Bomex), and the International Decade of Ocean Exploration (1970–80).

Research and Exploration Vessels

The traditional platform for oceanographic research has, until recent years, been described as any sturdy, seaworthy vessel capable of carrying oceanographic winches and a variety of measuring and sampling devices. In the 1950s a fleet of research ships designed specifically for oceanography began appearing. Their varied characteristics reflected the design requirements of their respective owners. The international listing exceeded 500 in the early 1970s. Large ocean vessels are operated by academic institutions or government agencies, while smaller vessels used for coastal work are operated by virtually all oceanographic groups.

The need for long-term investigations with fixed equipment led to the construction of fixed platforms of various sorts. Among these are fixed towers installed in moderate depths of water and instrument-supporting platforms moored to the ocean floor. Large oceanographic buoys and their associated sensors are also classified as platforms. The largest is a moored, 40-foot-diameter platform that can measure and record 100 separate channels of data, sending the data on command by radio to shore stations thousands of miles away.

The U.S. Naval Arctic Research Laboratory at Point Barrow, Alaska, operates numerous field stations, including research platform stations on ice floes. One such ice island drifted approximately 5,000 miles in four years from near

Point Barrow, through the Arctic Ocean, almost over the North Pole, and through the Greenland Sea to a point near Iceland, where it was evacuated.

One of the most unusual research vessels was developed by the U.S. Navy to fulfill a need for an extremely stable and yet mobile platform from which accurate acoustical measurements could be made at sea. This Floating Instrument Platform (FLIP) is a long pole-shaped platform towed in a horizontal position to the research area. On station, ballast tanks in the after two-thirds of the 355-foot vessel are flooded. As the stern gradually sinks, the prow rises. Ultimately the vessel is completely vertical with approximately 55 feet of prow above water and pointed skyward. As the hull is only 12½ feet in diameter some distance above and below the waterline, the rise and fall of the waves cause a very small percentage change in the displacement. Consequently, the vertical motions that do occur are extremely small when compared with those of a conventional ship. Stability, coupled with the unusually deep draft in the vertical position, makes FLIP an ideal platform for many sea experiments.

The descent of the bathyscaphe *Trieste* to 35,600 feet (10,850 meters) in 1960 was a major event in the deep-submersible field. The family of vehicles that has evolved since ranges in size from small one-man submarines for exploration of the continental shelf to vehicles capable of routine operation at great depths. In the early 1970s new materials were being fabricated and tested, and techniques of life support, navigation, communications, bottom mapping, photography, direct viewing, and in-place measuring were being studied to improve vehicle capability.

Buoys serve as effective instrument platforms that can remain unattended at a given location for extended periods. Simple can and spar buoys, decked-over skiffs, boat-shaped hulls, and giant saucer-shaped buoys are a few examples of unmanned buoys.

The Remote Underwater Manipulator (RUM) is a remotely controlled, tracked seafloor work vehicle with mechanical arms and pincers developed as a research tool. Its hull, tracks, and suspension system are those of a surplus U.S. Marine Corps vehicle. Equipment includes two television cameras, a scanning sonar, an acoustic transponder navigation system, and numerous other instruments to monitor operational conditions.

To explore details of seafloor topography and related char-

The Floating Instrument Platform (FLIP) is towed in a horizontal position (top) to its destination, then "flipped" (center) to the vertical position by flooding its ballast tanks. When completely vertical (bottom), the vessel is ready to be used for sea experiments.

acteristics, instrumented vehicles called Fully Instrumented Submersible Housing (FISH) are towed by a research ship. The FISH usually consists of a pressure-resistant enclosure to protect the electronic gear. A FISH system is a powerful research tool for studying details of the ocean floor, permitting the close correlation of magnetic, topographic, subsurface sediment, and photographic data.

Basic Methods of Measurement

Oceanographic observations are made from a surface ship while under way, on station, or at anchor. Observations taken while under way are generally limited to meteorological and bathythermographic observations with occasional shallow-water bottom sampling. For special surveys, hull-mounted recording devices for obtaining continuous data of water temperature, salinity, and conductivity are used. The greater portion of oceanographic work at sea is carried out while lying to on an oceanographic station.

Outboard from most oceanographic winches is a platform, with an A-frame over it. From the A-frame a meter wheel is usually suspended as well as a special block that will quickly receive a cable. The amount of oceanographic wire that passes over the meter wheel in or out is registered on dials, indicating the depths to which the lead-weighted wire has been lowered. The wire is used, variously, for carrying water-sampling bottles with attached thermometers to desired depths or to make a series of plankton tows, or for lowering either an underwater camera or a coring device to the bottom.

Among the most common pieces of oceanographic equipment are the Nansen bottle and the bathythermograph. The Nansen bottle, developed by the Norwegian Arctic explorer and oceanographer Fridtjof Nansen, is the most widely used water sampler. It is a metal vessel with a 1.25-liter capacity, intended to bring an uncontaminated water sample from a desired depth to the surface. The bathythermograph is an instrument for obtaining a permanent graphic record of water temperature at various depths as it is lowered and raised in the ocean.

Physical Oceanography

Physical oceanography embraces a number of disciplines. They include studies of the tides, currents, sea and swell, temperatures, densities, origin and circulation, sound propagation, optical transparency, sea ice, and other physical properties of seawater. Of major importance is the acquisition of knowledge of surface and subsurface currents, their origin, their speed and direction, and their influence on other oceanic factors. Determinations of subsurface currents may be made by direct measurements with current meters or by mathematical computations from the densities of the masses of water under study.

Depth information is an essential part of every oceanographic expedition and is a fundamental reference for all sampling. The echo sounder is an electronic instrument that automatically and continuously measures ocean depth by transmitting and receiving acoustic sound pulses. The use of high-energy electric discharges under water has directly augmented the echo sounder.

Oceanographers require thousands of temperature readings. The measure of seawater temperature both vertically and horizontally continues to be of great importance to oceanographers exploring the subtleties of ocean currents and physical forces related to them. Exploratory activities of physical oceanography profit from temperature-salinity measurements. Water masses can be classified on the basis of their temperature-salinity characteristics. A series sample of water, plus an accurate temperature measurement for each, provides one of the most valuable tools in physical oceanography.

Until recently, observations of deep-water waves were limited to visual data. Recently developed electrical wave staffs and pressure-operated wave indicators now provide recorded data for analyses.

The interaction of sea and air and the influence of one medium upon the other make up another important part of oceanographic studies. Prevailing winds in certain areas affect ocean currents, while in other areas the air temperatures are tempered by the sea surface. The types of meteorological information that must accompany all oceanographic observations include air temperatures, humidity, wind direction and speed, atmospheric pressure, cloud types, amount and visibility of clouds, and the oceanographic variables of sea-surface temperature, wind waves, and swell.

Surface ocean currents are a portion of a thin veneer overlying other currents that do not usually match the surface currents in any way. Probably more types of instruments are used for measuring currents than for any other single oceanographic operation. A simple, rugged, and accurate instrument that can indicate weak as well as strong current speed, direction, and depth is still one of the most important needs of oceanographic instrumentation. The physical relationships governing the penetration and absorption of light, the color, and the transparency of the sea are also of prime importance to both physical and biological oceanography.

Chemical Oceanography

Chemical oceanography is concerned with determining the various constituents of seawater and their distribution. The salinity of seawater is of major importance in computing its density and determining currents as well as sound velocities. Analyses of nutrient concentration (such as phosphate, nitrate, or silicate), the pH (acidity), and the content of dissolved gases (oxygen and carbon dioxide) provide information that aids in determining age, origin, and movement of water masses and their influences upon marine life.

One of the more rapidly expanding areas of interest in chemical oceanography is the study of dissolved gases. New, highly sensitive analytical methods that can be used aboard ship permit rapid accumulation of data on the distribution of dissolved gases. Analysis of such data is useful in tracing ocean-mixing processes, in studying the production of gases in the ocean, and in elucidating the natural cycles of atmospheric pollutants.

New and improved methods of trace-element analysis are being developed for use on shipboard. An electrochemical technique, for example, provides a means of investigating the unexplained fluoride concentration anomalies in certain parts of the deep ocean, the possible influence of submarine volcanism in causing such anomalies, and the physical chemistry of fluoride ions in seawater involving complex formation by elements such as magnesium. It is now possible to detect 25 parts per 1,000,000,000 of fluoride in seawater.

Marine Geology

The ocean floor has the same general character as the land areas of the world: mountains, plains, channels, canyons, exposed rocks, and sediment-covered areas. Because sound propagation is markedly affected by the ocean bottom and subbottom, extensive measurements have been made by means of an evolving series of geological or geophysical instruments of increasing precision and discrimination. These methods are providing increasingly accurate data on bottom topography and roughness. Investigators are using deep-ocean photography in conjunction with precision echo soundings to make detailed studies of bottom roughness and sediment structure.

Marine sedimentation embraces that phase of oceanography that is related to the deposition, composition, and classification of organic and inorganic material found on the ocean floor. Various sampling devices are utilized to obtain bottom sediments. Once obtained, samples are packed and shipped to a sedimentation laboratory to be analyzed and classified. Analysis of marine sediments generally includes the determination of size, shape, and percentage of component particles; identification of minerals and ratio of light to heavy minerals; wet density; pH; and calcium carbonate content.

Marine sediments are obtained by use of three basic categories of bottom samplers: corers, snappers, and dredges. Coring devices are essentially steel tubes that are driven into the ocean floor. Snappers are used to obtain small samples of the superficial layers of bottom sediments. The dredge is a sturdy piece of gear made of steel plate that is dragged over the bottom. The fore end is open, but the aft end has a grill designed to retain rock samples.

Biological Oceanography

Biological oceanography is concerned with both animal and plant life in the sea. Animal life is divided into three general groups—the benthos (bottom living), the nekton (swimming), and the plankton (floating and drifting life). The plankton are further divided into phytoplankton (plant forms) and zooplankton (animal forms). Little is known of the life cycles of most marine life. Oceanographers are interested in the distribution of plankton populations, from both quantitative and qualitative points of view.

Some of the most commonly used of oceanographers' samplers are plankton nets and midwater trawls. Nets have a mesh size capable of sieving microorganisms such as zooplankton and phytoplankton from water. The trawls have a net-mesh size that permits plankton to pass through but filters out larger forms. The midwater trawl is a specially designed net for rapid trawling at great ocean depths and at such speed that active, fast-swimming fish are unable to swim out of the net once caught.

A television camera and tripod are lowered into the water 1,200 miles off the California coast to search for manganese nodules on the ocean floor. The sedimentation sample basket hangs from the tripod by a chain.

Major studies are under way on the acoustical properties and behavior of marine organisms. Oceanic biologists record and analyze sounds produced by marine animals and their behavior as it relates to sound production. Concentrated effort has been made to identify sounds of biological origin.

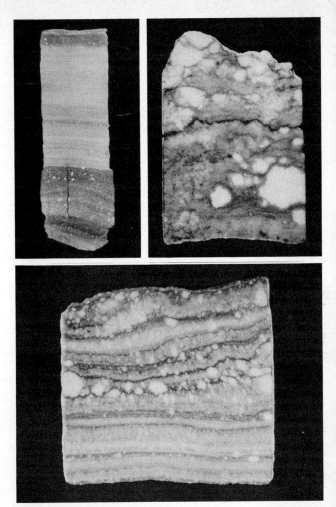

Deep-sea drilling has yielded new information about the history of the Mediterranean. A vertical crack in a rock salt sample (top left) taken from a depth of 10,000 ft. may indicate that the sea was once dry to that level; further evidence of the same possibility was provided by a piece of sedimentary rock (bottom), whose convex-upward lamination was caused by shallow-water algae, and by light-colored nodules (top right), which are anhydrites that are found in coastal desert areas.

Some fish and invertebrates make up layers of acoustic-scattering material that may exhibit daily vertical movement related to diurnal changes in light. The acoustical and biological properties of these layers have been studied for many years by scientists of several countries, partly because of their military importance in interfering with underwater target detection. The work of the biological oceanographer overlaps to a considerable extent with that of the marine biologist.

Future Oceanography

Important oceanographic prospects lie in increased drilling and core-sampling capabilities provided by improved technology utilized by such research vessels as the *Glomar Challenger*. The capability of drilling in the deep ocean will make available clues to the history of oceans, climates, mountain building, volcanic eruptions, life and evolution, and the movements of seafloor and continents.

Among the more important practical benefits that promise to accumulate from more sophisticated oceanographic research are more efficient use of potential marine food supply, fresh sources of pharmacological materials, and new mineral resources, including not only oil and gas but hard minerals. Salt, bromine, and magnesium are already being economically extracted, and submerged placer deposits on the inner edge of the continental shelf may presently be exploited. The seabed may also yield coal, potash, phosphatic rock, iron ore, bauxite, and possibly metallic vein deposits. Coal has already been mined from onshore shafts or artificial islands off the coasts of Canada, the United Kingdom, Japan, and Taiwan. The nodules and crusts that rise in certain places in the deep ocean contain manganese, copper, cobalt, and nickel. Rich brines have been discovered on the floor of the Red Sea.

In the not-so-distant future, manned habitats and diver-transport systems will permit scientists to work routinely at great depths. Operations at 2,000 feet appear feasible. Undersea tunnel drilling and a new technology for mating submersibles to a seafloor shaft entrance may provide a completely independent subseafloor installation for extended geophysical studies. As obstacles are overcome the oceanographer will have increased mobility to go where he wishes, at many depths, with greater convenience and safety.

4.
Biography and Topography

In possessing an ocean, bordered by continents, the Earth is unique among the planets and satellites of the solar system. To understand why this has come about, three questions must be answered.

Why Are There Ocean Basins?

The answer to this question is that the rocks making up the outer portion of the Earth's crust are not uniform in their properties or chemical constitution. Over large areas of the Earth's surface, the rocks are characteristically light in color and relatively light in weight. They are called granitic because among them granite is the major kind. Over other large areas the rocks are on the average darker in color and heavier in weight. They are called basaltic because among them basalt is the major kind.

It is known from studies of the propagation of earthquake waves that the core of the Earth at a depth of a few hundred miles below the surface has the properties of a fluid. The crustal rocks, many miles thick, in effect are floating on this liquid core. The areas of granitic rock, since they are lighter, stand higher than the surrounding areas of basaltic rocks, just as a cork floats higher than a piece of wood of the same size. The granitic areas thus form the continents, and the basaltic areas the ocean basins.

The concepts of plate tectonics and seafloor spreading have cast new light on the origin of the ocean basins. The theory holds that the Earth's outer shell is broken into a number of large, rigid, spherical caps, plus many small subplates. Except for the Pacific plate, which includes much of the Pacific Ocean, each major plate contains a separate continent embedded within it.

An ideal plate may be envisioned as rectilinear. Along one edge, where the plate is heavy, it dives into the Earth's mantle along a trench called a subduction zone. Opposing this zone of lithospheric descent, a rift is formed. As the rift grows larger, the void left behind is constantly healed by the upwelling of mantle rock that emplaces new ocean crust, a process known as seafloor spreading.

New ocean crust is presently being generated at about 0.6

square miles (1.5 square kilometers) per year, a rate sufficient to repave the entire ocean basin in 200 million years. The crustal plates and the continents embedded in them undergo drift; this condition provides the mechanism for continental drift. Typical drift rates range from one to several centimeters a year, a remarkably rapid geologic process.

Why Is There Water in the Ocean?

The answer to this question is threefold. In the first place, molten rock, such as lava, holds much more water when liquid than when it hardens and cools. As the Earth's crust solidified during geologic time, water vapor was given off to the atmosphere. Analyses of gases from volcanoes and fumaroles show that this process is still going on.

Something like this must have happened on the moon, which has suitable basins yet has no ocean. The explanation is that gravity is much weaker on the moon than on the Earth. Gas molecules in the Earth's atmosphere behave just as does any other moving body with respect to the Earth's gravitation field. The gravitational field of the moon, unlike that of Earth, is not strong enough to hold water vapor or the other light gases that make up our atmosphere and hydrosphere, and therefore it lacks an ocean. The second reason there is water in the ocean, therefore, is that the Earth's gravity keeps the water from escaping into space.

As the third reason, the pressure-temperature relationships on the Earth's surface are such that the water is mainly in liquid form. If the temperature and pressure were sufficiently high—705° F and 5,500 pounds per square inch—all the water could exist as water vapor. On the other hand, if the surface temperature of the Earth were sufficiently low, the ocean basins would become filled with solid ice. Since there still would be water vapor in the atmosphere, and snow still could fall, a vast continental glaciation might take the place of the present river drainage system. Since neither of these extreme temperature conditions exists, we have the ocean in its present form.

Why Is the Ocean Salty?

The salts in the ocean are one result of more than two billion years of disintegration of the igneous rocks of the Earth's crust. The soluble materials remain in the ocean; the insoluble precipitates have formed sedimentary rocks and the ocean sediments. The ocean contains all the elements

Seawater provides an abundant source of salt for human use as shown by this mountain of salt that was extracted from San Francisco Bay on the coast of California.

originally present in the igneous rock to the extent they are soluble, are not adsorbed on clay, or are not removed by biological activity.

Suspended material and dissolved salts, extracted from the rocks of the continents, are still delivered to the sea by rivers. Much of this eroded material is from sedimentary rocks that have previously passed through the same cycle. Equivalent amounts of new sediments are being laid down at the same rate. The result is that the sea is in a steady state with regard to the composition of its salt, and it has probably maintained a close approximation to this present composition for millions of years.

The Deep Ocean Floor

A classical view of natural philosophers held the oceans to be as deep as the mountains are high, which is roughly correct if only the greatest mountains are considered. The first deep-sea sounding was made in the central South Atlantic in 1840. A heavy plummet was lowered 2,425 fathoms (14,550 feet or 4,435 meters) on the end of a long line. The first generalized map of the ocean basins was fashioned in 1895, using the 7,000 ocean soundings deeper than 6,500 feet (2,000 meters) that were then available.

The advent of the echo sounder in 1920, with which precisely timed echoes are bounced off the bottom, revolutionized deep-sea soundings. A modern survey ship can obtain a sounding every second along its track. The problem of obtaining accurate position control, or fixes, under all conditions of weather and in any part of the world was finally solved through satellite navigation—determination of fixes continuously from low-orbited satellites. The bathymetry (depth measurement) of the entire ocean floor is rapidly being revealed and charted in the 1970s with literally millions of soundings.

Before about 1930 the ocean floor was regarded as flat, monotonous, and generally featureless. Charts since then show a topography remarkably varied in both shape and relief. Some seamounts (isolated conical submarine peaks) and escarpments (steep slopes) are higher and more rugged than any on land, whereas the abyssal (deep-sea) plains are the most level surfaces on the face of the globe.

Erosional landforms on the continents are sculptured by wind, ice, and running water, but only sluggishly moving water modifies the deep ocean floor. Terrestrial stream action is imitated beneath the sea by turbidity currents, mud-laden tongues of water that periodically pour down the continental shelves and slopes to the ocean floor. Weathering (rock disintegration by chemical and mechanical processes) and erosion proceed slowly beneath the sea, so that the sea-floor morphology (fault scarps, volcanic knolls, and other fractures) tends to retain a pristine appearance.

The major features of the ocean floor are deep-sea trenches, rifts, and fracture zones that are created by the interaction along their boundaries of shifting rigid crustal plates. The giant volcanic cones that create seamounts are especially spectacular. The smaller features represent a variety of volcanic topographic forms, related mainly to fissure eruptions and rifting of the ocean floor.

The major features are related because they are all as-

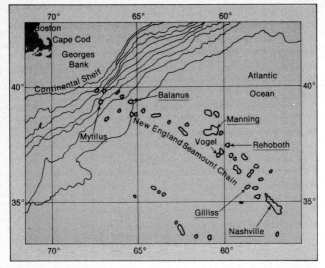

A chain of volcanic seamounts rises out of the ocean floor off the coast of Massachusetts. Like mountains or islands, the individual peaks have been given names.

sociated with the boundaries of the Earth's major crustal plates. These boundaries almost invariably lie within the ocean basins rather than on the continents. The trenches mark zones of underthrusting, associated with the descent of the crust into the mantle; the rifts, or midocean ridges, form along the pull-apart zones; and the fracture zones reflect lines of crustal disruption associated with great shearing action where one crustal plate has slid past its neighbor. The concept of plate tectonics—that the Earth's surface consists of a small number of crustal plates, the boundaries of which are the sites of major deformation—accounts for these three major types of features that dominate the ocean basins.

Oceanic Trenches

Oceanic trenches are long, narrow, arc-shaped depressions in the ocean floor. They occur principally around the periphery of the Pacific basin, but examples are also found in both the Atlantic and Indian oceans.

Individual trenches have lengths of thousands of miles, widths of roughly 60 miles (100 kilometers), and depths of one to two miles. Nearly all of the hadal regions, which are those deeper than 20,000 feet (6,000 meters), lie within trenches. Their continuity is remarkable. The Tonga Trench (30,000 feet or 9,000 meters deep) is about 3 miles (5 kilometers) wide, but is continuous for 400 miles (700 kilometers). Typically, trenches have an asymmetrical V shape with a steeper slope toward land and a gentle slope toward the ocean basin.

Trenches and their associated island arcs, surmounted by explosive volcanoes, are the most active geological features on the face of the Earth. The great earthquakes and tsunamis (under ocean, or submarine, earthquakes) generated from them are invariably associated with trenches.

The greatest depths of the ocean basins are found in trenches and so are near continental margins or island arcs rather than in the middle of the ocean basins. The deepest depression is the 35,600-foot (10,850-meter) Challenger Deep, discovered by H.M.S. *Challenger II* in 1948, in the Mariana Trench not far from Guam. Some other great deeps of the Pacific are the Tonga and Kermadec trenches, 35,400 feet (10,800 meters), and the Philippine Trench, 32,900 feet (10,030 meters). The greatest depth in the Atlantic is 30,200 feet (9,200 meters), found in the Puerto Rico Trench, just north of that island.

Rifts

The midocean-ridge system actually forms a continuous swell throughout the world oceans with an overall length of 40,000 miles (60,000 kilometers), or more than the circumference of the Earth. It is a broad arch 3,000 to 10,000 feet high, which may be either exceedingly rough or quite smooth. It is by far the largest and most extensive mountain range on the face of the Earth.

Nearly everywhere, the midocean ridge is deeply submerged, with only an occasional small island, such as Saint Helena or Ascension, marking its presence. Iceland alone is an exposed broad expanse of the spine of a midocean ridge. This broad swell in the ocean floor forms a median ridge through the Atlantic and Indian oceans. The median position is almost precisely true for the Atlantic, where the ridge faithfully follows the contours of the opposing continental slopes. The feature was first described and studied in the Atlantic and was appropriately termed the Mid-Atlantic Ridge. It is high, rugged, and marked by a prominent dorsal cleft, or rift valley. The ridge has a similar aspect in the Indian Ocean, although it is considerably more complex. Its overall form is like that of an inverted Y, but nevertheless the ridge maintains a roughly midocean position relative to the surrounding continents.

The midocean ridge system of the Atlantic and Indian oceans south of Australia joins with the East Pacific Rise (Albatross Cordillera). In the Pacific it is common practice to use the word *rise* rather than *ridge* because—although this rise is simply an extension of the midocean-ridge system of the other oceans—the Pacific swell has a smooth, low silhouette and generally lacks an axial rift valley. The East Pacific Rise also does not occupy a midocean position but runs north–south, paralleling South America and intersecting North America at the mouth of the Gulf of California. This rise remains deeply submerged, and its presence is suggested by only a single volcanic land formation rising from its crest, Easter Island.

Fracture Zones

Since the early 1950s, bathymetric surveys have revealed a large number of horizontal lineations of high and rugged topography called fracture zones. These are long, narrow ridges and depressions that usually separate oceanic ridges of different depths. The first to be described was the Mendocino Fracture Zone, extending westward for 2,100 miles (3,300 kilometers) from Cape Mendocino, Calif. Subsequently, three other almost parallel extensive fracture zones have been surveyed off western North America—namely, the Murray, Molokai, and Clarion fracture zones. These appear to be scarps associated with offsets of a former extension of the East Pacific Rise, which was overridden by the westward drift of North America.

In the Atlantic basin there are also numerous fracture zones that offset the axial rift of the Mid-Atlantic Ridge. These fracture zones also extend far beyond the limits of the offsets and, in some cases, can be traced nearly to Africa or North America before their trace is lost beneath the thick-lying blanket of sediments along the continental margins.

Seamounts and Guyots

A *seamount* is a mountain beneath the sea, generally in the form of an isolated, conical elevation of the seafloor at least half a mile (one kilometer) high. Seamounts are the most prominent and striking features on the ocean floor. More than 2,000 seamounts have been reported, and many more await future discovery. There remains no doubt that seamounts are nearly all volcanoes (mostly extinct) because when dredged the bedrock is always basalt, and seamount shapes and slopes are like those of a volcano on land.

The northeast Pacific basin is especially rich in seamounts that commonly trend northwest to southeast in long festoons. Many of these chains are entirely submerged, such as the Magellan Seamount Group in the far western Pacific. Others, such as the Hawaiian Chain, are mixed groups of islands, banks, and seamounts. Forming an extension of this chain is the giant, deeply submerged Emperor Seamount Chain off Japan. Each of these seamounts is named after a semimythical Japanese emperor.

Some large, deeply submerged seamounts, especially in the central North Pacific, are flat-topped and are named *guyots*, after Arnold Henry Guyot, a nineteenth-century Swiss-American geologist. An especially large cluster of guyots is that of the Mid-Pacific Mountains, which stretch from west of Hawaii to Wake Island. Guyots are thought to be drowned ancient islands that have subsided beneath the sea surface.

Abyssal Hills and Plains

Abyssal hills are protuberances smaller than seamounts rising from above the ocean floor in regions largely devoid of sediment. Extensive regions of chaotic roughness especially characterize the Pacific floor along the flanks of the mid-ocean ridges. Abyssal hills are caused by faulting of the oceanic crust, volcanic extrusions, and other kinds of deformation.

The abyssal plains are flat, featureless, sedimentary plains with slopes of less than one part in 1,000. Over broad reaches these plains will not vary in depth by as much as a meter. They are the most level regions on the face of the Earth. This nearly perfect flatness is derived by the long-continued deposition of sediments by muddy bottom flows, which pond in the deepest hollows, burying any existing irregularities. Abyssal plains are found in all ocean basins but are best developed near continental margins and in the Atlantic Ocean, where deposition rates are high. Fine examples off the eastern United States are the Hatteras and Nares plains, lying at 3.4-mile (5.5-kilometer) depth, which have been developed by sediments shed from North America. The world's

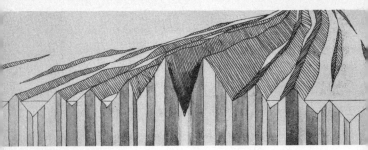

Along the crest of the mid-oceanic ridge, a rift valley opens to form what is thought to be a worldwide network of fractures in the crust. The valley is assumed to have been formed by the upwelling of molten rock from beneath the crust, repeatedly filling and opening. Moving outward from the rift, the ocean basins have been widening at the rate of about 2 to 3 inches (5 to 8 centimeters) per year, possibly contributing to the drift of continents.

greatest abyssal plain is probably that underlying the Bay of Bengal, which has been built up by the muddy Ganges and Irrawaddy rivers.

Sediments of the Ocean Floor

The ocean floor is blanketed in most places with a sedimentary cover. Two basic types of sediment are recognized: terrigenous sediments—sands, silts, and clays—shed from the continents or from islands; and pelagic, or open-sea, sediments, the finely suspended clays and remains of pelagic plants and animals that settled gently on the ocean bottom.

The terrigenous sediments generally are deposited near the base of the continental slope as sedimentary aprons or fans. They are mostly turbidites laid down by turbidity currents, a type of density current in which the density contrast arises because of the high sediment concentration of the flow. They attain great thickness.

Although covering a larger area, the pelagic sediments form a thinner blanket, up to about a mile thick. The most common pelagic sediment is globigerina ooze, composed of minute calcium carbonate shells of protozoans, mostly of the genus *Globigerina*. This ooze covers vast expanses of the Atlantic and Indian oceans. Calcium carbonate dissolves in the deeper portion of the oceans so that in much of the central Pacific basin calcareous oozes are replaced by red clay. Diatom ooze, composed of opaline siliceous shells of marine algae, is found mainly beneath colder waters.

Continental Slopes

The outer edge of the continental slope is marked by an abrupt brink where the seafloor plunges two to three miles to join the abyssal floor. The continental slopes are the longest, highest, and straightest boundary walls in the world. Only the lofty Himalayan rampart facing India attains the scale of a continental slope. If the ocean waters were removed, the continents would stand as pedestals.

Some continental slopes can be classified as accretionary because they were created by oceanic crust underthrusting the continental margin. This is the origin of most of the Pacific margin. Other slopes are modified scarps or faults related to continental breakup and drift.

The Continental Rise

In many parts of the world the continental slope is separated from the abyssal ocean floor by a broad apron. This is called the continental rise and is the top of a prism of sediments shed from the continents and laid down mostly by turbidity currents on the deep ocean floor. Such rises are particularly characteristic of the Atlantic and Indian oceans.

A particularly fine example of continental rise is developed off the eastern United States, extending as a smoothly sloping apron for about 150 miles (250 kilometers) from the 1,000-fathom (6,000-foot or 2,000 meter) level to the deep abyssal plain. This huge sedimentary prism is regarded as a potential major oil province of the future.

After initial deposition by turbidity currents, the sediments of the continental rise may be extensively reworked and are deposited by deep bottom currents. This condition is particularly true along the western sides of an ocean basin. The Blake Nose, a huge fan of sediment projecting outward from the continental rise off the south central United States, is an example of this bottom-current effect.

III. THE LIVING OCEAN

Ceaselessly moving, the waters of the ocean seem to have a life of their own, a life that affects every aspect of man's relation to the seas. Tides, currents, waves, tsunamis, upwelling, storm surges, and seiches are phenomena that men have struggled to understand through the centuries. Both the fisherman on his skiff and the admiral on his flagship must be attentive students of the sea.

An understanding of the life of the ocean has often been inextricably entangled with man's imagination. When the sea lies quiet, it is the Great Mother of Us All. When it responds to great storms or seismic shudders, it becomes the Great Destroyer that can wipe out the mightiest fleets of ships and entire island populations. Scientific study of the ocean has advanced knowledge and understanding, but many mysteries still remain.

5.
Tides and Currents

At most seaside places the water reaches its highest level twice a day. Living things along the seashore respond directly to this ebb and flow. Intertidal organisms such as barnacles, snails, clams, and oysters are most active when submerged by the rising tide. Others, like shorebirds and fiddler crabs, are specially adapted to feed on beaches exposed at ebb tide. For man a precise understanding of the tides and the currents they create can spell out the difference between a safe passage and a disaster for the sea captain entering a narrow strait or the small-boat sailor running for shelter in a land-locked harbor.

The Study of the Tides

The writings of various Chinese, Arabic, and Icelandic authors show that they paid some attention to the tides, but the theories advanced were quite fantastic. The writings of the classical authors of antiquity, however, contain only a few

Starfish are among the sea organisms that frequently become stranded on rocks and beaches at low tide.

references to the tides because the Greeks and Romans lived on the shores of the Mediterranean, which is an almost tideless sea.

In the early seventeenth century the German astronomer Johannes Kepler recognized the tendency of the water of the ocean to move toward the sun and moon, but his ideas were confused by his astrological beliefs. By calculating the attraction of both the sun and the moon on the waters of the Earth, the British physicist and mathematician Isaac Newton in 1687 laid the foundation of modern tidal theory, including the amplifying effect of narrow channels on the height of the tides. He accounted for many of the general properties of the tides, such as the phenomenon of springs and neaps, priming and lagging, and diurnal and elliptic inequalities. The only important factor that he did not mention is the dynamical effect of the Earth's rotation. Others who contributed to knowledge of the tides before the nineteenth century were Daniel Bernoulli, Leonhard Euler, Colin Maclaurin, Jean le Rond d'Alembert, and Pierre Laplace.

The connection between the tides and the movements of the moon and sun is so obvious that tidal predictions founded on empirical methods were regularly made and published long before mathematicians had devoted their attention to them. The best example of this kind of tide table was afforded by tables for Liverpool, England, based on twenty years of personal observation by a harbor master named William Hutchinson. The use of automatic tide gauges appears to have begun in about 1830.

William Thomson (afterward Lord Kelvin) became interested in the problems presented by tides by about 1863. In 1866 he took up the analysis of ordinary tidal observations and established the harmonic methods. He introduced the rotation of the Earth into the tidal dynamics of small seas, and in 1872 he designed a tide-predicting machine—the first analog computer. His theory, that the revolution of the Earth's poles in a 16-foot circle every fourteen months was the cause of small ocean tides, was confirmed by modern computers in the 1950s.

The first half of the twentieth century was notable for its meager advance in basic understanding of the tide and its geophysical implications. After about 1960, however, there was an increase of interest in tidal research along many different lines, resulting in a considerable contribution to knowledge.

The Movements of the Tides

The tides do not move regularly from day to day or from place to place. The average interval between two successive high waters is 12 hours 25 minutes, though this interval varies considerably during the course of a week. At certain places in the East Indian seas two successive high waters are separated by an interval of 12 hours, while at certain places in the China Sea the interval is often more than 24 hours. At certain places, such as Southampton, England, the high waters are often doubled (the water reaches a maximum height, falls a little, and then rises to a maximum again). At other places the low waters are often doubled. As one goes along any stretch of coast the time of high water generally becomes progressively earlier or later, while as one goes up an estuary from the sea the time of high water always becomes progressively later.

At most places, on the average, a high water is about as much above the mean level of the sea as the succeeding low water is below it. The difference in level between successive high and low waters is called the range of tide. The range of tide at any place may vary considerably from day to day. At most places it reaches a maximum once every two weeks and a minimum at times midway between two successive maxima. At London Bridge the greatest range of the fortnight has an average value of 21 feet, while the least range of the fortnight has an average value of 15 feet. The range of tide reaches 20 feet in the Gulf of Tonkin and 50 feet in the Bay of Fundy. At certain Pacific islands and over most of the Mediterranean, however, the range never exceeds 2 feet. At many places outside the Atlantic the heights of two successive high or low waters are markedly different, a phenomenon known as the diurnal intensity.

At a place in a strait or narrow sea the tidal current usually flows for about 6 hours 12 minutes in one direction and then for about the same time in the opposite direction. At the reversal of such a current there is the state of rest usually known as slack water. The speeds of tidal currents vary greatly from place to place; in the Seymour Narrows, British Columbia, the maximum current reaches ten knots, for example, while in the North Sea it rarely exceeds one. At some distance up certain rivers—as, for example, where the Colorado River meets the tide—a wave ten or more feet high travels up the river almost like a wall of water. This phe-

As the tide goes out, its high-water mark can be seen on this beach in Mozambique.

nomenon is known as a bore. Near a headland separating two bays there is sometimes a swift current known as a race.

Relationship to Moon and Sun

The times of high water bear an intimate relation to the positions of the moon and sun. The average period of 12 hours 25 minutes is half that of the moon's apparent revolution around the Earth. The length of time between the moon's crossing of the meridian of a place and the next high water at that place is known as the lunitidal interval, or the high-water interval, for the place. Similarly, the length of time between the moon's crossing of the meridian and the next low water is known as the low-water interval.

For Philadelphia, Pa., the lunitidal average is 1 hour 30 minutes. In many cases, including those of British waters, the chief variation in the lunitidal interval is associated with the phase of the moon. The average value of the lunitidal interval on the days of new and full moon is "the establishment of the port." For London Bridge this is 1 hour 58 minutes.

The range of tide may be similarly correlated. In British

waters it reaches its maximum a day or so after new and full moon and its minimum a day or so after the quarters. In these circumstances the maximum tides are known as spring tides and the minimum tides as neap tides. At about the time of the equinoxes the tides are generally larger than usual, and at about the time of the solstices they are generally smaller.

Dynamics of the Earth-Moon System

The moon attracts every particle of the Earth and ocean. According to the law of gravitation the force acting on any particle is directed toward the moon's center—jointly proportional to the masses of the particle and of the moon, and inversely proportional to the square of the distance between the particle and the moon's center. If one can imagine the Earth and ocean subdivided into a number of small particles of equal mass, then the average, both as to direction and intensity, of the forces acting on these particles is equal to the force acting on that particle at the Earth's center. If every particle of the Earth and ocean were being urged by equal and parallel forces there would be no cause for relative motion between the ocean and the Earth. It is the departure of the force acting on any particle from the average, therefore, which constitutes the tide-generating force.

It is obvious that on the side of the Earth toward the moon the departure from the average is a small force directed toward the moon, and on the side of the Earth away from the moon the departure is a small force directed away from the moon. All around the sides of the Earth along a great circle perpendicular to the line joining the moon and Earth the departure is a force directed inward toward the Earth's center. The tidal forces tend, therefore, to pull the water toward and away from the moon and to depress the water at right angles to that direction.

Predicting the Tides

Probably the greatest achievement of tidal study is that it has made possible the prediction, with a fair degree of accuracy, of what the sea level will be at any desired time for a great number of ports. The method used is essentially the following: constants in the harmonic development of the tide at any place are determined by analysis of a long series of observations at that place, and knowing the values of these constants it is possible to reconstruct or synthesize the tide for any past, present, or future time. This "harmonic method" can be applied to any observable tidal quantity that depends linearly on the tide-generating forces, such as the north or east components of the tidal current (not the speed or the direction of the current), the tidal variations of gravity or atmospheric pressure, and other variables.

The theoretical problem of the tide in the oceans has still not been solved, and knowledge of the tide at any place depends on some observations having been made at that site. The prediction process may be loosely considered as one of extrapolation of the observations. It is possible that at some future time tidal theory will have been advanced sufficiently that full knowledge of the tide at a given place may be obtained theoretically without the need of previous observations at the site.

Observation of the variable elevation of the sea surface is carried out by means of an instrument known as a tide gauge, which usually consists of a float and pulley system so arranged that the height of the float determines the position of a recording pen on a moving chart. The chart is made to move at constant speed by means of a clock mechanism, so that, as a result, one obtains a graph, or marigram, of the height of sea level as a function of time.

After the marigram is obtained the usual procedure is to read off at hourly intervals the height of sea level and to correct these hourly tidal heights for any variation of datum that may have occurred. Vast quantities of these hourly tidal heights for many seaports are on file at the world's principal tidal agencies.

Tidal Power

The idea of using the rise and fall of the tides to produce power has long attracted the attention of inventors, who have suggested many ingenious schemes. The only practicable method so far, however, is based on the use of one or more tidal basins, separated from the sea by dams or barrages, and of hydraulic turbines through which the water is passed on its way between the basin and sea or between two basins.

The earliest use of tidal water as a source of power was by means of a tide mill, a kind of water mill. Some depended on the tide alone, others used a proportion of fresh water. A storage pond was formed by enclosing part of a creek or estuary or by damming a tidal stream at its entrance to an estuary. Automatic lock-type gates or flap valves were set in the wall or dam, enabling the tide to fill the pond as it rose. When the tide fell, the water could be released through a sluice in order to drive a water wheel.

The *Domesday Book* mentions what seems to have been a tide mill at the entrance to the Port of Dover, England. It was built after 1066 and was a danger to vessels entering the harbor. The first mills of record were both in England: Three Mills, Bromley-by-Bow, London, in 1135, and that at Woodbridge, Suffolk, in 1170. In the Netherlands there was a mill at Zuicksee in 1220. Tide mills were built on sites around the coast of Great Britain, along the west coast of the European continent from the Netherlands to the south of Spain, along the eastern seaboard of colonial America, and on the coast of Surinam. The first tide mill in colonial America was built at Salem in 1635. In Surinam tide mills operated from 1667 to 1860.

Construction was begun in January 1961 and completed in 1967 on the world's first large-scale tidal plant. This project is located on the Rance River estuary in the Gulf of St. Malo, Brittany, France. After excavations on the estuary were completed in 1963, the flow into the Rance at spring tide attained a maximum of 635,670 cubic feet per second (18,000 cubic meters per second) at both flood and ebb—about three times the amount of the flow of the Rhône at Avignon, France.

The plant has twenty-four specially designed 10,000-kilowatt turboalternators, each installed in an aperture in the dam through which the water flows. Each unit acts as both turbine and pump, in both directions of tidal flow and in both directions of rotation.

Maximum annual net production for the plant is 544 gigawatt-hours, or billion watt-hours—537 gigawatt-hours in the basin-to-sea direction and 71.5 gigawatt-hours in the sea-to-basin direction, less 64.5 gigawatt-hours of energy used in pumping. It was intended that maximum power be directed to the national electricity network at those times when it would be economically most useful; in the early 1970s the maximum production amounted to 470 gigawatt-hours.

In 1969 the U.S.S.R. completed construction of its first tidal plant. This small plant, of about 1,000 kilowatts, is located on the White Sea. Tidal power plants have been proposed for the Bristol Channel in Great Britain, the San José Gulf in Argentina, and at various points on the western Australian coast.

Ocean Currents

The horizontal movement of water is called a current. In the ocean there exist both tidal currents, or tidal streams, which are associated with the tidal rise and fall of sea level and result from the same causes, and nontidal currents. The nontidal currents show considerable regularity in their general flow, although they may be modified by a persistent wind that blows for several days in the same direction. The nontidal currents in a given season of the year are relatively stable.

In describing the motion of any particle on the Earth it is necessary to consider the Earth's rotation. Since a body once set in motion continues that motion relative to space, it has an apparent deflection relative to the observer on the rotating Earth. This deflecting force is known as the Coriolis force, after the French engineer Gaspard Gustave de Coriolis who first derived it mathematically in 1835. The direction of the Coriolis force is to the right (clockwise) in the northern hemisphere and to the left (counterclockwise) in the southern.

The water discharged to the sea by a river is fresher and therefore lower in density than the seawater so it tends to turn in the direction of the Coriolis force along the coast. Thus, along the Atlantic coast of the United States, which has numerous rivers producing an appreciable lowering of the coastal salinity, the general inshore current sets to the south as far as Cape Hatteras. On the coast of California, where rainfall and runoff of the coastal rivers is confined chiefly to the winter months, the California current sets south in the summer. In the winter, however, a well-defined north-setting inshore current, the Davidson, makes its appearance.

Tidal currents exist in the open sea as well as in restricted channels. In deep water their effect is small and almost immeasurable, but on the continental shelves they are usually the predominant current. When not confined by coastal barriers, tidal currents generally change direction continually with the Coriolis force and, where the tide is mainly semidiurnal in character, a drifting object completes a roughly circular path every twelve hours.

Whenever the wind blows over a stretch of water for an appreciable time the frictional drag between wind and water and between the layers of water will set the water in motion. Swedish oceanographer Vagn Walfrid Ekman showed in 1902, as the result of observations of the drift of pack ice

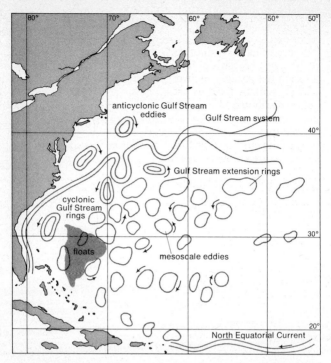

The Atlantic Ocean off the coast of North America is characterized by a complex system of currents and eddies, many of them associated with the Gulf Stream.

made by Norwegian explorer Fridtjof Nansen in the *Fram*, that in water of sufficient depth the surface wind current is directed 45° from the wind direction.

On each side of the equator each ocean has its own virtually closed surface circulation, that of the Antarctic being to the eastward around Antarctica and that of the Arctic entering from the Atlantic in the Barents Sea, proceeding northeastward, circling the pole, and leaving down the east coast of Greenland. In comparison, the exchange with the Pacific through Bering Strait is much less important. It is particularly noteworthy that in the surface circulation of the ocean little water crosses the equator, except where the South Equatorial current impinges on the bulge of South America. This flow makes up for the water that sinks below the surface in the northern North Atlantic in winter and crosses the equator near the ocean bottom.

Numerous means, direct and indirect, have been developed for measuring ocean currents. If the navigator of a ship keeps careful records of his course and speed the difference between the position so given (the dead reckoning) and the position actually fixed by astronomical or electronic means can be attributed to the effect of the current. Hundreds of ships report daily observations of this sort to the world's hydrographic offices, and although the results of necessity average the current over fairly large distances sufficient observations are available to permit averaging out of all random errors.

A somewhat similar method involves the dropping of bottles or cards (bottle post or drift cards) at known positions and noting the position of recovery. This method is excellent when practical applications are desired, such as the fate of sewage or oil disposed of at sea or the drift of fish eggs. An elaboration of the bottle or card is a drogue, or other object, which will be acted on by the current at a predetermined depth and will tow a light or radar reflector floating on the surface. Such a drogue can be followed from a boat for days or weeks and its successive positions determined.

Vertical Water Movements

When a persistent wind blows along a coast that lies to the left of the wind direction (in the northern hemisphere) the net transport of water in the wind-induced current is offshore. Since the coast acts as a barrier, water to replace that blown offshore can only come from the deeper layers. This phenomenon is known as upwelling, and it exists along the coast of northern California in summer and off Morocco, Peru, and southwest Africa. The replacement water comes from a depth of 600 to 1,000 feet, where the water is both appreciably colder and richer in plant nutrients than the water it replaces. Zones of upwelling, therefore, considerably modify the climate of the coasts where they occur. The coastal fogs of California result from this cause, for example. Such zones are also productive fishing areas.

In the open sea, areas of similar upward water movement are found in regions of divergence—lines along which the currents tend to flow away on both sides. Again the continuity is maintained by water that rises to the surface. Generally the vertical movement is less than 1,000 feet, as along the Pacific equator and along the northern boundary of the Equatorial countercurrent, but in the Antarctic, particularly south of the Atlantic, deeper water rises to the surface.

Convergences are lines toward which currents flow from both sides and where water, therefore, must be sinking. The water sinks only to the depth where water of corresponding density is found, which in most regions is not far below the surface, and there it spreads out sideways. The bottom water of the Mediterranean, however, is renewed by surface water that sinks in winter along its northern coasts; the Arctic Ocean is filled with water that has been cooled in the Norwegian Sea; the deep water of the North Atlantic is renewed from the surface just to the south of Greenland; and the rest of the ocean derives its bottom water mainly from the Antarctic, where the densest water is formed in winter along the continental shelf. Lines of convergence exist all around Antarctica, as well as in the subtropics, the tropics, the equatorial current system, and the North Pacific.

6.
Waves, Storm Surges, Seiches, and Tsunamis

Waves are irregular moving bumps and hollows caused by the wind blowing over the water, by submarine earthquakes, and by the effects of both sun and moon. By far the major portion of the waves that attack shore and harbor areas are those generated by the wind. Waves may also be generated by a sudden change in barometric pressure over a limited area of water surface or by an underwater seismic or volcanic disturbance or earthquake. The latter are called seismic waves or *tsunamis* (a Japanese word meaning "harbor waves"), often mistakenly referred to as tidal waves. Barometric pressure changes or seismic disturbances usually create only a small number of relatively low waves.

Wave Characteristics

The distinguishing characteristics of a wave are its height (the vertical distance from a trough to a crest), its length (the horizontal distance between successive crests), and its period (the time between the arrival of successive crests at a fixed point). These characteristics are determined by the velocity of the wind, the length of time that the wind continues at this velocity, and the distance over which the wind is in contact with the water (fetch). In general, the greater the velocity and duration of the wind and the larger the fetch, the greater will be the height and period of the waves.

Waves and the Shoreline

For people living along the seacoast, waves are notable principally for their assaults on the open coast—assaults that eat away the shoreline itself. Historical records show that wave erosion has made appreciable inroads in some coastal areas. Along a 30-mile stretch of the Yorkshire coast in eastern England, for example, waves have cut inland 2½ to 3 miles since the Roman occupation, sweeping away the sites of many villages. Whether wave work is effective in reducing a land area depends on exposure of a shore to prevailing storm winds, kind of bedrock, depth of water near shore, location and direction of currents, relation to streams that carry large

Giant waves, as this one at Waimea, Hawaii, are often spectacular in appearance but can be dangerous to boaters and swimmers.

volumes of sediment, and other variables.

Wave motion extends to a moderate depth in the surf zone, and in the lower part of the layer of agitated water there is little energy. As storm waves plane inland, energy is absorbed by friction on the wave-cut platform, so that with each advance the ability to erode decreases and the eroded surface slopes upward to an intersection with sea level.

The Scientific Study of Waves

Wave motions on the surface of a liquid have been the subject of theoretical investigations since the days of Sir Isaac Newton. Prior to about 1950, however, there was a discrepancy between the theoretical study of waves and the practical observation of waves. The theory of wave motions yielded results for regular, highly idealized waves, and the actual waves on the ocean were highly variable and did not resemble the theories. Also, there was no really good explanation for how waves were generated by the wind.

This unfortunate situation was remedied by the availability of new theoretical tools that were developed in the areas of probability and statistics. The concepts of generalized harmonic analysis, time series analysis, and random processes permitted much of the earlier results to be extended in a way that described many of the essential features of real waves on the ocean.

The full theory for the generation, propagation, dissipation, refraction in shallow water, and breaking on beaches of waves is so complex that the wave properties have to be described and forecast by means of high-speed electronic computers. The problem of wave forecasting is to describe the "spectrum" of the waves as it varies as a function of position and time over the oceans as the winds change from place to place and from day to day. Typically a wind-generated sea contains waves with periods ranging from about 15 to 20 seconds all the way down to capillary periods of a fraction of a second. The lengths of the waves range all the way from 300–500 meters to fractions of a centimeter. The waves travel in a wide range of directions even up to and past 45° to the wind direction. The higher the wind, the longer the time interval between the bigger waves, the larger the significant height, the more extreme the highest waves, and the rougher the sea surface.

To forecast waves by means of an electronic computer it is first of all required that a good forecast of the direction and speed of the winds over the ocean be available. Also required is a description of what the winds were like over the ocean for a week or so in the past. From the past-observed winds the characteristics of the waves at the time of the last available actual surface-weather charts can be computed. Surface-weather charts based on reports from ships at sea are prepared every six hours by the world meteorological services.

It is usually necessary to consider a large area of the ocean surface to compute what the waves will be like at a given point on the ocean. Waves generated near Australia and New Zealand have been tracked as swell all the way to the coast of Alaska. Distant regions eventually affect any given point of interest, and the waves have to be described over a close grid of points so as to be able to describe the waves at any given point.

Each of three important effects that modify the spectrum of the waves at a given point on the ocean has to be considered. These effects are the growth of the waves, the dissipation of the waves, and the propagation (or spread) of the waves.

Wave forecasting procedures by computers require that

these three effects be considered every three hours or so at each of many thousands of points over the ocean. If observed winds from past meteorological situations are used the result is a climatology of past wave conditions. If observed winds up to a certain time are used and if forecasts of the winds a day or two into the future are available from numerical weather prediction methods the result is a true forecast of wave conditions.

Wave climatologies and wave forecasts have many important uses. The wave spectra can be used to compute the

Refraction, diffraction, reflection, and surf are all seen in this aerial photograph of Morro Bay, Calif. Waves are approaching the coast from the northwest, but because of refraction their crests are lined up nearly parallel to the shore (bottom left). Waves are stopped by a breakwater, yet behind it they defract all the way to the beach (center). The rocky headland reflects waves in a circular pattern (upper left). Waves running into shallow water gradually lose their velocity of energy propagation, causing their height to increase and their crests to become narrower and steeper, until they disintegrate by breaking into surf (top center).

motions of ships in waves and to route ships more quickly and safely from one port to another.

Wave Refraction, Diffraction, Reflection, and Surf

As the waves from the deep ocean reach shallower water and approach a coast they are said to "feel" bottom when the depth of the water is half the length of the wave. Variations in the depth of the water cause the waves to speed up in the deeper water and slow down in the shallower water. This process of refraction is governed by the same law that describes the refraction of light. The refraction focuses the wave energy onto headlands and over shallow regions jutting out from the shore, and it turns the waves away from channels and bays. Particular offshore topographies can act like lenses and focus the wave energy onto a small portion of the beach. These effects can cause the breakers along a coast to differ in height over a small distance such as 10 to 20 miles by a factor of 10.

Waves on water can also be diffracted and reflected according to physical laws similar to those for light. At a breakwater entrance to a harbor, wave motions spread out into the geometrical shadow of the breakwater according to physical laws similar to the seventeenth-century Dutch physicist Christian Huygens' principle on the diffraction of light.

If there is no beach and the water lies against a nearly vertical cliff, or wall, the waves will be reflected. Locally, standing waves can then be produced that can be twice as high as the waves coming in from the deep ocean. Diffraction, refraction, and the basic randomness of the waves make what actually happens very complex; regions near cliffs and harbor breakwaters on the seaward side are not safe for small boats when the seas are running high.

Breakers put a tremendous volume of sand into suspension along the surf zone. Since the waves usually break at an angle to the beach there is a current produced parallel to the beach that transports the sand like a great river. Sandy Hook, N.J., for example, has been built up by sand transported to it by this effect so that now it is more than five times larger in area than it was in the eighteenth century.

The overall effect of breaking waves is to erode, on the average, about one foot of land from the entire coastline of the continental United States each year. The Coastal Engineering Research Center in Washington, D.C., is responsible for research on breakers and surf and beach erosion. Many ingenious ways to stop this erosion, or to preserve valuable beaches, have been developed. Plans to prevent erosion or to restore beaches must be coordinated over a considerable length of coast as the efforts of a single community are likely to be ineffective or even harmful to neighboring areas.

Much has been learned about such phenomena by building scale models of harbors, beaches, ships, and breakwaters, and then generating both regular waves and irregular random waves to see how the models are affected. Facilities exist throughout the world to study all of these problems in great detail.

Storm Surges and Seiches

Storm surges and seiches are larger scale wave motions caused by the large-scale pattern of the stress of wind on bodies of water. The length of a surge along a coast can be several hundreds of miles and it can last for many hours. A seiche is usually associated with a lake, but the equations and physical laws governing its motion apply equally well to bays and coastal regions.

If a strong wind blows across a lake for a while, it will pile up the water on the downwind side of the lake and cause a depression in the water on the upwind side. When the wind stops, the water will slosh back and forth in the lake a number of times as water does in a bathtub. The resulting seiche can be analyzed mathematically as a standing wave similar to the sound waves produced in organ pipes.

Many other standing-wave patterns can exist with antinodes at closed ends and nodes at openings. Continental shelves act like a node at the continental slope and an antinode at the shore and can therefore enhance the effects of strong winds from hurricanes moving up the coast over the water.

Hurricanes along the east coast of the United States and in the Gulf of Mexico, and their counterparts in the Bay of Bengal and off the coast of Japan, produce damaging storm surges. Onshore winds pile up the water in advance of the hurricane, and offshore winds blow the water away from the coast. Typically, storm surges can cause the water to be 10 feet deeper than it would be due to the usual astronomical tides, and if the storm surge peaks at high tide extensive flooding of coastal areas can result.

Extratropical cyclones of great intensity can also cause extreme storm surges. (The day-to-day variations in the wind also cause minor surges.) An intense storm surge in 1953 in the North Sea breached many of the dikes of the Netherlands, flooded about 25,000 square kilometers of land, forced more than 600,000 people from their homes, and drowned nearly 2,000 people. Warning services for potentially dangerous storm surges are provided by the meteorological services of the world.

Tsunamis

The Japanese word *tsunami* was adopted by the scientists of the world to avoid the misnomer "tidal waves," as these waves have nothing to do with the tides. Tsunamis are caused by earthquakes that occur under the ocean. They are confined mainly to the Pacific Ocean and are closely associated with the extensive seismic activity and the tectonics of the Pacific region. All tsunamis are caused by submarine earthquakes, but not every submarine earthquake causes a tsunami.

Seismic seiches are oscillations generated by earthquake surface waves in closed or partially closed bodies of water. In great earthquakes, seiches may be produced at large distances from the source. The great Lisbon, Portugal, earthquake of 1755 set up seiches all over western Europe, including the Scandinavian countries and Finland. In Scotland, Loch Lomond oscillated for an hour with an amplitude of about two feet. The 1964 Alaska earthquake produced seiches along the coasts of U.S. states bordering the Gulf of Mexico.

Some tsunamis are believed to be caused by vertical fault movements and others by submarine landslides initiated by earthquakes. In the open ocean the wave amplitudes are small, two or three feet at the most, but their wave lengths— distance from crest to crest—may be more than 100 miles. The wave periods—the time from crest to crest—usually range from 15 to 30 minutes. The waves travel at speeds ranging from about 150 miles per hour in water 1,600 feet deep to about 670 miles per hour in water 30,000 feet in depth.

Although the amplitudes are small in the open ocean they increase greatly upon approaching shore, especially in V-shaped bays where they may rise to 90 feet or more, and can produce great destruction and loss of life. The initial wave usually, but not always, begins with a recession that appears as an abnormally low tide occurring in a matter of minutes and exposing the ocean floor far beyond the limits of normal low tides. Residents of coastal regions subject to these waves recognize these abnormal recessions as the first movements of a tsunami and flee immediately to high ground.

Tsunamis travel great distances across the ocean with relatively little loss of energy. A tsunami originating in the Aleutian earthquake of 1946 produced waves up to 55 feet high in the Hawaiian Islands, where more than 150 lives were lost and 488 houses were demolished. The waves were 12 feet high on the California coast at Santa Cruz, where one man was drowned; tsunamis resulting from the Alaskan earthquake of 1964 hit Crescent City, Calif., with 10-foot waves, causing ten deaths.

The greatest tsunami of historic times occurred as a consequence of the great eruption of Krakatoa in Indonesia in 1883. The series of great tsunamis that were generated by the explosion and collapse of the volcanic island were recorded on tide gauges as far away as Hawaii and South America. The greatest was the wave that occurred just after the climactic explosion at 10 A.M. on August 27. The wave reached a height of more than 100 feet and took the lives of approximately 36,000 persons in coastal towns on the nearby shores of Java and Sumatra.

Severe seismic disturbances are now detected and located by the seismograph network of the world within a few minutes after they happen. If the epicenter is over water there is the threat of a tsunami. Since tsunamis travel at speeds of only 400–500 miles per hour, however, there is ample time to warn most populated areas. The tsunami of 1946, for example, originated at about 2 A.M. on April 1 near the Aleutian Islands but took about 4.5 hours to travel to the Hawaiian Islands.

The severity of a particular tsunami at a particular location is difficult to predict. For seismic disturbances of comparable Richter scale the associated tsunamis can vary markedly in their destructiveness as they approach a coast. The usual procedure is to monitor the path of the tsunami as it radiates in ever expanding circles from its source and determine how high it is on the various islands in its path. If it is high on these islands then the populous areas are warned. The Coast and Geodetic Survey of the National Oceanographic and Atmospheric Administration has this responsibility for the United States, and similar organizations serve other countries. Japan, in particular, has a well-organized, highly efficient disaster-warning service.

7.
The Ocean and the World's Climate

Climate has a history of its own that has had a clear impact on human history and on the distribution of animals and plants throughout the world. The factors that determine climate are the balance of incoming and outgoing radiation at any place; the temperatures of the surface and of the atmosphere that result partly from the radiation balance and partly from the heat transported into and out of the area by winds and ocean currents; the horizontal and vertical motion of the air; and the moisture cycle—evaporation of water from the sea and land surfaces, the transport of this moisture over great distances and to great heights by winds, and its ultimate precipitation as rain, hail, or snow. All of these elements are affected by the presence of the oceans on the globe.

Ocean Circulation and Currents

The circulation of the oceans is part of the apparatus that produces the observed climates. Ocean currents that have a northward or southward component, like the warm Gulf Stream in the North Atlantic or the cold Humboldt Current off South America, effectively exchange heat between low and high latitudes. In tropical latitudes, the oceans account for a third or more of the transport of heat toward the poles; at latitude 50° N, the ocean's share is about one-seventh.

Because warm water of Gulf Stream origin enters and occupies the eastern part of the Norwegian Sea, warmth is imparted to the winds blowing over the water, and the average air temperature over the year at Tromsø, Norway (69° 40' N), is above the average for its latitude by a margin of 25° F. (about 14° C.). In winter the excess is even greater.

The mean annual temperature at Quito, Ecuador, on the equator, is nearly 14° C. below the average for the latitude. This is an extreme departure found only close to the almost perpetually cloudy coast, where the drift of the current westward into the ocean causes water even colder than the Humboldt Current surface waters to well up from below.

The oceans, particularly in areas where the surface is warm, also supply moisture to the atmosphere. This, in turn, contributes to the heat budget of those areas in which the water vapor is condensed into clouds, liberating latent heat in the process, often in high latitudes and in places remote from the oceans where the moisture was taken up.

The great ocean currents are themselves wind-driven—set in motion by the drag of the winds over vast areas of the sea surface, especially where waves increase the friction. At the limits of the warm currents, particularly where they abut directly upon a cold current, the strong thermal gradients in the sea surface result in marked differences in the heating of the atmosphere on either side of the boundary. (These conditions occur at the left flank of the Gulf Stream in the neighborhood of the Newfoundland banks and at the subtropical and Antarctic convergences in the Southern Hemisphere oceans.) These differences tend to position and guide the strongest flow of the jet stream in the atmosphere above and thereby influence the development and steering of weather systems.

Ocean-Atmosphere Interactions

Interactions between ocean and atmosphere proceed in both directions. They also operate at different rates. Some interesting lag effects, which are of value in long-range weather forecasting, arise through the much slower circulation of the oceans. Enhanced strength of the easterly trade winds, for example, over low latitudes of the Atlantic north and south of the equator impels more water toward the Caribbean and the Gulf of Mexico, producing a stronger flow and greater warmth in the Gulf Stream some six months later.

Anomalies in the position of the Gulf Stream–Labrador current boundary, producing a greater or lesser extent of warm water near the Newfoundland banks, so affect the energy supply to the atmosphere and the development and steering of weather systems from that region that they are associated with rather persistent anomalies of weather pattern over the British Isles and northern Europe.

Anomalies in the equatorial Pacific and in the northern limit of the Kuroshio current seem to have effects on a similar scale. Indeed, through their influence on the latitude of the jet stream and the wave length (spacing of cold trough and warm ridge regions) in the upper westerlies, these ocean anomalies exercise an influence over the atmospheric circulation that spreads to all parts of the hemisphere. In the case of sea-temperature anomalies in the equatorial Pacific— anomalies that are traceable, at least in part, to variations in the South Pacific trade winds and the upwelling they produce at the coasts of Peru and Ecuador—the character of the atmospheric circulation over both hemispheres is affected.

Certain regions of the world's ocean may, therefore, be identified as peculiarly sensitive climatically because variation of the prevailing conditions is likely to have wide-ranging, or in some cases global, effects. The neighborhood of the nose, or oceanward projection, of Brazil near Pernambuco (7° to 8° S) is one such region. If for some time, through a southward displacement of the pattern of prevailing winds, the westward-moving South Equatorial current in the South Atlantic is similarly displaced, the proportions going into the two branches into which it splits at this point will be altered and the supply of warm water to the Caribbean, and ultimately to the Gulf Stream, will be reduced.

A southward displacement of the ocean-current pattern in this sense seems certain to have occurred in the ice ages and can be traced in more recent periods of cold climate. Recovery from this situation may require a period of unusual warmth over side areas of the tropical Atlantic.

Surface Salinities and Ice

Another sensitive point appears to be the surface layer, only 330–660 feet (100–200 meters) thick, of relatively low salinity on the surface of the Arctic Ocean in which the pack ice forms that largely covers that ocean today. Salinities observed in this layer are between 20 and 30 parts per thousand, as against 34 to 37 in most of the world's oceans and in the deeper levels of the Arctic Ocean itself.

Salt ocean water increases in density as its temperature falls, right down to its freezing point (about 28° F. or –2° C.). Therefore, cooling by the atmosphere and by the radiation regime in high latitudes normally causes the cold water to sink and to be replaced by other water from below the surface. Convective overturning would have to cool the whole depth of the ocean before its surface could freeze.

This convection is presumably the reason why the Norwegian Sea and the saltwater regions of the Barents Sea, as far north as 75° N, never freeze. Similarly, deep convection presumably also goes on in the central Arctic under the ice.

In the regions of variable ice cover around Greenland and Labrador, and elsewhere, advances and retreats of a surface layer of fresher water and consequently lower density can be traced. Fresh water has its maximum density at about 39° F. (4° C.); it expands as it is cooled, and so the coldest water tends to stay at the surface. Hence, the extent of the Arctic Sea ice can be expected to vary with any variation in the supply of fresh water to that ocean from the rivers draining the surrounding continents, from such glaciers as flow into the Arctic basin, and from precipitation over the ocean itself.

Influence of the Arctic Ocean

The surface of an ice-free Arctic Ocean would be approximately 20° to 30° F. (about 10° to 15° C.) warmer than at present, averaged over the year as a whole and 35° to 55° F. warmer than it currently is in winter. The strength of the existing thermal gradients—and therefore the intensity and the pattern of atmospheric circulation development and the steering of surface weather systems—would all be affected.

It has been found from studies in the North Atlantic-European sector that in years when the pack-ice limit is unusually far south the eastward-traveling, rain-giving cyclonic depressions in summer and autumn generally pass several degrees of latitude farther south and extend their influence toward central Europe. In years when the pack-ice limit is far north the depressions travel on more northern tracks and much of Europe is likely to escape their influence.

It seems probable that the great ice sheet covering Antarctica will occasionally be subject to forward surges, like most glaciers. Such an event must produce an extension of the surface layer of low salinity on the surrounding ocean and tend to bring about a widening of the pack-ice belt.

Icebergs and Pack Ice

The extreme positions at which stray icebergs have been recorded depend on the original size of the berg when it calved (or broke) off the front of a glacier or floating ice shelf. They also bear witness to the vagaries of wind-driven ocean currents and to the occasionally great spread of denser cold water beneath the warmer portions of the surface.

Icebergs or smaller pieces of floating ice have been reported about 60–61° N 0–10° W, in the vicinity of the Shetland and Orkney islands, about three times in one hundred years and have occasionally reached 35–37° N in the central and western Atlantic. In the middle part of the South Atlantic, one berg was sighted at 26.5° S in the last century, and others reached 36° S, off the mouth of the Río de la Plata (Buenos Aires) and 34–35° S near the Cape of Good Hope.

Around 1900 the Antarctic pack ice is believed to have

A U.S. Coast Guard icebreaker approaches a tabular (flat) iceberg, three-quarters of a mile long, off the coast of Greenland. Some scientists believe that it might be feasible to tow such icebergs to the coasts of desert countries to be used as sources of fresh water.

reached within 100 miles of Cape Horn, and in 1968 (as in 1888) Iceland was for a time half surrounded by the Arctic pack ice. The usual limits, however, are well short of these.

Oceanic Climate

The differences between oceanic (or maritime) and continental climates, though operative in all latitudes, are most apparent in the middle latitudes. The most obvious features are the windiness, relatively small temperature variations, and even distribution of rainfall in oceanic climates. Because westerly winds prevail in middle latitudes, oceanic climate characteristics spread farther into the continents from the western than from the eastern coasts, except where a mountain barrier stands in the way. Even at the eastern seaboards the climates are more continental, and in winter much more severe, than at the western limits of the continents.

Over and near the oceans the frequent strong winds and gales are the most severe element of the climate, hampering the activities of man. Gales (defined by a Beaufort wind scale force number of eight or more—in excess of 39 miles per hour) blow on approximately seventy days a year over the wide Southern ocean, near Cape Horn, and also near the coasts of Greenland; and between thirty and sixty days a year over the North Atlantic and the coasts bordering it between Nova Scotia, Scotland, and Ireland. By contrast, the frequency of such winds in inland Europe is usually under ten days.

The climate of coastal regions and islands differs from that of the open sea chiefly through the frequent development of diurnal land and sea breezes. These are caused by the convective overturning of air due to the unequal heating of land and sea surfaces. This results in a marked tendency to develop a belt of clear sky along, or parallel with, the coast where the descending air motion suppresses cloud development.

There is, therefore, more sunshine on the coastal area than out at sea and generally more sunshine than inland, where convective cloud development by day and fogs and haze caused by ground radiation cooling overnight restrict the hours of sunshine. There is also, however, more rainfall over the coastal area than over the open sea because of the forced uplift of air over the coast, particularly over mountainous coasts. Mountainous coasts and fjords are also liable to stronger winds than the open ocean owing to convergence effects where the windstream is channeled by mountain walls.

Hurricanes and Typhoons

Severe cyclonic disturbances of the atmosphere in low latitudes are called tropical storms. In the western Atlantic they are known as hurricanes, and in the western Pacific they are known as typhoons. They are distinguished from other weather disturbances in the tropics by the fury of their weather, which every year is responsible for much damage.

Tropical cyclones have caused many deaths and incalculable losses of property. In terms of human life one of the most catastrophic cyclones known hit Calcutta on October 7, 1737, causing a 40-foot (12-meter) storm surge ("wall" of water) and killing about 300,000 people. During an 1876 cyclone the storm surge blocked the ebbing tide and the Megna estuary near Chittagong, flooding 2,800 square miles (7,800 square kilometers), drowning about 100,000 persons and causing diseases that killed another 100,000. The fatalities caused by the cyclone that swept all the low-lying islands in the same area in November 1970 will never be known; estimates of the death toll were as great as 500,000.

A disastrous hurricane hit Galveston, Texas, on September 8, 1900, killing an estimated 6,000 people and causing about $20 million worth of damage. A seawall was built, and when Galveston was hit by a 1915 hurricane there were only 275 fatalities, though the damage ran to approximately $50 million. On September 21, 1938, a hurricane that had departed from the more normal storm track produced catastrophic winds, storm surge, and river floods in New England. It killed 682 persons and caused damage of more than $400 million. Even with continuous tracking by radar, satellite, and aircraft, a hurricane in September 1965 knocked out New Orleans' power, communications, and water purification systems and caused nearly $1,420 million worth of damage.

A cyclonic whirl is called a hurricane or typhoon if the surface winds exceed 75 miles per hour (125 kilometers per hour) or force 12 on the Beaufort scale. As a result of the Earth's rotation the rotation of the vortex is clockwise in the southern hemisphere and counterclockwise in the northern. The area covered by a hurricane's high winds may have a diameter of only 10 miles when the storm is in its early stage. In fully grown storms the diameter is rarely less than 50 miles and may attain 150 miles. The entire area affected by a large storm may exceed 500 miles in diameter.

Tropical storms generally originate between latitudes of 5° and 30° in either hemisphere. All tropical storms develop over the ocean. Long before the turn of the twentieth century, it was known that most such storms develop along a narrow zone of air convergence, where the trade winds of both hemispheres meet. This zone, which girdles the globe, has been variously called doldrums, intertropical front, and equatorial low-pressure trough. The zone penetrates to about latitude 15° N between July and October and to latitude 10° to 15° S from January to March or April. These months, then, represent the principal cyclone seasons of the respective hemispheres. In the northern hemisphere the peak month of activity usually is September.

Tropical storms can also develop in the absence of the equatorial trough, although they do so less frequently. The storms of the western North Atlantic and the Gulf of Mexico are the outstanding examples of formation without equatorial trough. High-atmospheric observations taken over the oceans have shown that tropical weather is greatly dependent on the atmospheric flow in the middle latitudes. In order to predict the formation of a tropical storm in the West Indies, for instance, a weather forecaster must have knowledge of weather conditions over all of the North Atlantic and the United States, besides the information as to conditions over the tropics themselves.

There are regions of the Earth where tropical storms principally form. On the average, about twenty tropical storms

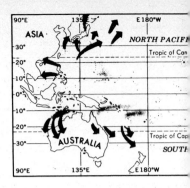

The principal regions of tropical storm formation around the world are indicated by the shaded areas; arrows show the usual paths taken by the storms, which are rare in the south Atlantic and southeastern Pacific areas.

form in the western North Pacific Ocean each year. The cyclone frequency of the South Indian Ocean is thought to be almost as high. Compared with these areas, other hurricane areas of the world have few storms. In the western North Atlantic, the Caribbean, and the Gulf of Mexico the mean annual frequency is about seven.

Natural History of Hurricanes

Young developing storms will give little or no advance notice of their arrival, except to the meteorologist. A mature cyclone is preceded by a distinct ocean swell with a frequency several times less than normal waves. In the Gulf of Mexico, for example, waves normally reach the shore about every four to five seconds. The presence of a hurricane may be expected if they arrive only every 12 to 15 seconds and if the swell is correspondingly higher.

The barometer often does not drop until 12 hours before the arrival of the storm center. Appearance of a sheet of cirrus clouds, gradually thickening, frequently supplies an earlier warning. In addition the inhabitants of the tropics often rely on other abnormalities of the local weather, such as brilliant red sunsets and winds from unusual directions as precursory signs of a cyclone. Satellites, which transmit photographs of the Earth and its cloud systems, give the most reliable and comprehensive coverage of cloud patterns and reveal storm systems from remote areas where other methods of detection (such as radar and air patrols) may not always penetrate.

The arrival of the storm area itself begins with a gradual picking up of the wind and increasing gustiness. This is followed by a thickening of low clouds in the sky and intermit-

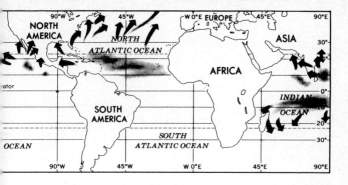

tent squally showers. Sometimes the main wall of cumulo-nimbus clouds can be seen approaching in the distance. It is called the bar of the storm.

When a storm is observed from a point that is not on the path of the center itself it will be noted that the hurricane winds gradually change direction. They will not let up materially, however, until the cyclone passes. Should the "eye" of the cyclone pass over, however, it will be noted that the winds drop from hurricane force to light breezes within a few minutes. At the same time the rain ceases and the clouds lighten. After passage of the eye the winds and the rain resume with full force, but the winds come from the opposite direction.

The amount of rainfall on tropical islands and coastal areas of continents during the passage of a storm depends on the speed, size, and intensity of the rain-producing center and on the topography of the land. A great storm passing over Puerto Rico in 1928 produced 10 to 15 inches (25 to 38 centimeters) of rain near the coast and up to double that amount in the mountainous interior. Precipitation of more than 20 inches in one day has occurred on several occasions along the southern coast of the United States and in various parts of the tropics. At Baguio in the Philippines 42 inches (107 centimeters) fell within 24 hours in 1911. A rainfall of 10 to 15 inches should be expected during the passage of a fully developed cyclone over coastal regions.

The duration of the hurricane winds depends on the size of the storm and its rate of movement. If the high winds extend over 100 miles and the storm moves 10 miles per hour, then the gales will last for ten hours. If the cyclone advances at 15 miles per hour the winds will last for less than

During a hurricane, such as this one in the West Indies, coastal areas are frequently lashed by heavy rains and high winds.

seven hours. The same consideration applies to the eye; the central calm may remain for only a few minutes or stay for one to two hours. Dissipation of tropical storms over the tropical oceans is rare. Most disturbances eventually enter the middle and high latitudes, where they are absorbed into the prevailing westerly circulation of those regions.

Tropical storms normally lose intensity when striking land, irrespective of latitude. Even passage over smaller islands of the tropics can result in great reductions of their strength. Within 24 hours after striking land, the winds of a severe hurricane may have been reduced to 20–30 miles per hour. Over flat ground, such as Florida, the dissipation is far slower than over rugged country. It should be noted, however, that tropical storms passing into the temperate zone occasionally encounter conditions favorable for regeneration as strong extratropical cyclones.

Life and Property Damage
The loss of life and property on tropical islands and the coastal areas of continents is caused by high winds and excessive rain. The pressure exerted by the air on solid objects (for instance, houses) is proportional to the square of the wind speed; an increase of the wind from 40 to 50 miles

per hour creates far less added danger to buildings, therefore, than a rise from 90 to 100 miles per hour. (In the first case the factor of increase is 1.6; in the second, 12.3.) Moreover, the resistance capacity of many structures appears to become exhausted rapidly when the winds exceed 75–80 miles per hour. In industrial and city areas, danger to industrial and electrical installations is great. Short circuits in the midst of a raging storm and the explosion of gasoline tanks have led to uncontrollable fires.

Some of the most disastrous losses of life and property have been caused by a sudden rising of the ocean and widespread inundations of low-lying poorly protected coastal areas. The abrupt increase of the water level, referred to as the storm wave or surge, is caused by the action of the wind on the water. The storm surge appears so quickly and is carried with tremendous force so far inland that often there is not time for the coastal inhabitants to rescue themselves.

The heavy rainfall often accompanying tropical storms frequently causes landslides in mountainous and hilly areas. Because of the great and sustained intensity of the precipitation the runoff of the water is extreme and produces rapid and excessive rises of the water levels of the rivers.

Hurricane Warning Services

In Australia a cyclone warning station was set up on Willis Island, off the Queensland coast, in 1921. Special hurricane forecast centers have been maintained by the U.S. Weather Bureau since 1935. Pioneer flights into a hurricane took place in 1943. Regular aerial hurricane patrols began in 1945, reporting location, characteristics, and movements of any likely disturbance. In 1955 the National Hurricane Research Project was started, and since then a great expansion of hurricane study and warning services has taken place.

Flights can now be made into, through, and above storms. Radar units are installed at suitable points to give warning of any storm within range; the characteristic spiral banding of dense clouds and rain makes cyclonic storms easy to identify. And satellites have greatly expanded surveillance.

IV. SHIPS AND OCEAN COMMERCE

For Western man the history of the ship begins in the eastern Mediterranean, where Egyptians plied the Nile River (and, later, the sea itself) on craft made of bundles of reeds. In the Mediterranean and along the shores of Asia the dugout canoe was the prototype of the square-rigged sailing ship and the Chinese junk respectively—both representing high points in the technology of using the wind as energy.

Without such ships, man would have remained a prisoner of the shoreline, his seagoing restricted to daylight cruises within sight of land. As the art of navigation kept pace with the capabilities of larger and stronger ships, man became at last a world citizen and developed a civilization whose prosperity and variety depended on ocean commerce.

Even in an age where the jet plane has taken over from the liner in carrying passengers across the oceans the world's merchant fleets continue to grow—the increase in tonnage since the end of World War II being about 300%. The future will see even larger fleets of bigger ships built to serve the international oil trade and, to a lesser degree, the trade in ore and other bulk cargoes.

8.
From Dugouts to Supertankers

During 8,000 years the technology of the ship has advanced from craft built of reeds and dugout canoes to supertankers —oil-carrying leviathans (some say monstrosities) that may reach a million tons displacement before the twentieth century is over. Yet there is a thread of constancy in the history of the ship; not everything changes. Canoes, both in the single-hulled form and the outrigger, are still paddled and sailed throughout the world for pleasure and commerce. Kayaks and coracles can still be found afloat. The Chinese junk, ungainly as it appears, is still one of the most splendidly efficient sailing vessels devised by man. The Tall Ships assembly during the U.S. Bicentennial Year in 1976 called forth an upwelling of emotion, compounded partly of nostalgia and partly of sheer admiration for the towering, graceful vessels. The love of ships is truly in man's blood.

Egyptian and Minoan

From rock drawings dating from 6000 B.C. in Egypt and from descriptions in legends and stories, we know that relatively large ships were first developed in the eastern Mediterranean. On the Nile River in Egypt ships were built of bundles of reeds, the ends of which were bound together and bent upward to form the bow and stern of the ship. This kind of construction was dictated not by choice but by the material available.

Further to the east, across the Red Sea, where there were large trees, early shipbuilders used a different method. They started with a canoe dug out from a stout log and graduated to building slanted sides fastened to a bow and stern boards to keep out the water and increase the carrying capacity. The result was a flat-keeled boat with square corners at the ends. Such ships were immortalized in rock drawings.

By 3000 B.C. the reed boats of Egypt were venturing into the Mediterranean as far as Crete and Lebanon to bring back logs and other materials. Because these ships had no keel, they were held in shape by a taut cable, running on deck from the bow to the stern, which could be tightened as required. They were rowed and were steered by long oars over the stern. Later, sails were devised to move the ships when the wind was from the stern, which in the Nile was an advantage because the wind normally blew upriver, so that the ships could sail up against the current and either pole or row down with the current.

By about 2000 B.C. in Crete, the Minoans had made an advance without which Western ship development would have ceased. This was the development of the keel to provide strength and stiffness to the ship's hull. The Minoan ships used a long keel with ribs and planking on the sides joined at the stem and stern.

Phoenician

The great merchants of the Mediterranean world, the Phoenicians of Tyre and Sidon, found that galleys were inefficient for trading voyages because the large crews needed were expensive to feed, and the long, narrow hull provided little space for cargo. The first merchant ships were descendants of the old Egyptian reed boats in that their hull form was broad and short. They were built up from a heavy keel and carried a single large square sail for propulsion. Such ships may have sailed around Africa, and it is known that they sailed in the Atlantic as far north as Britain to trade for tin.

Greek and Roman

The Greek galley developed from an open, undecked craft up to 100 feet (30 meters) long and driven by a single row of oars, 25 on a side, to the ships used in the Battle of Salamis (480 B.C.), which were about 150 feet (45 meters) long with an outrigger on which the oarlocks were fixed. The oars were arranged in two banks (biremes) or three banks (triremes). Larger galleys were tried but were found to be too cumbersome to maneuver. The final development of the war galley produced a ship of about 150 feet in length with a full deck or decks and a strong ram. They were called quinqueremes— a name for which the meaning is still in dispute.

The Romans brought little change in ships except the addition of the *corvus,* a bridge at the bows of the war galleys to accommodate boarding parties. Roman grain ships grew in size, reaching 90 feet in length. These ships could carry about 250 tons of cargo and more than 300 passengers. Such heavy oared ships required more sail to drive them as well as to help in maneuvering. Though Roman ships could still not sail into the wind, they were able to take the wind on the quarter (about 45° from dead astern), an important step forward. These ships proved their seaworthiness in regular commerce with the British Isles.

Oriental

While the peoples of the Mediterranean were developing ships from those of the Egyptians, China, with its vast land areas and poor road communications, was also turning to water for transportation. Starting with the dugout canoe the Chinese joined two canoes with planking, forming a square punt, or raft. Next, the side, the bow, and the stern were built up with planking to form a large, flat-bottomed wooden box. The bow was sharpened with a wedge-shaped addition below the waterline. The stern was built to a high, small platform, later called a castle in the West, so that in a following sea the ship would remain dry. In spite of what to Western eyes seemed an ungainly shape, the Chinese junk was an excellent hull for seaworthiness as well as for beaching in shoal water.

In rigging, the junk was far ahead of Western ships with a many-paneled sail that could be hauled about to permit the ship to sail somewhat into the wind. By the fifteenth century, junks had developed into the largest, strongest, and most seaworthy ships in the world. Not until about the nineteenth century did Western ships catch up in performance.

Northern

In the European north, where the seas were cold and unfriendly, the peoples of the Scandinavian countries developed still another form of ship. Because they also started from the log, some scholars have argued that in early times Minoans fleeing invaders had taught the northern people to build ships. In any case the first northern ships were similar to the Minoan ships. Because the northern ships had to weather higher seas, however, the Vikings developed double-ended ships, having both a sharp bow and a sharp stern, built high against following seas. The hull form in the center (amidships) was much broader than that of the galleys of the south. Overall there was a smooth, flowing curve from the high bow through the well-rounded midships to the high stern, a good design still used in lifeboats and whaleboats today.

Even more important was a northern merchantman, the *knorr*, broader and deeper hulled than a long ship and the first northern ship to sail into the wind. In about the four-

The Viking long ship, with both a sharp bow and a sharp stern, was used for raiding and warfare by the Norsemen between the seventh and the tenth centuries A.D.

teenth century the knorr developed into a standard merchant ship, the design of which governed northern European ship-building for more than four hundred years. This later version, the *cog,* was given a true stern rudder for better handling and a long spar, or bowsprit, extending forward. Modified by a built-up castle in the stem or stern to provide a platform for soldiers, the cog became the standard man-of-war.

Medieval Developments

Meanwhile in the Mediterranean a change in rigging had permitted ships to sail closer to the wind. Traders may have observed Chinese junks with their lug rig or the Arab dhows of the Indian Ocean, where the monsoon winds blew toward India in the summer and Africa in the winter. For this situation the Arabs had developed the dhow, with a long stem and a sharp bow to run well before the wind and a square sail with only a top spar. This sail could be placed so that the spar was nearly vertical, allowing the rest of the sail to lie near-ly in the fore-and-aft plane of the ship for sailing with the wind. It could also be placed horizontal to support the square sail for sailing before the wind. This rig became known as the lateen after an innovation that produced a triangular sail.

About the ninth century the Byzantines built ships with

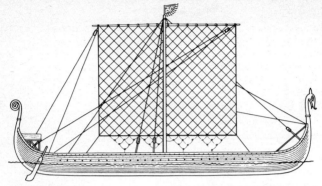

When William the Conqueror invaded England in 1066 he used vessels that were descendants of the Viking long ships.

the new lateen rig that could sail to within about 60° of the wind, giving them a great maneuvering and navigational advantage over earlier ships. This development was the final stage of the southern ship, which had inherited six thousand years of Mediterranean experience.

Full-Rigged Ships

In about the thirteenth century the sturdy square-sailed cogs of the north appeared in the Mediterranean and met the lateen-rigged ships of the south. Over the next years the features of the two types merged in the carrack, which became the prototype for the western European ocean ship. The carrack was a three-masted ship with carvel hull planking (smooth sides). It had the centerline rudder and the graceful rounded lines of the northern parent. Its rig was a mixture of north, south, and ancient Roman. By happy coincidence, at nearly the same time, the magnetic compass made its appearance, equipping the carrack with a fundamental navigational aid.

The swift evolution of the carrack into the classic ship that served as both warship and merchantman for the Western world consisted mostly of details. The drudgery of handling the large square sails brought forth sets of smaller sails on the forward masts, with the lower being the driving sail, called the course sails, then upper and lower topsails, resulting in the full-rigged ship.

Clippers

The last period of the wooden sailing ships produced some of the fastest and most beautiful ships of the entire era. The Industrial Revolution brought pressure for speed in shipping, while trade among Europe, North America, and the Orient was expanding, particularly in tea, which had become the staple beverage in England. Grown almost solely in China, tea was a seasonal crop, its leaves being picked each summer. Rivalry developed between ships to bring the first shipment each year to England and North America. As a result the sailing ship achieved its finest development in the form of the China clipper.

The word *clipper,* first applied to a class of small, swift Chesapeake Bay schooners and brigs, was used in 1833 for a larger ship being built in Baltimore (the *Ann McKim*), which became the prototype of a new type of ship for the North Atlantic packet service. Built for speed and stability to handle the greatest possible area of sails and to offer the least resistance to the water, the clippers had a radically new set of hull lines, a sharp cutwater at the bow widening gradually toward the midship section, giving actually a concave shape to the waterlines.

The British clipper ship *Cutty Sark* recorded consistently fast passage in all weather conditions.

Some of the clippers reached speeds of 21 knots, or 21 nautical miles per hour, and even averaged 16 to 18 knots for a full day's sailing. By the 1870s the Suez Canal had been opened, the transcontinental railroad was completed across North America, and the steamships were gaining dependability and acceptance. The day of the clipper ship was over barely thirty years after it started. With it ended the age of sail.

Steamboats

Though Robert Fulton is generally credited with the invention of the steamboat, it is well known that he had been preceded by several others. Salomon de Caus of France experimented with steam power for a boat as early as 1615, as did Denis Papin, a French Huguenot physicist, a century later. John Fitch demonstrated a steamboat in the United States in 1787, but he was unlucky in attracting backers and lacked the funds to continue development.

Fulton demonstrated his boat, the *Clermont,* on the Hudson River in 1807. The *Clermont* steamed up the Hudson under its own power at an average speed of five miles (eight kilometers) per hour. After a few improvements it was renamed the *North River* and went into regular service between New York City and Albany. Highly successful financially, it enabled Fulton to continue his work and produce many more ships.

For its first fifty years steam power was looked on with

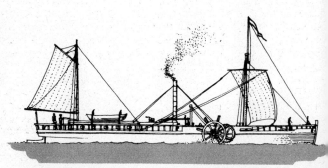

Robert Fulton's *Clermont,* constructed and demonstrated on the Hudson River in 1807, became a popular passenger boat between New York City and Albany.

mistrust, not totally unfounded in view of the wooden construction of the ships, yet the steam engines themselves were remarkably dependable, perhaps because of their simplicity. Nearly all ships of the period were equipped with sails as well as steam and relied mainly on sail to conserve their wood fuel supply. In later years the introduction of the steam turbine and reduction gearing met a continuing demand for greater speed and power.

From the introduction of steamships both the paddle wheel and the screw propellor were available for propulsion, and at first the paddle wheel predominated. The paddle wheel is, in fact, an efficient device and competitive even with modern propellors.

The victory of the screw propellor was signaled in a tug-of-war that the British Admiralty staged in 1845 between the H.M.S. *Rattler,* screw-propelled, and the *Alecto,* a merchant ship equipped with paddle wheels—the two ships being of about equal size and power. The *Rattler* towed the *Alecto* away at two and a half knots. Whether the paddle wheel would fare so badly at speed in an efficiency run was not determined, but from that day forward the screw propellor was favored. Nearly all ships are fitted with propellors today except for river steamers that are faced with shoal-water operation and some ships operating on sheltered lakes.

Transatlantic Liners

The changes in early steamships during the age of iron ships followed developments in power, propulsion, and hull materials. The rivalry for the record for the fastest passage of the Atlantic by steam spurred most of the developments in shipbuilding during the latter half of the nineteenth century, each company adopting new technology as fast as it proved practical.

By 1874 ocean liners of 5,000 tons had reached the speed of 16 knots and cut the Atlantic crossing time to seven days. By 1881 ships of 7,000 to 8,000 tons brought speeds of 20 knots. Steel had arrived as a hull material, and improved engines reduced fuel requirements by nearly 50%.

Between 1900 and 1914 all of the innovations in technology seemed to come into focus with the age-old principle that a larger, longer ship was easier to drive and more comfortable to ride. Ships grew to gigantic proportions. The largest of the prewar monsters was the German *Vaterland,* of 904-foot (276-meter) length and 54,000 tons. (Seized by the U.S. dur-

The first regular transatlantic steamship, the British *Great Western*, crossed the ocean in fifteen days on its maiden voyage in 1838.

ing World War I, converted to oil, refitted, and renamed the *Leviathan*, this ship dominated the Atlantic for years. It once set a new speed record of 27.48 knots for more than 25 hours.)

In 1929–30 the Germans launched the *Bremen* and the *Europa*, which, while moderate in size, had improved engineering and hull designs that gave them the transatlantic speed record. The next record holder was the giant 79,280-ton *Normandie*, which in 1935 reduced the transatlantic record to four days, three hours, and two minutes at an average speed of more than 30 knots. It used a turboelectric drive.

In the 1920s and 1930s the world's commerce was being hauled in many less glamorous ships, some with Scotch boilers and reciprocating engines. They were about 400 feet (120 meters) long and steamed at an economical 13–14 knots. The diesel engine had started to displace steam because fuel consumption and the crew requirements of the diesel made it more economical to operate, even though its maintenance costs were higher.

World War II Ships

World War II, with its tremendous production of new tonnage of all types, brought several important innovations. A military type of ship developed from a British prototype was introduced in several sizes during the course of the war. Its most widely used version was labeled the landing ship tank (LST), which could load or unload wheeled or tracked vehicles through a bow door, could transfer them to another deck through a ramp device, and could turn them around on a turntable. The great utility of this slow-moving, pedestrian-looking ship caused it to inspire many changes in ships of the postwar period.

The U.S. program to produce emergency ships got under way in April 1941; and the *Patrick Henry* was launched on September 27 of that year. In all, 2,610 Liberty (or Ec-2) ships were built. Many records were set in this effort, including the launching of a ship within ten days of the laying of the keel, with completion and delivery four days later. Altogether the U.S. shipbuilding effort in World War II produced 5,874 merchant-type ships of 57,205,407 deadweight tons.

After World War II the arrival of fast, dependable air

"France" (Compagnie Générale Transatlantique) approx. 60,000–70,000 tons, 1,035 ft

"Queen Elizabeth" (Cunard Steam-Ship Company, Ltd.) 83,673 tons, 1,031 ft

"Queen Mary" (Cunard Steam-Ship Company, Ltd.) 81,237 tons, 1,019 ft

"United States" (United States Lines, Inc.) 53,329 tons, 990 ft

The silhouettes of several post-World War II super passenger liners display their relative sizes. Though the *France* was the longest such ship in the world, the *United States* was the fastest.

travel across the oceans signaled the beginning of the end of the era of the super passenger liners. The speed differential between a jet aircraft and even the swiftest liners made performance differences between ships somewhat irrelevant. Significant postwar developments occurred with the development of containerships, tankers and supertankers, nuclear-powered ships, and hydrofoils.

Containerships

The military success of prepackaged shipments to overseas points and the rising costs of stevedore services and labor in general stimulated consideration of the use of standardized containers for shipping materials. Standard containers that fitted into cells created in containerships, on trailer trucks, and on rail cars were adopted. (These measure 20 by 8 by 8 feet or about 6 by 2.5 by 2.5 meters) The containers are fabricated of light, strong aluminum alloys, usually of corrugated construction to provide stiffness. These containers became the unit of transit in a complete transportation system from point of origin to destination.

Packed and sealed at the warehouse, the container is transmitted by road or rail to a port at which specially designed high-speed lifting cranes take it from the carrier either to temporary pierside stowage or directly to the containership. The ship is equipped with a cellular grid of below-decks compartments opening to the weather deck and designed to receive the containers and hold them in place until unloading.

At the port of destination, specially designed lifting gear removes the containers in a matter of hours and loads them onto trucks or trains or to temporary storage. In another few hours the ship can be filled with containers for another port and can be under way.

Other advantages of the containership are the low cost of the crew in port while loading and unloading, reduced pilferage and damage, better customer satisfaction, and greater facility of transshipping from sea terminal to land transportation. Furthermore, because each ship can make more trips than before, container fleets require fewer vessels.

Recent innovations include an increase in maximum size to 40 feet (12 meters) in length, with some ships able to carry large or small containers interchangeably. There are also refrigerated containers for perishables, open-top containers, and many other improvements.

Tankers and Supertankers

Perhaps the simplest ship to build and operate is the tanker. In essence, a tanker is a floating group of tanks contained in a ship-shaped hull, propelled by a machinery plant in the stern. Each tank is substantially identical to the next throughout the length of the parallel-sided middle body of the ship.

The first tanker, built in 1886, was the German *Gluckauf,* designed to carry oil in tanks against the ship's hull plating. (Before the *Gluckauf,* oil had been carried in barrels in ordinary merchant ships.) By 1900 the idea of the tanker was so well established that 99% of the oil carried at sea was carried in tankers.

Gradually, the size of oil tankers increased as the demand for the service grew and the need for economical operation to compete for cargo continued. The size of tankers built in the 1970s staggers the imagination. The Universe-class tankers, built in Japan, are of 326,000 tons deadweight. Dimensions are 1,132 feet (345 meters) in length and 175 feet (53 meters) in beam, with a loaded draft of 81 feet (25 meters), dwarfing the largest of the old ocean liners.

Complications arose with the introduction of such large ships; most of the harbors of the world are dredged to no more than 50 feet (15 meters) in the main channels, and special port facilities had to be arranged. One solution, used in Kuwait, where much oil is shipped, is to build an artificial island in deep water, connected to shore by a pipeline, to load and unload tankers.

Presumably, the length of tankers will ultimately be limited only by the strength of available materials. In the 1970s the monstrous Universe ships were surpassed by a new class of tankers ordered from Japan by a British firm and designed for 477,000 deadweight tons. A Netherlands company has developed an offshore buoy mooring and servicing system that will handle all ships now building or contemplated up to 1 million deadweight tons—three times as large as the largest now afloat.

Nuclear-powered Ships

From the end of World War II, when the power generation capability of nuclear energy was being developed, it was realized that, if a practical nuclear-power plant could be fitted into a submarine, a new type of ship could at last be realized

The Soviet nuclear-powered icebreaker *Lenin* was also built to serve as an Arctic weather station.

—a true submarine instead of merely a short-term submersible. A large number of such submarines have been built, with virtually unlimited underwater cruising range.

A few nuclear-powered surface naval ships have also been built. Civil applications of marine nuclear power, however, have been limited so far. The Soviet Union built a successful nuclear-powered icebreaker, the *Lenin*, in 1957, and in 1962 the potential of nuclear power for an ordinary merchant ship was explored when the *Savannah*, sponsored by the U.S. Atomic Energy Commission and the Maritime Commission, was delivered. A modern shelter-deck ship of 12,200 gross tons with accommodations for sixty passengers, the *Savannah* made about 20 knots on her 22,000-horsepower geared steam-turbine plant. Although *Savannah* performed reasonably well as a demonstration project, it could not compete with other dry-cargo ships and was never used commercially.

Hydrofoils

The search for speed on water has been frustrated by the combination of the resistance created by the ship in making waves and by the friction of water flowing past the hull. The combination of these factors makes the power demands of a ship at high speed prohibitive. One method of overcoming this situation is offered by the hydrofoil. This craft is designed so that the hull of the ship is lifted entirely out of the water as it gains speed and is supported on hydrofoils—wings shaped like those of an aircraft but much stronger and smaller. Because the density of water is about 600 times that of air, a relatively small lifting surface in water will lift as much as a large wing in air.

The first hydrofoil may have been described in a French patent application in 1897 by the Comte de Lambert, who drove a catamaran hull fitted with four transverse "hydro-planes." What was probably the first true hydrofoil was operated by Italian inventor Enrico Forlanini between 1898 and 1905.

Hydrofoils reached a pinnacle of performance and publicity when a boat built by Alexander Graham Bell and Casey Baldwin set the world's speed record in 1918 with a speed of 60 knots. The craft, the HD 4, was powered by two Liberty aircraft engines and was equipped with a set of ladder-type foils. In Germany during World War II craft of up to 80 tons and speeds of nearly 60 knots were built, but Allied bombs prevented this effort from reaching operational status. After the war, the United States, Canada, the Soviet Union, Britain, and Germany all launched development efforts.

By the early 1970s the technology was available to build and operate hydrofoils of up to 500 tons with speeds of from 40 to 50 knots. Several high-speed passenger ferries employed the hydrofoil principle; the *Meteor*, in the Soviet Union, had a capacity of 150 passengers. The U.S. Navy's *Plainview*, of about 300 tons, had a speed of more than 40 knots. Test craft have reached speeds in excess of 80 knots on foils under controlled conditions.

9.
Growth of Ocean Commerce

It has been said that commerce begins where civilization begins. Even the first great steps in the growth of civilization were dependent on the availability of essential materials, such as flint and metals, which usually had to be transported over long distances. The beginning phases of civilization known by such terms as the Bronze Age and the Iron Age were dependent on materials found only at a few localities and regularly carried over wide regions. In the near east and Europe, civilization at an early stage was based on the utilization of the dispersed resources of a whole continent and remained dependent for its preservation on the continuance of this trade. The history of commerce is closely connected with the development of the techniques of transportation and communication. Long-distance trading apparently developed first along desert routes over which comparatively large groups of men and beasts of burden could travel together in caravans, defending themselves against marauders. Oases were used as ports of call and depots. Caravan trade retained its essential characteristics for centuries. In the course of time, however, it became subordinate to commerce by sea routes.

The Ancient World

The first people to exploit the advantages of transporting bulk cargo by sea were the Phoenicians. From their bases on the Syrian coast they carried goods to Cyprus and Rhodes and then, step by step, found their way to the western Mediterranean and beyond. The original cities of Tyre and Sidon and the colonies they founded, of which Carthage became the chief, were true commercial centers. Glassware, textiles, and metal articles were exchanged for tin, copper, and silver in the west.

Athens exported olive oil, figs, honey, pottery, and small quantities of metal and textile goods. Its trade with the ports on the Black Sea was an early example of dependence for essential food supplies (mainly wheat) on regular communication by sea. The fortified harbor of Piraeus also attracted a considerable volume of trade, being used by the merchants of Asia Minor and Syria as a distribution center in their dealings with the rest of Greece and with the countries of the west. Greek commercial enterprise was offered new opportunities when the conquests of Alexander the Great opened the way into the heart of Asia. The consequent stimulus to long-distance trade was reflected in the growth of Antioch and Alexandria as great commercial seaports.

The series of events which led to the destruction of Carthage (146 B.C.) and the assertion of Roman supremacy over Greece revealed the possibilities of commercial development. When Augustus put an end to civil dissension and inaugurated a period of peace these possibilities were fully explored. The main currents of trade continued in the direction determined by the Greeks. The chief caravan routes from the east ended at Antioch, and the commodities thus secured were shipped from its port, Seleucia Pieria, to all parts of the Mediterranean. They were the traditional articles of trade—spices, drugs, silks, and other luxuries—that supplied the demand of the wealthier classes.

The commerce of Alexandria was of a more complicated nature. Oriental luxury goods from Arabia and India reached Egypt by way of the Red Sea. Augustus took steps to protect this trade by forcing the Arabs and Ethiopians to desist from piracy and by having the navigation canals repaired. The discovery of the periodicity of the monsoon winds of the Arabian Sea in about the middle of the first century A.D. made a direct voyage to India possible, eliminating the need to call at Arabian ports.

Rome became dependent on the importation of grain from Egypt, from which it shipped about 20 million bushels annually. Elaborate precautions were taken to safeguard the supply. There were many dangers. Ships that were not part of a convoy were in danger of being attacked by pirates. Weather conditions in the Mediterranean made winter sailing perilous. With favorable winds the voyage between Alexandria and Rome could be accomplished in eight or nine days. When winds were contrary, however, the recourse was to coast from point to point. Weeks could easily be consumed.

When the Roman Empire in the west collapsed under the successive blows of the barbarian invasions the volume of trade was greatly reduced. Commerce was virtually confined to the eastern Mediterranean, where Constantinople enjoyed preeminence as the capital of the east Roman or Byzantine empire. The rising Muslim tide swept over Egypt, and Alexandria itself capitulated in 640. Constantinople, however, did not fall into the hands of a Muslim conqueror until 1453. Until then it attracted to itself the commerce between Asia and Europe. From the fall of Rome in the fifth century to the age of the Crusades it was the great intermediary center of long-distance trade.

The Middle Ages

The heirs of Constantinople were the Italian trading towns. They had developed under the aegis of the Byzantine Empire, and they profited from its decline. Venice in particular rose to splendor in the Middle Ages. Situated amid the lagoons at the head of the Adriatic Sea, it was at first a place of refuge in the troubled days of the barbarian invasions. A position could hardly have been better chosen to serve as a transshipment point through which the trade of the Levant could pass into central Europe as conditions there became more settled.

From the early part of the fourteenth century a fleet of galleys was dispatched to the countries of the western Mediterranean, making its way by easy stages through the Strait of Gibraltar as far as the Low Countries. The voyage, usually annual, generally ended at Bruges, Belgium, the chief mart of northwest Europe. A ship might, however, detach itself to call at the British ports of Southampton, Sandwich, or London.

By this means such commodities as pepper, cloves, indigo, ginger, and other spices were carried to the west at a lower cost than if they had gone by the overland route. As a return cargo the galleys carried wool, hides, and metals that were then worked up in Italy for export to the east.

The fact that the Venetians found it worthwhile to make a direct sea voyage to the Low Countries shows that good markets for long-distance trade by sea had grown up by the fourteenth century. The peoples of northwest Europe had contributed to the process. The Norsemen found their way by river routes from the Baltic to the Black Sea and obtained supplies of oriental goods. By the eleventh century, German towns had taken the initiative; the merchants of Cologne were particularly active. The towns of northern Germany entered into agreements with one another to cooperate in suppressing robbery on land and piracy at sea.

The powerful Hanseatic League ultimately emerged from such understandings. It was a confederation of towns, mostly though not exclusively in Germany, formed to benefit their common commercial interests. They were successful in obtaining special trading privileges from other countries. There was a factory at Bergen, Norway, from which trade with Iceland could be carried on, and another at Novgorod, Russia, where goods were exchanged for Russian products. In London the league had its establishment called the Steelyard. Still more important was the position the league occupied in Bruges, where the merchants of northern Europe and the Mediterranean came into direct contact with each other.

From the Mediterranean to the Atlantic

The conquests of the Ottoman Turks in the fifteenth century threatened to close the route by which oriental goods had reached the Levant. Venice itself was involved in a series of wars with the Turks in the sixteenth century and suffered heavily from the exhaustion of its resources and the loss of territory. The question naturally arose whether the commodities could be obtained by some other route.

The pioneer work of Prince Henry of Portugal was rewarded by the rounding of the Cape of Good Hope by Bartolomeu Dias de Novais in 1488 and by Vasco da Gama's successful voyage from Lisbon to Calicut, India, in 1498. Meanwhile Columbus sought India by sailing west and found a new world lying across his path. These discoveries were destined to effect a revolution in commerce, but their consequences were not apparent for some time.

The Portuguese aimed at controlling for their own advantage the existing Indian trade routes to Africa, the Red Sea, the Persian Gulf, the Cambay ports, and the Spice Islands. The center of their power was Goa in Portuguese India, but they had important settlements at Hormuz, Persia, and at Calicut and Cochin, India. In 1580 the crowns of Portugal and Spain were united in the person of Philip II. This meant that the Portuguese possessions were at the mercy of the enemies of Spain. The position of the Spaniards in the new world had already been challenged by English sea captains. Spain had concentrated its main attention on the silver mines of Mexico and Peru. The treasure obtained in those countries by forced labor was carried by galleons to Europe and expended in buying commodities from other countries and in the conduct of wars.

In the last decade of the sixteenth century the English and Dutch turned their attention from the search for the northwest passage to the cape passage to India. An English expedition of 1591–94 reached the Indian Ocean, while a Dutch

Oceanica Classis

A drawing of one of Christopher Columbus's first ships was published in a book that announced his discoveries.

voyage of 1595 succeeded in getting a valuable cargo of spices from Bantam, Java, which became the site for the first Dutch settlement in the East Indies. These voyages were the beginnings of the great English and Dutch ocean commerce with Asia and their hegemony over the Indian subcontinent and the islands of the East Indies until modern times.

The strength of the Netherlands as a maritime power rest-ed primarily on the degree of organization it applied to the herring fishery, for this gave it experienced sailors and a commodity for which there was a great demand in the European markets. The fishing season was so arranged that a great fleet was kept constantly at sea and its wants supplied by other ships that returned with the herrings already salted and packed in barrels. Amsterdam, it was once said, was built on herring bones. Fishing led to improvements in shipping and gave the Dutch the proud position of being for a time the chief maritime carrier in the world.

Writing in 1665 Sir Josiah Child gave a list of trades that the English had lost—the Russian, the Baltic, the Spanish, that of the Spice Islands and the Far East, even that of Scotland and Ireland—all had fallen to the Dutch. In spite of English efforts to damage the Dutch carrying trade, it survived with little diminution into the eighteenth century.

With the colonization of America, trade flowed across the Atlantic. Routes sailed in order to take advantage of the prevailing winds were necessarily long and often involved triangular or even quadrangular voyages. As a result, cargoes were collected and exchanged en route, metalware being traded in Africa for slaves and ivory to be left in the West Indies for sugar, rum, and cotton, with return cargoes from America of tobacco and animal skins. The American colonies built up their own merchant fleet, at first principally to carry fish.

With the ending of the British East India Company's monopoly in trade with India in 1813, competition was renewed and speed became more important. The Americans, who had always built for speed, made the fastest times on the Far East runs. The great trade revival that followed the ending of the Napoleonic wars and the American War of 1812 emphasized the need for faster speeds and prompter deliveries in order to ensure profitable operations.

Modern Ocean Commerce

Technological advances in the late eighteenth and early nineteenth centuries—particularly the coming of steam and the building of ships of iron and, later, of steel—brought about changes that were to lead to the emergence of the world's merchant fleets as they existed up to World War II. Early in the nineteenth century the successful harnessing of steam for ship propulsion was exploited by traders who were quick to realize the advantages of speed. Yet the advantages of sail for long voyages on which steamships had to be able to carry large amounts of fuel, kept a considerable sailing cargo fleet alive into the twentieth century. World War I was the final blow to sail.

With the screw replacing the paddle wheel, the fitting of water tanks for ballast, and the great increase in coal-bunkering stations along the trade routes, the type of services provided by shipowners underwent a change. Before then the steamship had been built for definite, regularly scheduled services operating on defined sea routes, whereas bulk cargoes were mainly carried by ships chartered for the purpose. To these liner and chartered services a third was now added—tramping. The tramp cargo ship became available to transport cargoes between ports as required on a negotiated contract basis.

With the opening of the Suez Canal in 1869 and the consequent shortening of the sea route to India and the Far East by about 3,500 miles (5,600 kilometers), a great stimulus was given to world trade. Shorter voyages combined with the reduction in distance between bunkering stations enabled more of a ship's capacity to be given over to cargo. Consequently, one-third more traffic could be carried by the same vessels. As their coal-bunkering costs fell, steamers were able to successfully challenge the clipper. Shipowners were slow at first to take advantage of this new route, but by the 1880s the Suez Canal had a substantial impact.

The Panama Canal, opened in 1914, shortened the distance from the Atlantic to the Pacific by 7,000–9,000 miles (11,000 –14,000 kilometers), and had as great an effect as the Suez on world trade routes. The traffic flow through the Panama Canal is greater from the Atlantic to the Pacific than in the reverse direction, and the cargoes differ. The closing of the Suez Canal by the Arab-Israeli War in 1967 greatly increased traffic through Panama to the Far East. In 1976 nearly 44% of the westward traffic was petroleum products, coal, and coke. Ore, metals, and lumber constituted more than 21% of the total going in the other direction, with the remainder being made up of a great miscellany.

Between World War I and World War II world seaborne trade rose by 1929 to 35% above that of 1913 but declined during the depression of the early 1930s. Seaborne trade did not recover to the 1929 level until 1937. During that period, important technological changes had taken place, including

The 38,000-ton supertanker *W. Alton Jones*, launched in 1954, was built to carry a cargo of 336,000 barrels of oil.

conversion from coal to oil and the development of diesel motor ships. Steam turbines were favored for greater speed for long voyages but diesel was preferred for intermediate and short distances.

After World War II, shipping underwent several major changes resulting from rapid technological progress in ship construction and port handling and in the greater development of specialized ships, including the cellular vessel built to carry cargoes in standard containers. World trade expanded, and with it the volume of goods and the variety shipped increased and was accompanied by changes in directional flow. Shipping routes were altered to meet the new requirements. With competition from the air, passenger traffic declined sharply, particularly on the North Atlantic and on the long voyages to the Far East. Of all the changes, however, the most significant were the strides made in the construction of special-purpose vessels for specialized trades to handle the widening range of commodities often carried in entire shiploads.

In 1974, petroleum transport accounted for 45% of the world's total seaborne trade. The three principal bulk dry commodities—iron, coal, and grain—accounted for another large percentage of all movements.

Generally speaking, more manufactured goods were imported by three regions during this period: North America, Western Europe, and Japan. Fuel and raw materials imports to Europe and North America fell, but rose slightly in Japan. In the mid-1970s Japan was becoming the second most important region in terms of seaborne import tonnages, although its total imports by value were far behind those of North America.

International Conventions

Ships operate in an international field, the high seas, and are subject not only to the laws of the country in which they are registered and the laws of the country in whose territorial waters they may be but also to a series of international conventions, the principles of which are incorporated into the domestic legislation of most maritime countries. There has grown up, particularly in the years since the expansion of steam navigation, a body of international maritime law—"the common law of the sea"—that has been developed through international agreement. Nearly all the world's maritime countries, for example, have adopted the International Regulations for Preventing Collisions at Sea, originally based on British rules formulated in 1862 and made internationally effective after a series of meetings culminating in a conference in Washington, D.C., in 1889. These rules specify in great detail how ships must navigate in respect of each other, what lights must be shown, and what signals must be given in accordance with circumstances.

Similarly, the internationally accepted requirements for the protection and safety of life at sea, as far as the ship and its equipment are concerned, are embodied in the International Convention for Safety of Life at Sea. The sinking of the liner *Titanic* in 1912 gave rise to a general desire to raise the standards of safety of life at sea. Conventions setting safety standards were drawn up in 1914 and 1929; the most recent International Convention for Safety of Life at Sea became effective in 1952.

In 1958 the Inter-Governmental Maritime Consultative Organization, a specialized agency of the United Nations, came into existence. The purpose of this advisory organization was to promote international cooperation in maritime navigation. By late 1976, membership had grown to 99 and 1 associate member.

The UN proclaimed the 1970s an International Decade of Ocean Exploration, and research projects were begun on environmental quality, environmental forecasting, and sea-bed assessment. A series of international UN Conferences on the Law of the Sea, organized in 1958, continued to meet throughout the 1960s and 1970s to draft a convention creating a comprehensive international legal regime for the oceans and seabed.

The World's Merchant Fleets

By 1939, before the outbreak of World War II, world merchant shipping totaled more than 69 million tons gross. Despite enormous war losses the world fleet reached more than 80 million tons by 1948 and exceeded 100 million tons gross by 1955. In 1975 the world merchant fleet totaled more than 342 million gross registered tons, more than one-third of which consisted of tankers. Ore and bulk carriers totaled almost 62 million tons, and fully cellular container ships totaled more than 6 million tons gross.

Among the merchant fleets of the world, that of the Commonwealth, the world's largest until 1972, has declined steadily in importance in percentage terms. In 1886 the Commonwealth owned 63.6% of the mechanically propelled fleet of the world, but by 1939 its share had fallen to 30.7%. By 1975, though total tonnage amounted to more than 51 million tons gross, making the combined Commonwealth merchant fleet still the second largest in the world after Liberia's, its proportion of world tonnage had fallen to about 15%.

The geographical situation of Japan is favorable to the development of a large shipping industry, and that in fact is what Japan has built up during the last century. In 1971 Japan's merchant fleet was the third largest in the world (after the Commonwealth and Liberia), totaling more than 30 million tons gross. It reached 40 million in mid-1975. Japan's world import share by value of the three most important raw materials carried by tramps—iron ores, coking coals, and cereals—increased from 18% in 1963 to about 40% in 1974.

Although the overseas trade of Norway itself is not sufficient to maintain a large merchant fleet, Norwegian shipping grew to large proportions through the enterprise of Norwegian shipowners in the worldwide tramping trades. A number of liner groups also developed, but the recovery and expansion of the fleet after World War II to more than 26 million tons gross in 1975 (about half being tankers) was again due to the enterprise of tramp-tanker owners.

By mid-1975 the total seagoing merchant fleet of the United States consisted of more than 4,300 ships totaling more than 14.5 million tons gross. Of the oceangoing fleet, 327 vessels, totaling more than 5.2 million tons gross, were tankers. Container ships totaled more than 1.7 million tons. U.S. shipping on the Great Lakes reached a peak in 1934 and nearly matched that peak in 1956. Thereafter, prospects began to decline with the decrease of the iron-ore deposits in the area and with the completion of the Saint Lawrence Seaway, which opened the Great Lakes to intense competition from oceangoing foreign-flag vessels.

The merchant fleet of the Soviet Union registered a phenomenal growth after World War II, amounting in 1975 to more than 19 million gross tons—approximately equal to that of the United States. One-fifth were tankers. A program was announced in 1971 for the construction of container ships for both international and coastal trade. The Soviet Union is experimenting with gas-turbine-engine ships; one, the *Paris Commune*, built in 1968, had by 1971 successfully sailed more than 70,000 miles (110,000 kilometers) and carried 150,000 tons of cargo across the Atlantic. Other countries having merchant fleets of more than 5 million tons are France, Germany, Greece, Italy, the Netherlands, Spain, and Sweden.

Liberia and Panama are both countries with "flags of convenience." In 1975 the Liberian fleet was the largest single-flag fleet in the world, totaling more than 65.8 million tons gross. The Panamanian flag flew over 13.6 million tons gross. Of the Liberian fleet nearly 65% consisted of tankers, with the remainder dry-cargo ships or bulk carriers engaged in international tramping; 40% of the Panamanian fleet also consisted of tankers.

The fleet of the People's Republic of China exceeded 1 million tons gross for the first time in 1971. That figure had almost tripled by 1975.

10.
Sea Power and Naval Warfare

Throughout the course of recorded history a tremendous amount of the energy (and sometimes genius) that man directed toward the ocean was channeled into the development of fighting ships and naval tactics. That this should have been the case was mandated by the political and commercial rivalry of the great powers—Greece and Persia, Rome and Carthage, Great Britain and Spain, Great Britain and Holland, Russia and Japan, and the United States and Japan. More than once, the course of history was decided by a sea battle. The command of the ocean often implied the command of the land as well. Furthermore, the necessity of the naval strategist to achieve the greatest possible mastery of the ocean frequently led, often by a circuitous route, to naval leadership in global exploration and scientific discovery. James Cook's magnificent voyages of discovery were made while he was a captain in the Royal Navy. H.M.S. *Challenger*, the first oceanographic survey ship, was a converted corvette manned by naval officers and men. Matthew Fontaine Maury carried out his pioneer work while a U.S. Navy lieutenant in charge of the Depot of Charts and Instruments. Jacques-Yves Cousteau, whose invention of aqualung diving apparatus revolutionized man's relation with the sea, is a *capitaine de corvette* in the French Navy.

Sea Power

The main purpose of sea power has always been to protect friendly shipping from enemy attack and to destroy or hinder the enemy's shipping. According to a time-honored phrase it has aimed at "using the sea for oneself and denying its use to the enemy." When one belligerent or the other has virtual control of surface shipping in portions of the seas, the situation has traditionally been known as "command of the sea." In a great naval war, each side may command different areas of the sea, but large areas may be so generally in dispute as not to reflect a condition of command at all.

There are five major functions of sea power in wartime. It protects the movement over water of military forces and supplies to coastal areas where they may be landed and used against enemy forces. It also protects from enemy attack the friendly shipping that carries raw materials and industrial goods that support a war economy. It prevents the enemy from using the sea to transport its own military forces. It exerts pressure on the enemy by preventing the importing of commodities necessary for the war effort. Naval forces can also be used to bombard land objectives—a function that grew enormously in importance in the twentieth century.

Beginnings of the World Navies

The first warships ever recorded sailed on the Nile River. Hieroglyphics recount the dispatch of forty armed ships to Byblos on the Phoenician coast in about 2900 B.C. to buy cedarwood (from the famous cedars of Lebanon) to build ships. The development of the Egyptian war galley was essentially a process of modifying a merchant hull. In the twelfth century B.C. planks were fitted to the gunwales to protect the rowers, and a small fighting top, built high on the mast, accommodated several archers. Some galleys carried a projecting ram, well above the waterline, that may have been designed to crash through the gunwale of a foe, ride up on deck, and swamp or capsize the enemy ship.

By about 2000 B.C. Crete had evolved into a naval power exercising effective control of the sea in the eastern Mediterranean. Little record exists of Minoan sea power, yet these maritime people are known to have had an organized navy that cooperated with Egypt in suppressing piracy. Sometime during the second millennium B.C., fast fighting craft developed both to prey on and to protect maritime trade and coastal cities. This "long ship" was narrower, faster, and more agile than the tubby cargo ship, which was called a "round ship."

During the Phoenician domination of the Mediterranean, they appear to have built ships primarily for trading but with a capacity to fight effectively if necessary. Because the ram was the principal weapon, fine lines and great rowing power were important in providing speed for the decisive shock of battle. Coins of Sidon and sculptures of Assyria show the staggered-bank oar arrangement that the Phoenicians probably introduced.

The earliest warships built by the Aegean peoples may have been large dugouts, perhaps 65 feet (20 meters) long, fitted with outriggers for stability. They and their successors for centuries were used more to carry attack personnel than to fight at sea. No mention is made in the *Iliad*, for instance, of sea warfare. Even the pirates of the time were sea raiders, seeking their booty ashore like the later Vikings.

The first Greek galleys mounted their oars in a single bank and were undecked or only partially decked. They were fast and graceful with high, curving stem and stern. In Homeric times some carried an *embolon*—a beak or ram—that became standard in succeeding centuries.

In the battle of Salamis (480 B.C.) an outnumbered Greek fleet engaged a Persian squadron in the channel between the island of Salamis and the mainland. The Greeks engaged the enemy fleet in the narrow channel and proceeded to ram the Persian ships, which fell into disorder in the narrow space as reinforcements pressed up from behind. The Greek victory was decisive at sea, for the Persian navy never tried to reverse the verdict of Salamis.

The galley rowers in the ancient world, and into early Roman times, were free crewmen rather than slaves. The captain of a Greek trireme was usually a wealthy man, a political appointee who could afford to fit out and operate the warship for a year. The navigator was an experienced seaman. A voyage usually consisted of short hops from island to island or headland to headland. Even the largest triremes put into shore and beached, stern first, for the night, resuming the passage in the morning, weather permitting.

As Rome expanded southward, its interests collided with Carthage's ambitions in Sicily, leading to the First Punic War, which began in 264 B.C. Unlike their seafaring opponents, the Romans were not a naval power. When in the fourth year of the war Carthage sent a fleet against Sicily, Rome realized its fatal disadvantage and moved to remedy it.

The Greek city-states Rome had conquered had long seagoing experience. Employing the subjugated shipbuilders and learning also from the foe, Rome built a fleet of triremes and quinqueremes, the latter patterned after a Carthaginian warship that had grounded on Roman territory. While galleys were being built, oarsmen trained on dummy rowing benches ashore.

The Romans took land warfare to sea and forced the Carthaginians to fight on Roman terms. Each Roman galley had fitted in the bow a hinged gangplank with a grappling spike or hook in the forward end, thus providing a boarding ramp. They added many more marines to the crews than warships usually carried. Later Roman warships carried catapults and ballistae to serve as "artillery," and it was under their fire that

The Roman triremes of the third century B.C. were manned by slaves who were chained to three massive banks of oars.

Julius Caesar's legions landed in England.

Early Roman warships were large. To escort merchant-men and combat pirates Rome found need for a lighter type, the *liburnian*. Probably developed by the pirates themselves, this was originally a light, fast unireme—a galley with one bank of oars. The Romans added a second bank. In the Battle of Actium (31 B.C.) Octavian's skilled fleet commander, Agrippa, used his liburnians to good effect.

With the breakup of the western Roman Empire, naval organization and activity in the west decayed. In the eastern Roman Empire, however, the need for sea power was well appreciated. During the eleven centuries that the Roman Empire centered on Constantinople, the Byzantine rulers maintained a highly organized fleet. Their original type of warship was the liburnian.

War Vessels in Northern Europe

Like the Homeric Greeks the Vikings at first made no distinction between war and cargo ships, the same vessel serving either purpose. Later, however, they built larger ships specifically designed for war. By A.D. 1000 they sailed three categories of these: those with less than 20 thwarts (40 rowers), those with up to 30 thwarts, and "great ships" with more than 30. The latter, considered the battleships of the time, were expensive and unhandy. The middle group, maneuverable and fast, proved most valuable.

These long ships played an important role in exploration (reaching Greenland and America before Columbus), in the consolidation of kingdoms in Scandinavia, and in far-ranging raids and conquests. It was in them that the Norsemen early invaded the British Isles and established themselves in Normandy, whence their descendants under William the Conqueror crossed the Channel in 1066.

The employment of guns afloat, bringing a slow but progressive revolution in warship construction and naval tactics, had its first small beginning by the fourteenth century in the English, French, Spanish, and other navies. Most of these guns were relatively small "man-killers" located in the castles fore and aft. Later, heavier guns were added.

Henry VII of England created the first true oceangoing battle fleet. The "king's ships" carried many guns but most of the impressively large numbers were small breechloaders. Then Henry VIII initiated gunports in English warships, a development that was to have a far-reaching effect on man-of-war design and, indeed, on world history. Henry's introduction of gunports, at first low in the waist of the ship and afterward along the full broadside, made possible the true heavy-gun warship.

The coming of mighty men-of-war, like the 1514 *Henry Grâce à Dieu* (or "Great Harry"), did not mean the immediate end of oared warships. In fact, some types of galleys and oared gunboats continued to serve into the nineteenth century. Venice had galleys when conquered by Napoleon. Throughout the eighteenth century Russia and Sweden employed galleys and, toward the end of that period, oared gunboats. Russian oared gunboats were built in 1854 and engaged in action that year. The United States employed "row galleys" in the War of 1812 and in the Mexican War of 1846–48.

The climactic action of the age of oar was Lepanto, fought off Greece in 1571, in which a combined European fleet defeated the Turkish fleet in an action that differed little from traditional galley warfare. There were two exceptions. First, galleys carried guns, and second, the European line of battle included six Venetian galleasses, a cross between a ship and a galley, having both rowers and lateen sails.

A second critical sea battle was fought later in the century. When the Spanish Armada arrived off the coast of England in 1588 the British sought and fought a naval battle with ship-killing guns rather than the conventional engagement

The H.M.S. *Victory*, launched in 1765 with 100 guns, served as Lord Nelson's flagship at the battle of Trafalgar in 1805.

of the past that concentrated on killing men, ramming, and boarding. With superior ability and long-range culverins they punished the invading fleet outside the effective range of the heavy but shorter cannon the Spanish favored. This historic running battle of July 1588 closed one era and opened a greater one of big-gun sailing navies.

Ships of the Line

The late Elizabethan galleon that began the true fighting ship of the seventeenth and eighteenth centuries reached its culmination in England's *Prince Royal* of 1610 and the larger *Sovereign of the Seas* of 1637, along with similar great ships in other European navies. These floating fortresses became standardized according to the number of guns carried. The frequent hard-fought battles of the seventeenth century between fleets closely matched in size and skill, particularly in the Anglo-Dutch wars, led to the column formation of heavy warships known as *line ahead*, a tactical concept that survived until modern times.

Frigates, faster and more lightly armed than ships of the line, and smaller vessels undertook blockade, escort, commerce raiding, and other duties. (The U.S.S. *Constitution*, the only sailing frigate still under commission in the U.S. Navy, is the best-known example of its type.) Converted merchantmen, such as John Paul Jones's *Bonhomme Richard,* often took part in combat.

Steam and Iron

As the Industrial Revolution unfolded in the nineteenth century, the age of wood and sail gave way to that of steam and iron in navies as well as in the world's merchant fleets. Phenomenal changes took place in nearly every aspect of warship design and naval operations and tactics. These changes ended the reign of the majestic ship of the line by the mid-1800s but another half-century elapsed before it was clear what form her replacement as the backbone of the fleets would take.

These nineteenth-century changes may be summarized under two headings: construction and armament. Changes in the construction, design, and propulsion of naval ships paralleled the changes made by the merchant ships. In armaments the principal change was the development of breech-loading rifles firing explosive shells (rather than solid shot).

The U.S. Civil War produced several spectacular developments, including pioneer submarines, the first aircraft carriers (to handle balloons for observation), and the torpedo boat, one of several means the Confederates explored in trying to break the Northern blockade. These little craft, called Davids, had weak steam engines and mounted a torpedo lashed to a spar projecting from the bow. They frightened the blockaders and might have sunk a wooden ship, but the one successful attack struck the armored *New Ironsides.* The explosion caused considerable damage, requiring shipyard repairs, but did not lift the blockade.

Ironclad warships were crucial, perhaps decisive, in the North's victory. Partial ironclads appeared early on the western rivers and spearheaded General Ulysses S. Grant's victories in 1862. Most memorable of the combats was the duel between the U.S.S. *Monitor* and the C.S.S. *Virginia* (formerly the U.S.S. *Merrimack*). When the federal forces lost Norfolk Naval Shipyard in April 1861 they burned several warships, including the heavy steam frigate *Merrimack.* The Confederates raised *Merrimack,* installed a ram and slanting casemates made from railroad track over thick wooden backing, and renamed her *Virginia.* The *Monitor,* less than a third the size of the *Virginia,* had a boxlike iron hull supporting an iron-plated wooden raft on which revolved the turret.

The battle of the two ironclads off Hampton Roads ended in a draw with neither ship seriously injured, but the repercussions swept the world. Less than a month after the celebrated duel, Great Britain ordered the 131-gun ship of the line, *Royal Sovereign*, to be cut down, armored, and fitted with turrets. Only three and a half weeks later the Royal Navy laid down its first iron-hulled turret ship.

Prophet of Sea Power

The name of Alfred Thayer Mahan, who as a young naval officer fought in the Civil War, became synonymous throughout the world with the doctrine of the strategic importance of sea power. An indefatigable student with a prodigious memory, Mahan steeped himself in the strategy of Napoleon and Lord Nelson and made critical analyses of the conclusive battles of the world, both on sea and land.

The Influence of Sea Power Upon History, 1660–1783, which was published in 1890 after Mahan had served as president of the Naval War College, was inspired by a conviction that the historic significance of the control of the sea had never been fully revealed. This and succeeding works were widely acclaimed by naval men, statesmen, and scholars and have been credited with stimulating the growth of navies between 1900 and 1914. No previous writer had so convincingly argued the case for the dominating influence of sea power.

Mahan, who excelled as a strategist rather than as a tactician, attempted chiefly to make clear the paramount importance of the sea as a decisive factor in history. He analyzed the elements of sea power in all its bearings—military, national, territorial, and commercial. He stressed the interdependence of the military and commercial control of the sea and held that commerce dominates war.

The World Wars

As the nineteenth century turned into the twentieth, the trend toward the all-big-gun, heavily armored battleship became clear. The lessons of the Spanish-American (1898) and Russo-Japanese (1904-05) wars were incorporated in the British *Dreadnought*, completed in 1906, which gave its name to an era of naval design. *Dreadnought* had ten 12-inch guns, turbine drive, and a speed of 21 knots.

The battleship saw little combat in World War I as compared to its predecessor, the ship of the line, and as compared

Two turn-of-the-century steel battleships, the *Minneapolis* and the *Columbia*, reflected the U.S. Navy's "New Look."

to the role it was destined to play in World War II. Yet World War I was in many ways the zenith of the battleship's influence. Despite submarines, aircraft, and destroyers the outcome of the war still hinged upon control of the sea by the battleship. Had superiority in battleships passed to Germany, Great Britain would have been lost, and the Allies would have lost the war.

The one moment when this might have happened was the single large-scale clash of battleships, the Battle of Jutland. Fought in May 1916 in mist, fog, and darkness, the British advantage in battleships was decisive. Germany turned to the submarine as a means of countering the Allied blockade.

The largest battleships built in the era between the two wars were the Japanese *Musashi* and *Yamato*. Displacing 70,000 tons, mounting 18.1-inch guns, with armor capable of withstanding projectiles of equal caliber, these two giants were never surpassed in battleship construction.

Although battleships performed many useful functions

Huge landing ships were used by the U.S. Navy during World War II to get troops and equipment ashore quickly.

during World War II, the era of the battleship was clearly at an end. The sea war in the Pacific, particularly, was dominated by the aircraft carrier.

Carriers played a dominant role in every aspect of the war at sea. The Pacific conflict began with the Japanese strike against Pearl Harbor in Hawaii and ended with U.S. and British carriers operating with impunity against the Japanese homeland. In between, the Battle of the Coral Sea (May 1942) was the first in history in which opposing fleets fought without ever coming in sight of each other. A month later, off Midway Atoll, carriers again played the decisive role in the U.S. victory.

The Battle of Midway reinforced a conviction already clear, especially from British operations in the Mediterranean, with and without air support, that control of the sea now also meant control of the air over the sea. For the rest of the war this axiom ruled with increasing force.

World War II was also to a great extent a submarine war. The new submarines were larger and faster, could dive deeper, and had longer endurance than their World War I predecessors—and they carried more powerful torpedoes. The fall of the Low Countries and France in May 1940, providing long, open coastline for submarine bases close to British shipping routes, enabled a handful of German U-boats to become highly effective. Although Germany put a tremendous effort into belatedly building up its submarine fleet, massive antisubmarine measures defeated its usefulness.

Both the United States and Japan made extensive use of submarines in attack roles in the Pacific. As the war progressed, U.S. submarines played a key role in the air-naval blockade of the Japanese home islands. They sank many warships and were responsible for 55% of Japan's merchant ship losses.

Sea Power in the Nuclear Age

Perhaps the most significant development in the years after World War II has been the evolution of the nuclear-powered submarine of virtually unlimited cruising range and its mating with the ballistic missile. In 1959 the United States launched the nuclear-powered *Halibut* as the world's first submarine exclusively designed to fire guided missiles. While working with guided missiles the U.S. Navy had begun the development of an even more significant naval weapon, the ballistic missile. In December 1959 the complex and power-

The *Nautilus*, the U.S. Navy's first nuclear-powered submarine, was launched in 1954 and was 319 feet long.

ful fleet-ballistic-missile submarine U.S.S. *George Washington* was commissioned, constituting a weapons system generally said to be without parallel for power, accuracy, concealment, range, and effectiveness. Other major navies—including those of the Soviet Union and China—launched similar vessels.

Though the future of navies is unclear it is possible to speculate on the basis of current trends. Manned-satellite space stations may come into use to perform or monitor naval missions. Unmanned satellites will also become more widely used. Advances in vertical- and short-takeoff-and-landing planes will cause a proliferation in numbers and kinds of warships carrying high-performance supersonic planes. As a consequence, super aircraft carriers may have reached their maximum size.

The Soviet Union, China, and other countries will begin or continue light-carrier programs. Helicopters will become widely used for such missions as antisubmarine warfare, reconnaissance, enemy-missile warning, and midrange guidance of friendly missiles.

The principal menaces to ships will continue to be undersea weapons and long-range missiles from ships and planes. Antimissile systems and weapons will grow in complexity, speed of reaction, and effectiveness. Antiballistic-missile ships will appear, capable of intercepting hostile missiles over the ocean. Ballistic missiles will probably go into some surface ships.

Hydrofoils and air-cushion or surface-effect war vessels will make striking advances in size and usefulness. Nuclear-propulsion plants will become smaller and cheaper, though remaining costly for initial installation.

Submarines will run faster, quieter, and deeper and will be armed with larger, longer-range missiles. Measures to combat them will include super-quiet attack submarines, helicopters on small ships, other airborne efforts, distant-detection devices, and many more advanced weapons.

V. BIOLOGY OF THE OCEAN

The fossil record shows that a rich and diverse marine fauna has persisted on the Earth since the beginning of the Cambrian period (at least 570 million years ago). The present oceanic fauna—clearly and smoothly traceable from that period—is incomparably richer than the fauna of any lake or river.

The living creatures of the ocean range from microorganisms that are essential links of the oceanic food chain to great whales that may reach a weight of 150 tons. Fish are found in every possible marine habitat, from the nutrient-laden upwellings off the continental coasts to the darkest abysses of the ocean basins. Evolution has created more diversity among fish than among any other class of vertebrates.

Fish are important to man because they represent a major source of protein for his nourishment; the great marine mammals are important to him because they represent his closest relatives that live in the sea, breathing air as he does and bearing their young alive. The great whales and the dolphins in particular continue to excite man's interest and admiration even as they risk extinction at his hands.

11.
Life in the Ocean

The ocean contains a vast assortment of living things, including the smallest and the largest that inhabit the world. The smallest life forms that can definitely be called living are the bacteria that perform the important function of decomposing the dead bodies of larger organisms, which then release their elementary substances as primary nutrients for plant growth. Plant life includes the algae, the seaweeds, and the flowering plants such as the eelgrasses and the salt-marsh grasses. The animal kingdom presents a spectacular array of forms and sizes, from the worms, mollusks, and crustaceans that teem on the ocean bottom to reptiles, birds, fish, and mammals. The vertebrates range from tropical fish less than an inch long to the great blue whale. Marine biology is the science that deals with these animals and plants, both those that live in the sea and those that depend directly on bodies of salt water for food and other necessities of life. In the broadest sense it attempts to describe all vital phenomena pertaining to the myriads of living things that dwell in the vast oceans of the world. Some of its specialized branches concern natural history, taxonomy, embryology, morphology, physiology, ecology, and geographical distribution. Knowledge of marine biology is essential to certain aspects of human welfare. Intelligent regulation of the commercial marine fisheries would be impossible without a thorough understanding of the biology of commercial fish. The prevention of fouling of ships depends on the knowledge of factors that interfere with biological processes of fouling organisms. Survival at sea on life rafts and lifeboats often depends on using various kinds of marine life for both food and water. Most importantly, the rapid increase in the human population of the world has pointed to the need for greater use of marine products, which may be made available through contributions of the study of marine biology.

Benthos, Nekton, and Plankton
The marine environment is divided into arbitrary zones for means of convenience, and the organisms are classified into categories determined by habitat and locomotive behavior.

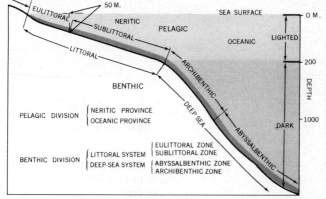

For man's convenience, the marine environment is arbitrarily divided into zones.

The two main divisions into which the ocean's living creatures are divided are the benthic and the pelagic. The benthic division consists of the entire deep sea bottom; the pelagic division, all the overlying water. All organisms that burrow through the mud, attach to solid surfaces, or crawl on the bottom are ecologically classified as living in the benthos. Organisms inhabiting the pelagic water are classified as nekton if they are strong, active swimmers and as plankton if they are weak swimmers or passive drifters.

Planktonic plants such as diatoms, photosynthetic dinoflagellates, and other floating algae are known as phytoplanktons. Planktonic animals, which include a host of drifting forms, comprise the zooplankton.

Life on the Sea Floor

The benthic division is divided into a littoral (coastal) system that extends from the shore to a depth of 200 meters and a deep-sea system extending down to the greatest depths. The littoral system may be further subdivided into a eulittoral zone, extending from the high-tide mark to the 50-meter contour, and a sublittoral zone, to the edge of the continental shelf. (The 50-meter depth is chosen because it represents approximately the greatest depth at which attached plants can grow.)

Barnacles are marine crustaceans that attach themselves to rocks, ships' hulls, driftwood, or to the bodies of larger sea creatures.

The kinds of things that grow in the littoral system depend to a considerable extent on the type of bottom and on the degree of exposure to wave action. Exposed sandy coasts generally have sparse populations, especially between the tide lines, and the few organisms inhabiting wave-swept rocky shores are generally firmly cemented to the substratum.

Protected bays and inlets often develop rich populations. Protected rocky shores are generally covered with seaweeds, mussels, and barnacles—with various kinds of crabs and worms crawling among them. Sandy and muddy bottoms teem with burrowing mollusks, worms, and echinoderms in localities where headlands and projections protect the environment from violent wave action.

The sublittoral zone, which receives a considerable amount of organic matter from the shoreward area and from the waters above, is particularly rich in animal life. It is there that important ground fisheries are located.

More than 90% of the ocean bottom is included in the deep-sea system. A detectable amount of light penetrates the shallower (archibenthic) zone, but it is in such reduced amounts that no plant growth can occur. Beyond the 1,000-meter contour the abyssal-benthic zone remains in perpetual darkness. The entire deep-sea system depends on food produced in the upper lighted zone; this food drifts downward in limited quantities, restricting the numbers and kinds of animals that can depend upon it for existence. Most deep-sea animals are therefore small and inconspicuous.

Life in the Open Ocean

The pelagic division may be divided into the neritic province, which overlies the littoral area, and the oceanic province, which occurs over the deep-sea system. The entire neritic province receives sunlight and may develop rich blooms of phytoplankton, aided by contributions of nutrient salts from the nearby land and the shallow bottom. The zooplankton, which feeds on the phytoplankton, is characterized by the presence of a number of temporary forms, including the

Plankton is composed largely of microscopic marine plants and animals that drift under the influence of sea currents. In time, it may become an important source of human food.

larval stages of benthic animals. These are scarce in the oceanic province because of their distance from adult populations and also because of the scarcity of such animals in the deep-sea system.

The upper illuminated section of the oceanic province is known as the upper pelagic. There the phytoplankton may develop in abundance in places where oceanographic features bring up nutrient salts from the deeper waters below. Animal life may become so abundant that tuna and other pelagic fish may be profitably pursued. In the unlighted abyssal-pelagic zone the animal populations become sparse. The fish of this region are generally small, dark in color, and often equipped with light-producing organs.

Adaptation to Life in the Sea

The principles of general physiology of marine organisms are essentially the same as those that apply to freshwater and terrestrial organisms. All living things extract substances from their surroundings to provide materials for growth and for energy to maintain the processes of life.

In the plant kingdom the marine bacteria and microscopic algae reproduce by simple cell division. Favorable conditions may increase the rate of reproduction to such an extent that dense local accumulations known as "blooms" may occur. Abnormal blooms of certain poisonous dinoflagellates are not uncommon in the warmer seas where, as "red tides," they color the water and kill vast quantities of fish with their toxic secretions. These substances are of such virulence that shore resorts are at times made uninhabitable because respiratory irritations result when these poisonous substances are transferred to the air by breaking waves.

The life histories of marine animals are remarkably varied. Most sedentary forms reproduce sexually by liberating eggs and sperm into the water, where fertilization takes place. Typically, this is followed by a larval stage with the swimming larva quite unlike the adult. After a free-swimming existence, a period of days or weeks, the larva undergoes metamorphosis and assumes the adult form. Fertilization is internal among the majority of the crustaceans. The younger grow by molting, or shedding their shells, and pass through a number of successive larval stages before the adult form is attained.

As a rule the reproductive and developmental patterns of

marine animals fall into one of three general categories: internal fertilization, with parental protection of the early stages of development, the offspring numbering in the hundreds or less, as in certain gastropods; internal or external fertilization, with some provision for the early helpless stages, the offspring numbering in the thousands, as in many bottom-dwelling crustaceans; and external fertilization, with no provision for protection during the early stages, the offspring numbering in the millions, as in most mollusks, echinoderms, and many fish. (Mollusks are shelled animals —including chitons, snails, and the bivalves—but also include the squids and octopuses. Gastropods are the class of mollusks comprised of snails, limpets, whelks, and slugs. Echinoderms include the starfishes, sea urchins, and sea cucumbers. Crustaceans include lobsters, shrimp, and crabs.)

The type of fertilization determines to a considerable degree the extent to which populations of any animal may fluctuate from time to time. Certain snails lay small numbers of eggs in resistant capsules that protect the embryos until they become well enough developed to cope with their environment. Populations of such snails tend to remain relatively constant, with only gradual fluctuations over long periods of time.

Many of the bottom-dwelling crustaceans fertilize the eggs internally and attach the fertilized eggs to special appendages. The eggs are then carried on the mother through the early stages of development and are finally hatched as free-swimming larvae in an advanced stage. To ensure survival in the precarious free-swimming state the eggs usually number from the hundreds to the tens of thousands.

Most mollusks, echinoderms, and many commercial species of fish produce millions of eggs per female. These are fertilized externally and then are abandoned to fend for themselves through a prolonged period of helpless developmental stages. Survival during this period depends on the presence or absence of predators, the strength and direction of currents, and the suitability of the physical and chemical factors of the environment. So many factors or combinations of factors may influence the survival of each generation that populations of organisms with this mode of reproduction tend to exhibit extreme variations from one year to the next. Occasionally circumstances may permit such a high degree of survival of a single generation that its constituents may outnumber all other members of the population for several years. Such a generation is known as a dominant-year class and is of considerable importance to the commercial fisheries.

Maintaining Saltwater Balance

The water content of living matter and the concentration of various mineral salts must be maintained within narrow limits. Marine organisms manage this maintenance in a number of ways.

Most naked or thinly covered marine organisms have little difficulty in coping with their environment because the composition of their blood approximates that of seawater with respect to the major salts. They are thus able to carry out their living processes without expending large amounts of energy in concentrating or eliminating water and mineral substances.

The blood of many of the fish, however, is less concentrated than seawater, and special mechanisms are necessary to prevent loss of water through the body membranes by osmosis. In most fish the walls of the digestive tract are permeable to solutions of mineral salts, so that seawater with its salts ingested by these species can pass into the bloodstream. Special organs on the gills extract the excess mineral salts from the blood and excrete them into the waters outside the body. The salt concentration of the blood is thereby reduced to an optimal level.

Certain species of cartilaginous fish (sharks, skates, and rays) accomplish the task of regulating their salt concentrations in a different fashion. Instead of expending energy in secreting salts against the osmotic gradient, they conserve their nitrogenous wastes in the form of urea, which is retained in the blood in concentrations sufficient to make it the osmotic equivalent of seawater.

A number of crustaceans that invade the variable dilute waters of the estuaries are faced with a problem of surviving in a medium that is less concentrated than their blood. Consequently water flows into their bodies by osmosis. These forms are generally protected over most of the body surface by impermeable shells, and the excess water entering through the reduced permeable area is eliminated with considerable expenditure of energy by means of special kidney-like organs.

The cellular fluids of many marine plants differ considerably from the surrounding seawater in their relative concentrations of sodium and potassium. In effect, these plants appear to concentrate potassium, and in doing so they must eliminate sodium in order to maintain the total salt concentration of the cellular fluid at a level equal to that of seawater. The elimination of excess sodium is accomplished by means of a "sodium pump" that operates in an unknown manner.

Oxygen Levels and Metabolism

Organisms that live between the tide lines, such as clams and oysters, are deprived of oxygen-bearing water at each low tide. The end products of metabolism formed during this period are acidic. These acids are temporarily prevented from injuring the organism by being neutralized by the calcium carbonate of the shell, at which time the organism incurs an "oxygen debt." This temporary debt is paid off by an increase in oxygen consumption when the oxygen-rich waters flow over the organism at high tide, the accumulation of metabolic products then being eliminated by oxidation.

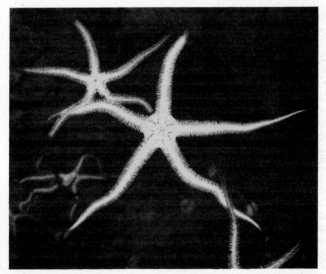

Brittle stars, echinoderms that live on the seafloor, are extremely fragile. When handled, they may throw off all their arms in pieces.

Rhythmic Behavior

Certain tidal organisms exhibit rhythms in behavior, or rates of metabolism, that correspond to tidal periods. These peculiarities persist even when the organisms are transferred to situations where there is no tide. The oxygen consumption of some mollusks varies as much as tenfold with the phases of the tide. This variation continues in a rhythmic manner even when the organisms are maintained under constant conditions in laboratory aquariums. Such organisms collected from separate localities where the phases of the tide differ will maintain their intrinsic rhythm. Fiddler crabs

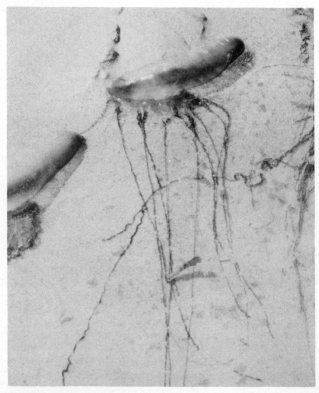

The Portuguese man-of-war is an invertebrate, jellylike marine animal that floats in groups of thousands in warm oceans. Its painful sting can seriously disable a human victim.

The many-colored tentacles of the sea anemone look somewhat like the petals of a blossoming flower.

The octopus is an eight-armed mollusk. Some varieties are less than two inches long; others have tentacles with a thirty-foot spread.

that live in the intertidal zone and alter their color patterns as the tides rise and fall, for example, continue to exhibit the same rhythmic color variations under constant conditions in the laboratory.

Brittle stars, sea cucumbers, and other voracious animals dwell on the sea bottom in dense accumulations. They require such enormous quantities of food that each generation of immature food organisms would be entirely exhausted if eaten immediately after settling to the bottom. To make efficient use of their food supply the brittle stars and cucumbers enter a quiescent stage during the period when the food organisms are settling and maintain their metabolic activities at a low rate until the food organisms have increased in volume through growth. In this way the food supply is extended, eliminating starvation.

Floating and Swimming

Most marine animals are heavier than the surrounding seawater; therefore, special adjustments have appeared among the various forms to offset the tendency to sink. Among these adjustments are the flotation processes of diatoms and dinoflagellates; the oil droplets in the protoplasm of many protozoa; the gas traps in some radiolarians, some jellyfish and notably in some large seaweeds; and the swim bladder in some fish.

Many larger marine animals actively swim about by adaptations of appendages (fish, whales, and seals) or by ejecting water (octopods, scallops, and some jellyfish). Those confined to the bottom may flip about, creep, and swim to some extent, but some are sedentary, such as sea anemones, corals, and many large seaweeds attached to intertidal rocks. The great bulk of living substance of the sea, however, is passively adrift as plankton.

The Food Web

The marine environment is essentially a closed system in which life proceeds in a cycle determined by the nutritional requirements of the various kinds of organisms. The marine plants undergo continual grazing by hordes of herbivorous animals. Since the bulk of the plant material produced in the sea is included in the phytoplankton, the majority of the herbivorous animals are filter feeders, endowed with special structures for straining the tiny plants out of the water.

Crustacea possess filter nets of closely spaced bristles on the appendages adjacent to the mouth. Clams, oysters, and mussels strain their food out of the water by means of their gills. Some worms employ mucous nets capable of extracting particles of extremely minute size from the water. These herbivorous animals, which perform the important function of converting plant materials into animal substance, are in turn subject to predation by the primary carnivores.

These carnivores include a vast array of forms, from the tiny arrow-worms, which snap at individual organisms with their formidable jaws, to the great baleen whales, which strain vast numbers of organisms for food by means of their whalebone plates. Beyond the primary carnivores are successive layers of carnivorous forms ending with the top predators. When the latter die they are decomposed by bacteria, releasing the elementary substances for the use of the photosynthetic plants and completing the food cycle.

Within this general cycle of life there are a number of events that make the system complex. Death and decomposition occur at every phase of the cycle. Phytoplankton drifting down into the deep, unlighted zones of the oceans may die and decompose. Their elementary substances are then beyond the reach of their photosynthetic relatives until such time as turbulence or upwelling may return the nutrients to the illuminated water. Shrimp, fish, and other forms dying from causes other than direct predation may sink to the bottom to be eaten by scavengers such as crabs and worms before bacterial decomposition is completed. Incomplete decomposition of any dead organism may result in the production of organic detritus, which is particulate matter of indeterminate nature included in the diet of many filter-feeding species. Lastly, the general system is made complex by the fact that the metabolic activities of all organisms continue to release elementary substances through respiration and excretion, helping to maintain the supply of basic nutrients for the photosynthetic plants.

The great demands for energy made by living organisms in order to maintain the fundamental processes of life necessarily limit the amount that is available to be transferred from one step to the next in the food cycle. In general every organism uses 90% or more of its food intake merely to sustain its metabolic activities and transfers less than 10% into its own substance during growth. Thus the rate of pro-

Marine mussels, which are bivalved mollusks, are prized as a nutritious and appetizing food in many parts of the world.

duction of marine life depends upon the position of a particular species in the cycle with respect to the primary source of supply, the photosynthetic plants.

In the pelagic division the tiny herbivorous copepods and euphausiid shrimps are produced at a rate fast enough to support the feeding requirements of the giant baleen whales. Mussels, clams, and oysters—which are also herbivorous filter feeders—have proved to be a dependable source of food for coastal peoples throughout the ages.

The bulk of the world's catch of commercial fish consists of certain pelagic species—including the herring, mackerel, and menhaden, all primary carnivores—that subsist on small crustaceans and other similar organisms. At the other extreme the very large fish and other top predators seldom reproduce and grow at a rate fast enough to permit catches of a size approaching those of the herring and mackerel.

Research Methods in Marine Biology

During the last half of the nineteenth century, when emphasis was placed mainly on the collecting and cataloging of marine organisms, the methods employed in marine biology were directed toward the capture and preservation of specimens for study. Various kinds of dredges and trawls were used to collect specimens from the bottom, and hoop nets of different sizes were employed in securing pelagic specimens. The vast multitude of marine species has made it necessary to continue to use such methods up to the present time. The first half of the twentieth century, however, saw a shifting of the emphasis toward quantitative and dynamic aspects of the science, for which refined methods and the use of more complex tools were required.

Equipment to determine the physical features of the marine environment was developed with a considerable degree of precision. Among the instruments devised were thermometers to determine the temperature at any desired depth and containers that close automatically to bring water samples to the surface for analysis. New analytical methods made possible immediate determinations for salinity, oxygen, nutrient salts, and plant pigments on shipboard. Also developed were photoelectric devices for measurements of light penetration and a variety of coring instruments for collecting bottom sediments.

Even the collecting apparatus underwent a high degree of refinement. Qualitative hoop nets gave way to quantitative samplers that may be lowered in a closed position to any desired depth, opened, towed, and closed again. The exact amount of water filtered through the fine silk netting is accurately determined by propellers and counters. Continuous sampling is accomplished by a filtering device whereby a band of fine netting is moved across an opening and then is rolled up in a tank of preservative. Such samplers may be towed long distances behind commercial vessels and require only a small amount of attendance by unskilled personnel.

Direct observation of marine organisms in their natural habitats has been made possible by underwater cameras, television, and improved diving equipment. Cameras have been devised that function in the greatest depths by means of light produced by commercial photographic flash bulbs or xenon-gas discharge tubes. Underwater television provides the observer with a continuous picture of events that occur within the field of a submerged camera. The development of self-contained diving equipment made it possible for the investigator personally to inspect marine organisms in their natural habitat.

The rate of production of primary foods by the photosynthetic plants is determined by dark and light bottle experiments and by the use of radioactive isotopes of various elements. Dark and light bottles filled with seawater of known oxygen concentration and containing a normal population of organisms are suspended in the sea for a given time. Photosynthesis that occurs in the light bottles is determined by the increase in oxygen. A comparison is made between the oxygen concentration in the water in the light bottle, determined after a finite time, and that of the water at the time of filling. The result gives an indication of the amount of food produced.

Corrections for losses of oxygen by respiration are determined from the oxygen content of the dark bottle. More direct determinations of this primary productivity are made with the aid of radioactive isotopes. Light bottles filled with water containing normal populations are supplied with small quantities of salts of radioactive carbon and suspended in the sea. After a period of photosynthesis the organisms are filtered off and the amount of carbon fixed in their bodies is determined by Geiger-Müller counters.

The properties of isotopes have also been used to determine climatic conditions in earlier times. It was discovered that the ratio of the commonest isotope of oxygen, 0^{16}, to 0^{18} in the calcium carbonate of shell-forming organisms is influenced by the surrounding temperature at the time of the formation of the shell. The climate in which a number of prehistoric organisms lived can therefore be determined by analyzing their fossil remains.

Morphological and taxonomic studies of marine organisms are generally performed on preserved specimens in connection with research programs in museums and universities. Physiological and embryological investigations requiring the use of living material are generally pursued at biological stations situated on the seacoasts in order to facilitate the rapid transfer of specimens to the laboratory where they may be maintained in seawater provided by special circulating systems.

12.
Some Creatures of the Ocean

Except for a few regions that are barren of life, animals are found throughout all seas and at all depths. The diversity of animal forms in the sea is much greater than on the land. Ignoring purely parasitic types, of all the classes of free-living animals, only four—Onychophora (caterpillarlike animals), Chilopoda (centipedes), Diplopoda (millipedes), and Amphibia—are completely absent from the sea. At least twenty-seven classes seem to be confined to the ocean. Despite the greater variety of types, the number of species of marine animals is only about one-fifth of the total number of animal species known to scientists. This is correlated with the relative uniformity of habitat conditions and the comparatively minor barriers to dispersal in the oceans. Only in shore areas and estuaries do conditions fluctuate widely, where species are found with limited geographic range because of their restricted dispersal capabilities.

Plankton

Planktonic organisms comprise the comprehensive section of marine life that drifts under the influence of sea currents. Planktonic life is important because almost all animal life in the sea is ultimately dependent on it for existence. The great majority of planktonic organisms are microscopic plants and animals; by definition, plankton also includes bigger organisms, even the largest jellyfish.

Little was known of any except the largest species of plankton until in 1845 the German physiologist Johannes Peter Müller towed a small conical net of fine-meshed cloth behind a boat and collected a sample of the minute plants and animals. Many forms new to science were soon collected in this way, even in coastal waters, although it was not until 1872–76, when the *Challenger* expedition explored the great oceans of the world, that a real impression was obtained of the almost infinite variety hidden in the sea.

Nearly every important group of animals, from the fish downward, is represented in zooplankton. Only one major plant group (the algae), however, is found in the phytoplankton.

The best-known members of phytoplankton are the dia-

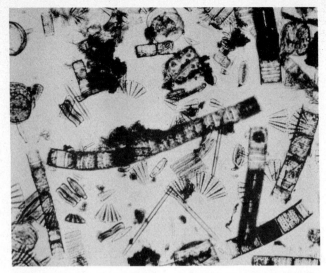

Marine diatoms, as seen through a microscope, have a general preference for cold water and are most abundant in the Arctic and Antarctic oceans.

toms, unicellular greenish-brown plants enclosed in a transparent shell of silica. They range in size from forms like the large *Coscinodiscus*, just visible to the naked eye, to the most minute species of *Nitzschia*. Diatoms were long believed to be the chief food producers in the sea, but it is now thought that far greater numbers of smaller algae, mainly flagellates, may play a more important part.

The colored flagellates, with their animal movements and plant nutrition, have been studied by both zoologists and botanists. Two other unicellular plankton groups, both related to amoebae but far more striking, are the Radiolaria and Foraminifera. Both have elaborate skeletons and have accumulated in such numbers over certain parts of the oceans as to give their names to distinctive oozes on the seabed.

Most marine animals are represented in plankton for a time by their eggs and larvae; few are without at least one wholly planktonic representative. Among the most beautiful are the ctenophores, siphonophores, and jellyfish, as well as the medusoid larvae of the bottom-living coelenterates, such as anemones and corals.

Some fish, such as herring and mackerel, feed largely on plankton all their lives, as do the whalebone whales. Other fish, as they grow, feed more and more on larger animals, either fish or animals that live on the seafloor, such as crabs and whelks. This life of the seafloor in turn is largely fed by the shower of dead and disintegrating plankton that is continually falling from the upper layers of the water. The whole system forms a network of feeding chains that, as the salts and carbon dioxide are returned to the sea by excretion and death, is seen to be one part of an elaborate chemical cycle.

The vast resource of plankton is only beginning to be developed and exploited by man. It may in time be the chief food supply of the world in view of its high biological productivity and wide extent. In addition, phytoplankton may become increasingly important in the space age as a source for food and for gas exchange. The carbon dioxide released during respiration of the crew of a spaceship would be transformed into organic substances by the algae, while the oxygen liberated during this process would support human respiration.

Starfish

Starfish and *sea star* are names given to radially symmetrical, more or less star-shaped, bottom-dwelling animals found on the margins of almost all seas. Sea stars, which range from the tide lines to depths of 19,700 feet (6,005 meters), are particularly abundant in numbers and species along the rocky coasts of the North Pacific. In size they vary from ½ inch to 3 feet (0.9 meter) in diameter. The commonest colors are shades of yellow, orange, pink, or red, but gray, green, blue, and purple forms are also known.

The body of the starfish is more or less flattened, with the mouth located centrally on the underside. From the body project a number of radially arranged arms, usually 5, but in a few species up to 44, as in a South American genus (*Heliaster*), which looks like a giant sunflower. In the tropical cushion star *Culcita* and in the many cookie stars, the body is simply pentagonal, whereas in other species the arms may be long and snakelike, as in some of the deep-water forms that live on mud. The sex glands of the starfish open by pores between the arms. In most forms enormous numbers of eggs and sperm are set free. After a period during which it may be carried afar by ocean currents the free-swimming larva undergoes a drastic metamorphosis and settles down as a bottom form. Many species, particularly cold-water forms and those from deep water, have large eggs that undergo direct development. Some of these "brood" their young by crouching over them. In one species the eggs are taken into the mother's stomach, where the young develop.

The sea star's ability to open a bivalve by pulling the shells apart has been known for centuries. The feat is accomplished by the sea star affixing itself by its tube feet to the two shells, applying "pull" to separate the shells—a fraction of an inch is enough—and squeezing part of its eversible stomach into the interior. The victim, adversely affected by the stomach fluid secreted by the sea star, opens its shells wider, allowing the predator to insert more of its stomach and to complete the digestion of the soft tissue.

Coral

Coral is the common name for a variety of invertebrate marine organisms that are characterized by skeletons—external or internal—of a stonelike, horny, or leathery consistency. The name is also applied to the skeletons of these animals, particularly to those of the stonelike corals.

The body of a coral animal consists of a polyp—a hollow, cylindrical structure attached at its lower end to some sur-

A starfish seeks out food on a stony coral colony.

face. At the free end is a mouth surrounded by tentacles. The tentacles, which gather food, are more or less extensible and are armed with nematocysts, or stinging cells, that paralyze prey.

Eggs and sperm, usually produced by separate individuals, develop as outgrowths in the body cavity and are expelled through the mouth into the open water. The larva, a ciliated form known as a planula, swims about for several days or as long as several weeks, then settles onto a solid surface and develops into a polyp. Reproduction also occurs by budding—a fingerlike extension of the body cavity. The bud remains attached to the original polyp. A colony develops by the constant addition and growth of new buds. As new polyps develop, the old ones beneath die, but the skeleton remains.

Stony corals, the most familiar and most widely distributed forms, are both colonial and solitary in habit. Stony, black, and thorny corals differ from the sea anemone chiefly in having an external skeleton. Stony corals occur in all oceans from the tidal zone to depths of nearly 20,000 feet (about 6,000 meters).

The famed precious red coral is found in Mediterranean waters and has been used for centuries as ornamentation. The Gauls decorated their helmets and weapons of war with coral. The Romans not only prized it for its beauty but also attributed magical and medicinal virtues to it; their children wore necklets of coral to ward off danger. It was also valued greatly in India and the Far East. The richest yields of coral come from the coastal waters of Algeria and Tunisia. Other profitable deposits are found off the coasts of Spain, Provence, Sardinia, Corsica, Sicily, and in the Bay of Naples.

Clams and Oysters

In the broad sense, a clam is any member of the invertebrate class Bivalvia—mollusks with two shells. More than twelve thousand species of bivalves are known, of which about five hundred live in fresh water; the others occur in all seas. Bivalves usually live on sandy or muddy bottoms.

In the strict sense, clams are bivalves with equal shells closed by two adductor muscles situated at opposite ends of the shell and with a powerful, muscular burrowing foot. Most clams inhabit shallow waters, in which they are generally protected from wave action by the surrounding bottom. One species of abra clam, however, has been taken in the Pacific at a depth of more than 16,000 feet (4,800 meters).

Clams draw in and expel water for respiration and feeding through two tubes, the siphons, or "neck." The water is impelled by the beating of millions of cilia (hairlike structures) on the gills; other cilia strain food from the incurrent water and transport it, entangled in mucus, to the mouth. Eggs are usually shed into the water and fertilized there by sperm released from the male. The eggs develop into larvae that swim briefly before settling permanently on the bottom.

In size clams range from pinhead-sized gem shells to the giant *Tridacna* of coral reefs of Australia and the East Indies. These giant clams, reaching lengths of more than 4 feet and a weight of 500 pounds, are unique in that during evolution the soft parts have rotated 180° within the shell, with the foot passing through a separate opening adjacent to the hinge.

Among the most widely used clams for human food are the quahog (or littleneck clam), ocean quahog, soft-shell or long-necked, and surf clams of eastern North America. On the Pacific coast are found the pismo, butter, giant razor, gaper, and jackknife or broad razor clams. The largest of the Pacific clams is the geoduck, weighing up to 6½ pounds.

The soft-shell or long-necked clam is much prized in America as steamed clams eaten with melted butter, and for chowder in which the ground clams are combined (New England style) with salt pork, onion, and potato in a rich cream sauce. Small quahogs are eaten raw as the so-called cherrystones. These and oysters on the half shell are perhaps the only animals eaten alive by North Americans.

True oysters (Ostreidae) have been cultivated since pre-Christian times as food. Pearl oysters (Aviculidae) also have long been valued for the precious pearls that often develop in them. (Pearls found in edible oysters are lusterless and of no value.)

The two valves of the oyster shell, which differ in shape, have rough surfaces that are often a dirty gray. The upper valve is convex, or higher at the middle than at the edges. The lower valve, fixed to the bottom or to another surface, is larger, has smoother edges, and is rather flat.

The valves are held together at their narrow ends by an elastic ligament. A large central muscle serves to close the valve against the pull of the ligament. As the valves are held slightly open, cilia draw water inward by means of wavelike motions. Two or three gallons may pass through the oyster in an hour. Minute organic particles, filtered from the water, serve as food.

Oysters, in turn, are eaten by invertebrates such as starfish and snails, as well as fish, including skates. A common enemy is the oyster drill, a widely occurring snail that drills a tiny hole through the oyster shell with its tongue, then sucks out the edible tissue.

Oysters breed in the summer. The eggs of some species are released into the water before fertilization by the sperm; the eggs of others are fertilized within the female. (The European flat, or edible, oyster is hermaphroditic, with functional reproductive organs of both sexes in the same individual.) The young are released as ciliated spheres known as spat, which swim for several days before attaching themselves permanently to a site.

Oysters are shucked and eaten raw, canned, or smoked. Small quantities are frozen. Popular varieties include the bluepoint and lynnhaven—forms of the North American or Virginia oyster harvested from Blue Point, Long Island, N.Y., or Lynnhaven, Va., regions—as well as the colchester of Britain and the marennes of France.

Pearls are formed in oysters by the accumulation of calcium-containing material around a solid piece of foreign matter that has become lodged inside the shell. The best natural pearls occur in a few Oriental species, particularly *Meleagrina vulgaris,* native to the Persian Gulf. Pearls are taken mostly from oysters more than five years old. Cultivated pearls are grown around bits of mother-of-pearl inserted manually into the oyster. Most cultivated pearls are grown in Japanese coastal waters.

Shrimps, Crabs, and Lobsters

The Crustacea include not only shrimps, crabs, and lobsters but also crayfish, sandhoppers, wood lice, barnacles, water fleas, and a vast multitude of less familiar forms that are not distinguished by any popular names. Crustacea have been described as the "insects of the sea." In the great oceans their teeming multitudes, the "things creeping innumerable" of the Psalmist, play a part not unlike that taken by the true insects in the life of the land. Curiously, these "insects" provide man with some of the most highly prized food that comes from the sea.

The most obvious features of a shrimp are the long legs,

The fiddler crab is so called because the male holds the larger of its two claws somewhat like a violin.

weak claws, and laterally compressed abdomen. Like other crustaceans, a shrimp wears its skeleton on the outside of the body and, in order to grow, must cast off this shell and replace it with a new and larger one. In the process of shedding, all of the hard structures of the shrimp are cast off and renewed.

The common shrimp swims in a forward direction by the use of the pleopods or abdominal feet. When frightened or when rapid movement is desired the shrimp can propel itself backward with remarkable speed by flexing its powerful, muscular abdomen. It can also leap clear of the water.

Shrimps occur on mud bottoms of inshore and offshore waters in many parts of the world. Important fisheries operate in European, North American, and Asian waters. Although often thought of as warm-water shellfish, shrimps are also found in northern seas, and there are commercial shrimp fisheries in the waters off Norway, Greenland, and Alaska. Considerable effort was expended in the search for new shrimp grounds in many parts of the world following World War II, and important new fisheries for the brown-grooved shrimp and the pink-grooved shrimp were developed in the Gulf of Mexico.

Shrimps are taken in a variety of ways—with hand or cast nets, baited traps, haul seines, stake or channel nets set in tideways, and boat-drawn beam and otter trawls. The trawls, which account for the major portion of the world catch, consist of large baglike nets that are dragged over the floor of the ocean, scooping up the shrimps in their path.

True crabs, or brachyurans, are distinguished from the long-tailed lobsters and shrimps by the small abdomen or "tail," folded up under the body. Most crabs live in the sea; even the land crabs, which are abundant in tropical countries, visit the sea occasionally and pass through their early stages in it. As a rule, crabs breathe by gills, which are lodged in a pair of cavities beneath the sides of the hard shell or carapace, but in the true land crabs the cavities become enlarged and modified so as to act as lungs for breathing air.

The peculiar sidelong gait familiar to most people in the common shore crab is characteristic of most members of this group. Some crabs, however, swim with great dexterity by means of their flattened, paddle-shaped feet. Like many other crustaceans, crabs are often omnivorous and act as scavengers, but many are predatory in their habits and some are content with a vegetable diet.

Though no crab, perhaps, is truly parasitic, some live commensally with other animals. Examples are the little pea crabs that live within the shells of mussels and a variety of other mollusks, worm-tubes, and echinoderms and share the food of their hosts. The coral-gall crabs irritate the growing tips of certain corals so that they grow to enclose the female in a stony prison from which there is no escape. Many of the sluggish spider crabs cover their shells with growing seaweeds, zoophytes, and sponges, which afford them effective disguises.

The giant crab of Japan and the huge Tasmanian crab are two of the largest known crustaceans. The former can measure 12 feet from the tip of one laterally extended claw to the tip of the other. The Tasmanian crab may weigh more than 20 pounds; its larger claw may measure 17 inches long.

Hermit crabs live in the empty shells of gastropod mollusks, which they carry about with them as portable dwellings. As the crab grows it changes its abode from time to time,

The spiny lobster, a member of the family Palinuridae, is found mainly in tropic and subtropic latitudes of the ocean.

often having to fight with its fellows for the possession of an empty shell.

The most important and valuable crabs are the edible crab of British and European coasts, the blue crab of the Atlantic coast, and the Dungeness crab of the Pacific coast of North America. Two varieties of swimming crabs related to the American blue crab are among the most important sources of seafood throughout the entire Indo-Pacific region.

Crabs are usually caught in baited traps or "pots," but the blue crab of the American Atlantic coast is frequently taken on baited lines and the king crab fishery of the North Pacific employs trawling vessels, accompanied by factory ships to which the catches are transferred for immediate freezing or canning.

In the United States the word *lobster* is used to describe both the American (or northern) lobster, which is a true lobster found from Labrador to North Carolina, and the spiny lobster (or langouste) of the Pacific coast. The spiny lobster is readily told from the true lobster by the lack of prominent pincers and the presence of a more or less spiny carapace or shield. The dark greenish common lobster of European coastal waters is closely related to the American lobster.

Although uncommon, giant American lobsters measuring about 2 feet long and weighing more than 30 pounds have been taken; a weight of 44½ pounds has been recorded. The average-sized lobster in a catch is about 9 inches in total length or 3½ inches in carapace length (from eye socket to end of dorsal shield). Conservation laws vary considerably, but most regulations require that a lobster of carapace length less than 3¾6 inches be returned to the sea.

The European lobster rarely reaches 10 pounds in weight, though individuals of 15 pounds have been found. A third species of true lobster, 4–5 inches long, from the Cape of Good Hope, is of no economic importance.

A true lobster is hatched from the egg in a shrimplike, free-swimming form. With the eighth molt it becomes quite definitely a bottom-dwelling juvenile lobster. Larval molts appear to succeed one another with considerable rapidity and without much difficulty; growth in the adult is a much more serious proceeding. The stout exoskeleton prevents increase in body size until there is a literal bursting at the seams. In the true lobster the "seam" that gives is the chitinous articulating membrane between the hinder margin of the carapace and the fore edge of the tergum of the first abdominal somite, or segment. Through that narrow opening passes the entire soft body of the animal, including the relatively huge claw.

The body, and the soft cuticle that in the premolt period was forming beneath the old shell, expands rapidly in size during the next few hours by the absorption of water. When this increase (about 12%) has reached its maximum, the cuticle begins to harden with a deposition of lime salts. Within an hour the new shell perceptibly hardens; in six to eight weeks it has the rigidity and strength of the old one. By the time an average American lobster is eaten it is about five years old and has shed about twenty-five times.

The principal foods of the omnivorous and scavenging adult lobster are fish, alive or dead, and bottom-dwelling invertebrates, especially small mollusks and such larger ones as can be crushed. Vegetable matter is eaten occasionally. Cannibalism is not unknown.

True lobsters are generally fished in relatively shallow water, 5 to 50 fathoms, from more or less rocky bottoms by means of lobster pots or creels, rectangular traps of wooden slats, or frames covered with netting and provided with a funnel or two permitting entrance but preventing escape.

Oily fish—fresh, salted, or partially decomposed—are the greatest attraction as bait. Lobsters constitute a multimillion-dollar industry in the United States, where about 30 million pounds are caught annually.

Sea Serpents

In the depths of the sea there may possibly still be gigantic creatures that are still unknown. Up to the present, however, no animal has been captured that has not been proved to belong to a previously well-known group.

Many possible explanations have been put forward to account for reports of sea serpents. A number of porpoises swimming one behind the other and rising regularly to take air might produce the appearance of a large serpentlike creature progressing by a series of vertical undulations. A flight of seafowl and a brood of ducks have been mistaken for a large snake swimming at the surface of the water. Basking sharks, which have a habit of swimming in pairs one behind the other with the dorsal fin and the upper lobe of the tail just above the surface, produce the effect of a body 60 feet or more long; even a simple, partially decomposed specimen that was cast ashore was reported in all good faith as a sea serpent.

Giant squids, which may attain a total length of 50 feet, are undoubtedly the foundation on which many accounts are based. They occasionally frequent those regions from which many accounts of sea serpents have come—Scandinavia, Denmark, the British Isles, and the eastern coasts of North America. One of these animals swimming at the surface with the two enormously elongate arms trailing along through the water would produce almost exactly the picture that many of the strangely consistent independent accounts require.

Sperm whales are known to kill and devour giant squid and similar cephalopods, and one of the most graphic accounts of a sea serpent tells of one in conflict with a whale, around which it had thrown two coils and ultimately dragged below the surface. Actually, it seems probable that the whale was eating a giant squid whose tentacles, thrown round the whale in the struggle, were mistaken for the coils of a snake, and that the whale, far from being dragged under, merely sounded with its prey in its mouth.

13.
Ocean Fish

Since earliest times the fish has appeared in the folklore of many peoples. This is not surprising in view of the ubiquity of fish and their importance as food. Among some African tribes the fish is taboo as food, but fish is recommended in the Talmud and is highly favored among many peoples as being beneficial to long life and to intelligence. (In fact, neither of these qualities is peculiar to fish or to any other single type of food.) The fish was adopted as a Christian symbol sometime in the second century. It stands for Christ, for the newly baptized, and for the Eucharist. It is frequently found in religious art in combination with bread and wine. In classical Greek and Roman literature and in early Christian art and heraldry the dolphin (both the fish and the mammal of that name) appears frequently, symbolizing diligence, love, or swiftness. As ichthyology emerged as a modern science it became apparent that the fish of the world comprise a family of animals of widely different appearance and behavior. There are more living species of bony fish than any other vertebrate animal; 30,000 is a conservative estimate. The smallest fish—less than one-half-inch long when mature—is said to be a tiny goby from a lake in the Philippines. The largest is probably the whale shark, which reaches 70 feet in length and weighs several tons. Although most fish swim, some fish fly (or, more correctly, glide), while others walk along the bottom, or even ashore, on their fins. Most fish "drown" when they are taken out of water, but some, such as eels and lungfish, can survive ashore for considerable periods of time. One most curious fish lives inside the hollow of the marine animal called the sea cucumber, darting in and out with impunity and apparently not harming its host in any way. Another lives among the poisonous stinging tentacles of the jellyfish called the Portuguese man-of-war.

What Is a Fish?
As popularly conceived a fish is any cold-blooded aquatic animal that swims by means of fins and breathes by means of gills. It is usually thought of as having scales. There are, however, many fish that do not thoroughly correspond to this conception: some do not have scales; some spend a consider-

There are thousands of living species of fish in the ocean, many of which live in dense schools.

able period out of water; some have vestigial gills and breathe by means of lungs or other specialized organs; and some are finless.

A more technical definition of a fish is based on anatomy: a fish, among other characteristic structures, has a skin with many mucous glands; a backbone consisting of vertebrae; eyes with no lids; and a heart formed of a single folded tube with several chambers. This definition excludes many aquatic invertebrates that have "fish" as part of their common names—cuttlefish, jellyfish, starfish, and shellfish.

The Fish in Nature

Fish are the principal free-swimming aquatic animals (nekton). Most of the vast number of aquatic invertebrates are either more dependent on the bottom or, because of lowly organization or small size, drift about in the currents. The molluscan squids, like the mammalian whales and porpoises, are exceptional in having invaded the fish's sphere. Removed from serious competition by other groups, fish are abundant everywhere. They have expanded into every conceivable ecological niche and have evolved a much greater diversity of forms than any of the other classes of vertebrates. Fish competition, one species balanced against another, made for evolutionary divergence in every direction; therefore, fish present a particularly fertile field for the student of evolution.

The basic food supply of all animals, including fish, is plant life. The mass of rooted vegetables, such as is found in terrestrial environments, is relatively small in aquatic environments. This is compensated by the great abundance of microscopic, planktonic plants (diatoms and other tiny algae) in water that is within the reach of sunlight. Although their mass is quite adequate, these plants are too tiny to be utilized directly as food by more than a few fish, but they do serve as pasturage for smaller animals that are eventually eaten by fish. Most important of these intermediate creatures are small, also planktonic, crustaceans (shrimplike animals), frequently so abundant as to cloud the water.

Some fish are omnivorous, feeding on both plants and animals; some are herbivorous, subsisting mainly on such water plants as there are in fresh water, along the shore, or adrift; but the majority are carnivorous, feeding exclusively or chiefly on animals. An increasing proportion of the larger

The barramundi dines on rainbowfish; though most fish are carnivorous, others are omniverous or herbivorous.

ones eat other fish smaller than themselves, simply because these are the most available food. The saying "fish eat fish" is by no means an invariable rule, but it is rather generally applicable. The carnivorous fish living in the dark, miles down in the ocean, subsist almost entirely on animal detritus showering down from sunlit waters.

The great divergence of fish depends, to some extent, on how far back toward the base of the food pyramid each group reaches for subsistence. The menhaden goes all the way and feeds on diatoms. The predaceous bluefish feeds on menhaden and other fish of comparable size. There is also a basic cause for the diversity of fish life in the vastness of aquatic environment. Fish of one heritage may have been superseded by those of another in centers of abundance and competition yet persist somewhere else—perhaps in fresh, deep, or isolated waters.

Fish utilize every available food resource. Many freshwater species eat insects that drop upon the surface by chance or eat the aquatic larvae of terrestrial insects (the rationale behind fly-fishing). Rivers wash the waste products of the land into the sea. Some of these products nourish fish or the marine animals on which the fish feed. It follows then that fish life is usually abundant off the mouths of great rivers.

Although fish are generally in competition, beneficial associations have also developed, as they have on land. These associations may be advantageous in securing food, shelter, protection, or relief from parasites. A well-known example is the remora (or pilot fish), which attaches itself to sharks and other large fish, thereby being assured of transportation as well as scraps of food that elude its host's mouth. "Cleaning stations" set up by certain small fish are visited fairly regularly by larger fish beset with parasites; oddly enough, many of these larger forms, which are predators that would in other circumstances devour these "cleaners," eagerly submit to the tendings of the smaller fish.

Fish Behavior

It is assumed, probably correctly, that fish behavior is more mechanical than that of the higher animals—in no way to be compared psychologically with man's behavior. Nevertheless, fish behavior has many features to suggest an anthropomorphic interpretation.

One underlying factor in fish behavior seems to be that the individual fish seeks to swim at a given distance from others of its kind, no more and no less. This distance varies according to the fish's condition and all the more according to its species. It is a very short interval in herring and mackerel, which swim in dense schools, and varies all the way to fish that are essentially solitary, such as pike. The fish school is a social organization whose members are bound by species-specific behavior patterns.

Many sedentary fish living in a circumscribed area at or near the bottom defend their property rights to the area, being domineering within its confines or driving intruders from it; these property rights, when asserted, tend to be respected by both neighbors and strangers. This behavior is most marked in, but not confined to, fish protecting their mates, eggs, or young.

Because sound does not pass readily from air to water, and vice versa, it was believed for many years that fish were mute. It has been definitely established, however, that some are, on the contrary, very vocal, and certain species are particularly vocal during the breeding season. The range of noises that they make is not great: grunting, tooting, chirping, clicking, rattling, humming, or drumming—the voice of one species differing from that of another.

Sea grunts produce grunting noises by grating their teeth. A school of sea drums in spring makes a considerable noise, which can be heard through the bottom of a boat lying at anchor in a quiet bay. They are easily recognized by man, and it may be assumed that they can be heard and recognized by others of their kind. Sea drums, also called croakers or pumpers, make soft drumming sounds or harsh froglike croaks by rapidly contracting and expanding muscles associated with the air bladder, causing the walls of the bladder to vibrate, the organ itself acting as a sounding board.

Lacking eyelids, fish cannot close their eyes. They recoup their strength by a behavior analogous to sleep in mammals. Some simply remain suspended motionlessly in the water; others settle on a surface, resting either upright or on their sides; and a few partially wriggle into the mud or sand on the water's floor. Fish that assemble in schools during the day often disperse at night to retire alone or in small groups.

Swimming, Gliding, and "Walking"

By far the greater majority of fish are capable of transporting themselves by swimming, some species being more efficient than others. The greatest swimming speed is likely attained by some member of the group of mackerellike fish, to which tuna and marlins belong. Exact knowledge is scant, but it is safe to say that, unless in short spurts, few attain 20 miles per hour. One may well be skeptical of records, however circumstantial, of speeds more than 50 miles per hour claimed for any fish.

Some fish have almost given up locomotion. Holdfast devices, or suckers, have been developed in some species. Examples are the remoras, gobies, and clingfish, which live between tide marks and fasten to objects to avoid being carried away by the rushing tide.

Besides swimming, other methods of locomotion have been employed by various fish. Many bony fish are able to jump out of the water; some of them, as the salmon, leaping as high as nine feet into the air. The devilfish, one of the large rays, also breaks the surface of the water, leaping a few feet. Individual fish of many species occasionally jump spontaneously out of water. This behavior may be an attempt to capture prey (in trout), to breech a barrier (in salmon), or to loosen parasites. Some have suggested that certain jumps are simply expressions of well-being or of illness. Many game fish, upon being hooked, break the surface before diving in an effort to free themselves.

Flying fish have the pectoral fins enlarged, a specialization that enables them to break the surface and, in some species, glide for several hundred yards over the water. Among a few families of bony fish (lungfish and others) the pectoral fins have been modified into lobed structures that allow these fish to "walk" on the bottom. Some, like the mudskipper, occasionally venture on land in an attempt to capture crustaceans and insects.

Migratory Fish

Birds are the only other vertebrates that migrate as regularly as fish. Fish migration, however, appears to be much more complicated than that of birds. It is usually similarly correlated with the change of seasons, but less predominantly with reproduction. Search for food and optimum temperatures are larger factors in it. Furthermore, a fish has three directions to migrate into a different environment—north and south (latitudinal), onshore and offshore (horizontal), and up and down (vertical). The migration of shore fish commonly combines the three.

Anadromous fish are those bony fish that grow in the sea

Chum salmon spawn in the rivers of Alaska.

but ascend fresh waters to spawn. These fish have appreciably fewer eggs than comparable species that spawn in salt water, an adaptation probably correlated with less wastage of eggs and fry (young). The Chinook and sockeye salmon wander an unknown distance in the Pacific from the mouths of the rivers in which they spawn, then later return to ascend these rivers for hundreds of miles to their spawning grounds. Like other Pacific salmon they spawn only once and then die. The return downstream and out to sea is made by the succeeding generation, after spending its early life in fresh water. There is thus a single, complete round-trip migration in the life of an individual Pacific salmon.

The anadromous shad runs up rivers to spawn, from Florida to New Brunswick, progressively later in the spring northward. There is an anadromous Chinese herring, corresponding to the American shad, and an equally prized food fish that runs up the Yangtze river 1,000 miles or farther from the sea.

A few species of fish are catadromous (live in fresh water but spawn in the sea), being quite the reverse of the anadromous fish. Among these the freshwater eels are preeminent. European and American eels, which are much alike, are

Grunions, a species of small smelt found along the California coast, breed along beaches at night, burying their eggs in the sand at high tide.

known to spawn in adjacent areas of the open Atlantic southeast of Bermuda, at a probable depth of 200 fathoms (1,200 feet) or more. Their young are larval, elongate but flattened, pelagic, and not eellike. They live near the surface of the Gulf Stream drift, on the first leg of the long two-way migration in the life of an individual. By the time they have reached the end of the larval stage, they have drifted to the shores of Europe and America. They work into shallow water, lose transparency, becoming dark in color, and begin to grow.

Migrations also occur entirely within the sea. The migrations of marine shore fish are largely determined by water temperatures and availability of food. Their breeding migrations are for the most part of lesser extent or are combined with the other migrations.

The common mackerel of the east coast of North America is an example of such a migratory fish. It is not known exactly where schools of this species spend the winter, perhaps at a considerable depth in the ocean, but they appear off the Carolinas in spring and work northward. They spawn in summer abundantly in favorable feeding grounds from Massachusetts Bay to the Gulf of Saint Lawrence and over offshore banks. It seems that they move into these grounds when water temperatures permit; their spawning there appears to be more or less incidental. The bluefin tuna and the swordfish, of the western Atlantic, invade the same grounds in summer but have certainly spawned elsewhere.

The shore waters between Cape Cod and the Carolinas are occupied by warm-water fish in summer and by cold-water fish in winter. Of the former, the tautog and striped bass may be little migratory, merely becoming less active in the winter months. Bottom fish such as the summer flounder and sea robins move offshore into warmer, deeper water when shore-water temperatures fall. To what extent they edge southward while doing so is uncertain. The arrival in spring and departure in fall of the menhaden is closely correlated with water temperature; its migration along the coast is probably combined with an inshore–offshore movement, but it is improbable that it goes to any considerable depth.

In winter, schools of cod, which normally wander considerable distances in search of food, invade the area from the northeast when shore-water temperatures fall to a suitable level and the warm-water fishes withdraw from it. As a rule only an occasional individual of the little tomcod is to be met with here in summer, but in late fall a wave of this species invades inshore waters, presumably coming up along the bottom from a greater depth to spawn in winter in shallow bays and estuaries. The long-horned sculpin, which is abundant in the colder months and spawns in late fall and winter, doubtless also comes up along the bottom, probably with little or no southward movement from northern shore waters where it is plentiful the year round. Much remains to be learned about the migration of any fish, even in this narrow and comparatively accessible area where a large part of the species are migratory.

Sexual Life and Development

All fish except those who bear live offspring are prolific, producing large numbers of eggs and sperm. This is an adaptation associated with life in a rigorous environment where mortality, especially of eggs, is high.

In the great majority of fish the sexes are separate, but among many groups, mainly saltwater fish, hermaphroditism occurs. The killifish seemingly has only males and self-fertilizing hermaphrodites with female secondary characteristics.

The *Monopterus albus* is protogynous—all individuals functioning at first as females and becoming transformed into males at about age three. Groupers exhibit both types of hermaphroditism.

The male fish produces sperm (or milt) in two more-or-less united testes located in the body cavity, posteriorly in the bony fish and anteriorly in the cartilaginous fish or sharks. From the testes a sperm duct passes to the urogenital aperture, an opening behind the vent (in bony fish), or to the cloaca (in cyclostomes and cartilaginous fish). Accessory organs, modified portions of certain fins, are used to transfer milt in most of those fishes that fertilize eggs internally. Examples of these organs are the claspers (parts of the pelvic fins) of sharks and rays and the gonopodia (parts of the anal fins) of guppies and swordtails.

In the females of most bony fish (oviparous forms) eggs pass from two united ovaries through the oviducts and uterus (if developed) through the urogenital aperture to the outside water. Among some cartilaginous fish and certain bony fish the ripe eggs are held inside the body, fertilization taking place internally. In these viviparous forms the developing embryos are nourished within the uterus and are eventually born alive.

Most bony fish reproduce themselves by means of small (often less than one-eighth inch), usually spherical eggs that are laid and fertilized in the water and then left to develop. Among these fish reproduction is effected simply: the males and females come close together and extrude their sex cells into the water. Some bony fish take part in courtship and nest-building activities before mating; examples are the sticklebacks and the bowfin, in which a nest of sorts is formed by the male to receive the egg-swollen female, which is often attracted by the male's graceful movements.

In the sea horses and pipefish, which have internal fertilization, a reversal of the usual mating procedure occurs: the female deposits eggs, by means of an intromittent organ, into a broad pouch of the male. In certain catfish and cichlids the males incubate the fertilized eggs in their mouths. In freshwater habitats such behavior appears to prevent infection of developing eggs, which float to the surface, where they are more secure from predators. Despite these examples, courtship and "parental concern" are not common among fish.

Newly hatched fish are still partially undeveloped and are called larvae until body structures such as fins, skeleton, and

The male seahorse has a broad breed pouch in which the female deposits her eggs.

some organs are fully formed. Larval life is often short, usually less than a few weeks, but it can be very long, some lampreys continuing as larvae for at least five years.

Young and larval fish, before reaching sexual maturity, must grow considerably, and their small size and other factors often dictate that they live in a habitat different from that of the adults. Larval food is also different, and they often live in shallow, more protected waters.

After the fish reaches adult size, the length of its life is subject to many factors, such as innate rates of aging, predation pressure, and the nature of the local climate. The longevity of a species in the protected environment of an aquarium may have nothing to do with how long members of that species live in the wild. Many small fish live only one to three years at the most. In a few large species some individuals may live as long as ten or twenty years or even longer.

14.
Ocean Mammals

The mammals that live exclusively in the ocean include the whales and porpoises, the sea cow, manatee, and dugong, and the sea otter. Other oceanic mammals—the seals, sea lions, and walruses—spend much of their life upon land. The vast size and inaccessibility of the great whales has always aroused men's curiosity and exercised their imaginations. The whale has become the symbol of everything huge, and the term is so used even in modern slang. It is, however, the smaller whales, the dolphins, that have been the subject of the most charming legends. Aristotle, Pliny, and other classical writers reiterated the belief that dolphins are the friends of man, and that they delight in bearing his ships company and running races with them however fast they sail. Dolphins were supposedly attached to boys, and there are many stories of tame dolphins that came to hand when called and even carried their young friends upon their backs to and from school. These legends are probably founded on truth

A killer whale was incised on a boulder—uncovered recently at Ozette, on the coast of Washington—more than three hundred years ago by a Makah Indian.

A sperm whale stranded on a beach created a sensation in the Netherlands in 1598.

because several modern instances are known of dolphins fraternizing with bathers and allowing youngsters to ride upon their backs.

Classification

At their uppermost range, the whales, which comprise the order Cetacea, are the largest of all animals, the blue whale exceeding in mass the elephant and even the largest dinosaur. In size they range from 4 feet to 100 feet (1.2 meters to 30 meters), with an adult range of about 100 pounds (45 kilograms) to 150 tons. They are warm-blooded, lung-breathing animals with skeletal, vascular, alimentary, respiratory, sensory, and reproductive features fundamentally the same as those in other mammals and not as in fish. They have exploited all the available aquatic habitats—the oceans and the seas connected with them, estuaries, and rivers; one species lives in a lake of the Yangtze River 600 miles from the sea.

The cetaceans are divided into two suborders, the baleen or whalebone whales (suborder Mysticeti) and the toothed whales (suborder Odontoceti). The baleen whales include the gray whale, the right whales, and the rorquals. The toothed whales include beaked or bottle-nosed whales, sperm whales,

Killer whales, which sometimes prey on other whales, display large conical teeth (above) and prominent dorsal fins (above right).

the narwhal, and porpoises and dolphins. (The mammal dolphin should not be confused with the fish of the same name.)

Anatomy of the Whale

The general body shape of the whale is fusiform, or spindle-shaped, with the head end modified variously into a more or less attenuated beak—rounded, bluff, or flattened. The tail end is always produced into two horizontal fleshy lobes, the flukes, which, by nicely adjusted inclinations of their sur-

faces and the mainly vertical movement of the tail stock, propel the body through the water. The forelimbs (flippers) are paddle-shaped and serve the functions of balance and steering. A fleshy dorsal fin is generally present.

Unlike the flippers, which enclose the recognizable elements of the mammalian forelimb skeleton, neither dorsal fin nor flukes have any bony support. No external trace remains of the hind limbs and no ear pinnae are to be distinguished adjacent to the inconspicuous entrance of the external ear tube. The nostrils (blowholes) are remote from the snout tip (except in the sperm whale), being situated near or on the highest part of the head. Eyes are present and usually fully functional, but vision is said to be reduced in some river dolphins. The skin is exceedingly smooth and devoid of hair, except for occasional remnants on the snout and lower jaw (mandible). Near the beginning of the hinder third of the body are found the reproductive opening and the vent.

The "telescoping" of the whale's skull, and the laminated bony structure so produced, together with a high, short, broad braincase result in a skull form that is far removed from the conventional mammalian pattern. To these features must be added the enormous development of the bony processes from the cranium and the unique asymmetry of the rostral and nasal regions of the toothed cetaceans.

The bones are spongy in texture, the cavities filled with oil.

The white whale, or beluga, found mainly in Arctic waters, attains a length of about thirteen feet.

The neck vertebrae, seven in number, are short and often blended together to a greater or lesser extent. The thoracic vertebrae vary in number from eight in the bottle-nose whale to seventeen in the pigmy right whale. In the baleen whales the ribs differ greatly from those of other Mammalia in their extremely loose connection both with the vertebral column above and the sternum below. In the toothed whales the ribs are long and slender.

The greatly reduced pelvis is represented by a pair of slender, irregularly curved bones, remote from the backbone, embedded in flesh in the vicinity of the reproductive opening. In some of the larger whales bony or cartilaginous remnants of the hind limb skeleton still persist as attachments to the pelvis. The brain is large and typically mammalian in general structure, but the globular shape, complex convolutions of the cerebral hemispheres, and large size of the cerebellum combine to distinguish the cetacean brain from that of any other mammal.

The reproductive system exhibits many adaptations to aquatic life. The testes lie just below the body surface, there being no need, as in most other mammals, to keep developing sperm cooler than the rest of the body. The penis in its flaccid state is curled and retracted into a pouch within the general contour of the body. On either side of the reproductive open-

Finback, which can be as long as eighty feet, are among the largest species of whale.

ing in the female is a mammary slit within which is an evertible teat. The uterus is bicornate, with provisions for two fetuses, but only one young is carried at a time.

Breathing

Although whales sometimes idle at the surface, blowhole above water, the normal respiratory pattern is one in which the whale, after a period of submergence, comes to the surface a number of times in quick succession, exhaling (blowing) and inhaling on each occasion. This period of successive respirations alternating with shallow dives is followed by a period that begins with the final inspiration of the preceding phase, includes a much deeper dive and a longer time of submergence and ends with the ascent to the surface again.

The blow (spout) of the bigger whales is conspicuous and can be detected at a considerable distance. Its shape, determined by the blowhole, is used by experienced whalers to distinguish different kinds of whales: in the rorquals it is single, vertical, and plumelike; in the humpbacks, low and bushy; in the right whales, double and directed obliquely forward; and in the sperm whales, single and directed obliquely forward. The blow is made visible by the condensed moisture due to sudden expansion and therefore cooling of the exhaled breath together with a certain amount of waste matter from the respiratory passages and adjacent air spaces. It is not, as is popularly believed, a fountain of water as such.

During submergence the whale is subjected to the pressure conditions imposed by the depth attained. The question of the whale's immunity from caisson disease (the bends) was answered by Swedish-U.S. physiologist P. F. Scholander, who showed that the essential difference between the cetacean and the human diver is that the former dives with only the air that is in its lungs, while the latter has a constant replenishment of air throughout the diving period, with all the implications of increased nitrogen solution in the blood under pressure and the subsequent gasification if relief from pressure is too rapidly achieved.

The myoglobin in cetacean muscles is an important reservoir for the storage of oxygen, in addition to the oxygen accumulated during successive respirations and stored in the blood and in the air contained in the lungs. Even these combined supplies are not believed to be adequate provision for the whale swimming actively and submerged for a period up to half an hour. It is suggested that the muscles may function anaerobically (without replenishment of oxygen) during the dive and that the *retia mirabilia* (a feature of the whale's vascular system) may act as a shunt, ensuring that while the muscles may be deprived of their oxygen supply, the brain is adequately supplied during the whole period of submergence.

Baleen and Blubber

The baleen whales are distinguished from others by the possession, within the mouth, of a double series of triangular horny plates, one set or "side" on each half of the palate. Since these plates do not consist of true bone, the word *baleen* should be used in preference to *whalebone* to avoid confusion. The baleen plates are anchored in the roof of the mouth and are spaced apart by a brief interval from one another, their plane surfaces being at right angles to the long axis of the head. The inner side of the baleen is frayed out into a fringe of bristles that combine to form a matted sieve or strainer for collecting planktonic animals on which baleen whales depend for nourishment. The plates are longest (to 12 feet) in the right whales and shorter, broader, and less flexible in the rorquals. A "side" may consist of upward of 300 plates. Essentially baleen does not differ from hair, and like hair, it has its origin in the skin.

The body of the whale is enveloped in a layer of subcutaneous fat called *blubber*. The blubber is white, rubbery, and tough and is composed of fat cells and fibrous tissue. It functions as an insulating layer for the retention of body heat in animals whose temperature is always higher than the water in which they live.

The internal temperature of a whale (92° F. in a stranded fin whale) is not much different from that of a man, but with the exertion of active swimming the heat generated beneath the insulating blubber layer tends to increase. In order to maintain its normal body temperature the whale must dissipate the mounting heat. The whale lacks the system of sweat glands common to land mammals and is deprived, by the intermittence of its breathing, of the cooling effect that, for example, a dog obtains from panting. It has been suggested, however, that the flippers, dorsal fin (when present), and flukes, being without blubber, act as radiators and that a system of arteries, each surrounded by a meshwork of veins, acts in combination as a countercurrent heat regulating arrangement, conserving the body heat when the whale is inactive and dissipating it from the surface of the appendages when vigorous muscular action tends to make the body temperature increase. In addition to its insulating function the blubber serves also as a food reserve in which fat accumulates when the whales are actively feeding and from which it is withdrawn when food is scarce.

Food and Feeding

The digestive tract and the feeding apparatus of the whale show several special features associated with feeding habits. Food enters the large gape and passes unchewed through the esophagus and into a specialized several-chambered stomach. This specialization of the stomach is related to the simplification of dentition, which requires that the food, swallowed whole, undergo prolonged digestion in the various chambers. The serrate-edged teeth of even the earliest of the archaeocetes (a now extinct suborder) may be said to be adapted for dealing with gregariously occurring macroplanktonic species such as the shrimplike crustaceans known as krill, or even smaller fish, rather than for a carnivorous diet of larger animals. In those cetaceans that are carnivorous (in the generally accepted sense) the teeth are simple, uniform, peglike, and single-rooted, frequently exceeding the primitive mammalian number, with the top teeth interdigitating, when the mouth is closed, with those of the lower jaw. The teeth are used for seizing prey, which is not chewed before being swallowed.

Generally, dolphins and porpoises eat fish, but the common dolphin at least also adds cuttlefish to a diet that includes herring and pilchards. Some of the larger dolphins—for example the false killer, the pilot whale, and Risso's dolphin—feed either exclusively or predominantly on cuttlefish.

The sperm whale, in which functional teeth are restricted to the lower jaw, eats large squids almost exclusively, but fish may also be taken. The killer is exceptional in eating marine mammals (dolphins, porpoises, and seals) and aquatic birds such as penguins in addition to salmon, sharks, and other large fish, but squid are also taken. The baleen whales are plankton feeders, including in their diet crustaceans such as krill and copepods and fish such as herring, sardines, and capelins. The nourishment of these great whales is dependent on the swarming habits of the food animals involved.

Ambergris, a waxlike substance formed in the intestine or stomach of the sperm whale, is a valuable fixative in the manufacture of perfumes. It is a debated point whether ambergris is a normal or pathological product and whether it is released during life or after death. Some believe that squid beaks cause an inflammation of the intestinal tract and stimulate the formation of ambergris.

Sound Production and Hearing

The sense of hearing is without question the dominant long-range perceptor, cetaceans depending principally on their ears for awareness of their surroundings. The reception of sounds is by a system of hearing comparable with that used by terrestrial mammals but with modifications of the structural components needed for receiving and transmitting waterborne instead of airborne sounds. The range of sounds perceived is much greater in cetaceans than in terrestrial mammals, with an upper limit of about 120 kilocycles. (The human upper threshold lies between 15 and 30 kilocycles.)

Cetaceans emit a considerable range of sounds, from low "creaking gate" noises to high-pitched whistles, which can be related to various activities such as feeding, breeding, aggressive display and communication. The dolphin calf starts emitting high-pitched whistles as soon as it is born. That some of the sounds emitted are used in echo-location has been proved, and it has been shown that bottle-nosed dolphins can range in, from a distance, on a comparatively small target in circumstances under which hearing is the only sensory means available for detection. The animal picks up its target by the transmission and reception of an intermittent pulse with a variable recurrence frequency, much as the bat locates its food and avoids obstructions while in flight in the dark. The dolphin may be said to obtain an assessment of its environment predominantly by auditory impressions as many of them live in turbid estuaries or river water. Some of the bigger cetaceans descend to depths of extreme light attenuation, conditions in which vision is of, at most, extremely limited use.

Breeding and Reproduction

Most whales are gregarious during certain times; for example during migration or at the breeding season schools numbering several hundred individuals may be seen. Smaller groups are referred to as pods or gams. Whales are often found alone as well. The Cetacea are in all respects mammalian in reproduction. Fetal life generally extends to about a year, but in the humpback whale it is eleven months and in the sperm whale fifteen months. The larger cetaceans are usually sexually mature in their fifth to sixth year and produce young in alternate years.

Many of the smaller cetaceans give indication that parturition and pairing are accomplished in the early summer; and although in the bigger whales these activities may occur over a wide period of months there are nevertheless indications, so far as parturition at any rate is concerned, of a period of maximum frequency. A single calf is normally produced, but twins occur, and there is fetal evidence of occasional larger numbers. The size of the newly born calf is large in relation to that of the parent; for example, in the common porpoise the calf is just over 2 feet long at birth from a parent of about 5½ feet. There is a recorded measurement of 24½ feet for a full-term fetus of a blue whale from a parent 93 feet long.

The calf is delivered in the water and is able to swim as soon as it is born. It is suckled for a period of several months, up to one year in humpbacks, keeping close to the mother until weaning time. Suckling is accomplished as in other mammals, but with the provision for doing so under water. Milk secreted by the mammary gland flows through large channels and collects in the lacteal duct. The mammary gland lies between superficial skin muscles and deeper body

Playful behavior that includes impressive leaps from the water, performed by some species of whales, is known as breaching.

muscles, which, by their contraction, force the milk out of the lacteal duct and through the nipple. Suckling can thus be accomplished speedily. Growth is fairly rapid; a sperm whale calf, for example, may double its length in the first year and may attain adult size in two or three years. The average life span is about half that of a human being.

Migrations

The principal movements of many whales are largely connected with feeding and reproduction. The large baleen whales, for example, are found in the high latitudes of the Arctic and Antarctic during the summer, when they become fat from the food they eat. Correspondingly, in the winter they disperse into the warmer subtropical waters where pairing takes place and where the young are born. Some of the migratory movements of the whales—as, for example, those of the Californian gray whale along the west coast of America and of the humpback along the coast of New Zealand on their journeys to and from the Antarctic—are predictable within fairly narrow time limits.

Seals

The seal is an aquatic mammal of the family Phocidae, suborder Pinnipedia, order Carnivora. The eared seals, consisting of the fur seals and sea lions, belong to the family Otariidae. The phocids are the true seals. They lack external ears and their bodies are torpedo-shaped. Their limbs are short, with the fingers of the forelimbs joined to form a flipper bearing separate claws and the hindlimb joined by a web. In swimming, the body is propelled by side-to-side strokes of the paddlelike hind flippers, each acting alternately in the power stroke. On land, progress is laborious, the body being hitched

Seals are gregarious and, especially at breeding time, assemble in enormous herds.

forward by the forelimbs and pushed along by the pelvic region alternately in a looping movement.

There are about eighteen kinds of phocids, those of temperate and polar seas being more numerous than those of the tropics, with one species confined to fresh water. They range in size from the small freshwater seal of Lake Baikal in southern Siberia (about 3 feet long) to the enormous sea elephant or elephant seal of the sub-Antarctic, the bulls of which reach a length of 16–18 feet.

Nearly all seals are gregarious, at least when breeding; some kinds assemble in enormous herds on sea beaches or floating sea ice. In species such as the elephant seal and gray seal the males take possession of harems of cows and drive rival bulls away from their territory. One young at a time is normally born to each adult cow and suckled for a comparatively short while; the pups gain weight rapidly on the diet of seal milk, which contains about 50% fat. During the period of suckling the cow remains ashore and does not feed.

The newborn pups are clothed in a coat of soft, silky fur, which is molted at about the time of weaning and replaced by coarser hair. In some species, such as the common or harbor seal and the sea leopard or leopard seal, the first molt is precocious and may take place partly or completely before birth. The fluffy birth coat is generally white but sometimes, as in the elephant seal, black. The cows are again impregnated soon after the birth of the pups. The gestation period is about eleven months or a little more; some species (possibly all) exhibit delayed implantation, in which the growth of the embryo is arrested at an early stage and renewed some months later, so that active gestation may actually occupy only about seven months.

Seals appear to be long-lived, with a potential span of thirty to forty years, but their average life in the wild is considerably shorter because of heavy mortality from accident and misadventure among the younger animals. Some kinds of seal—such as the common seal—inhabit coastal waters, but others—like the harp seal of the Arctic, the Weddell seal, and the crabeater seal of the Antarctic—are pelagic and live in the open sea, generally leaving the water only to lie on floating sea ice. The coastal species are more or less sedentary, but the pelagic ones make extensive, regular migrations.

Seals produce a variety of sounds, from the wailing bleat of the pup through snarls and barks to the windy roars of the elephant seal. The food of many kinds of seals consists mainly of fish; some species consume large quantities of squid, other mollusks, and crustaceans. The crabeater seal lives on planktonic crustaceans that it strains from seawater through the sieve formed by the serrated cusps of its side teeth. The leopard seal of the Antarctic feeds largely on penguins and other seabirds, as well as fish.

Seals have a thick layer of blubber under their skin, and some of the gregarious species are killed in large numbers by man for the sake of the oil that can be rendered from it. Their hides are sometimes used for leather, and the skins of new-born phocids in their fluffy natal coat are prized in the fur trade.

Sea Lions

Sea lion is a name given generally to all members of the eared seal family (Otariidae), also known as otaries. In a more restricted sense the term sea lion is applied to the larger forms, such as the northern or Steller's sea lion and to species of *Zalophus*, to which belongs the California sea lion. Otaries, along with true seals and walruses, constitute a suborder of Carnivora.

There are about fifteen species of otaries frequenting the North and South Pacific Ocean, the South Atlantic, and the southern oceans—but entirely absent from the North Atlantic. One of the southern species extends up the west coast of South America as far as the Galápagos Islands. Some species of otary undertake regular and extensive annual migrations; those breeding on the islands of the North Pacific Ocean journey as far as California every year. One of the smaller species, the California sea lion, is commonly kept in captivity and is the kind generally seen in circuses, trained to balance objects on its snout. All otaries have a thick layer of blubber beneath the hairy skin, and though fur seals are principally valued for their pelts the so-called "hair seals" are hunted for the oil obtainable from their blubber.

Otaries differ from phocids, or true seals, in having external ears and a longer and more distinct neck, and in the formation of their limbs. The limbs, as in true seals, are flippers with the digits joined, but the toes of otaries bear separate straplike extensions beyond the last joint. The locomotion of otaries is quite different from that of phocids. Their forelimbs are longer than those of phocids and their hindlimbs are long enough to be rotated forward under the body when the animal is on land. The body can thus be lifted clear of the ground; otaries can lope along at a clumsy gallop for a limited distance at considerable speed. In swimming the body is propelled by powerful strokes of the forelimbs, whose effective area is increased by a fold of skin joining the trailing edge to the body wall. The hindlimbs, unlike those of the true seals, are of secondary importance in swimming.

Adult males and females differ greatly in size. The mature bulls in some species are more than twice as large as the cows and have an enormous development of the neck muscles and of the mane on the head and neck.

The voice of an otary is harsher than that of a phocid and ranges from a sharp bark or honk to a growling roar. Otaries are strictly gregarious in the breeding season; some species gather on remote islands in herds numbering millions. They have a well-developed harem system, with the master bulls fiercely defending their territories and the younger, bachelor bulls gathering in segregated herds.

Otaries feed on squid and fish. During their time ashore the bulls fast for several months; but the cows leave the beaches at intervals, presumably to feed, after their pups are born. The gestation period is about ten or eleven months; but, as with true seals, there is probably a delay in implantation of the embryo.

Fur Seals

The otariidae also include the fur seals. These have a thick, soft fur beneath their coarse outer hair; the pelts of the young bulls and of the females form the seal fur of commerce. The wild herds are scientifically managed on their breeding grounds so that an annual crop of pelts is harvested without risking extermination of the animals—a possibility in former times, when indiscriminate slaughter was practiced.

Various kinds of fur seals are found in both northern and southern subarctic and temperate seas. The northern fur seal ranges along the North American coast from Alaska to the Mexican border and breeds in the Pribilof Islands. The southern fur seals range from sub-Antarctica to southern South America, Africa, Australia, and New Zealand.

Walruses

The walrus is a large seallike mammal in some ways intermediate between the otaries and the true seals, inhabiting the Arctic seas of Eurasia and America. The single species,

Male walruses reach a length of ten or eleven feet and may weigh more than a ton.

Odobenus rosmarus, constitutes the family Odobenidae.

Walrus males are much larger than the females, reaching a length of 10 or 11 feet and a weight of more than a ton. In both sexes the upper canine teeth form large tusks projecting downward from the mouth, the Pacific race having longer and more slender tusks than the Atlantic. The head is rounded, the eyes are small, and there are no external ears such as the fur seals have. The short, broad muzzle is covered with stiff, quill-like whiskers. The skin, which is thrown into deep folds over the shoulders, is covered with short, reddish hair, very scanty on old animals.

Walruses, unlike true seals, can turn their hindlimbs forward under the body when on land. The animals are sociable and live in groups. Young are born singly and remain with their mothers for a year or more, a habit quite different from that of most seals. Walruses usually frequent comparatively shallow water and haul out on beaches and ice floes. They feed largely on clams, which they dig out of the seabed with their tusks and shovel into their mouths with their stiff whiskers. Walruses are commercially valuable for the oil that can be extracted from their blubber, for their hides, and for their ivory tusks.

Manatees, Dugongs, and Sea Cows

The Sirenia, an order of aquatic placental mammals, is composed of the manatees, the dugongs, and the extinct (since the eighteenth century) Steller's sea cow. The name Sirenia was given in allusion to the supposed resemblance of these animals to mermaids. A manatee or a dugong as seen at a distance from the deck of a ship and especially if floating half upright, with its baby under its flipper, might well be mistaken for a mermaid, and many legends gathered around them in the early days of exploration of the Indian Ocean. Although highly specialized in structure, the Sirenia have certain characters that indicate they are perhaps distantly related to the elephants.

The manatees (genus *Trichechus*) inhabit the coasts and rivers of both sides of the tropical Atlantic. The body of the manatee is fusiform in shape, rather flattened dorsoventrally, with no externally visible neck. There are no hindlimbs; the forelimbs are small flippers without separate fingers, and the tail is expanded laterally to form a wide, rounded fluke, the principal organ of locomotion. The thick, fleshy upper lip, beset with stiff bristles, is cleft vertically in the center; the two halves can be separated or brought together and are used for seizing food and pushing it into the mouth. The body is covered with short, coarse, bristly hair, brownish or blackish according to the species. The total length usually ranges from 8 to 12 feet.

Manatees live singly or in small troops or family parties,

The manatee is an aquatic mammal that may be a distant relative of the elephant.

swimming about slowly and grazing on aquatic plants. They are quite inoffensive creatures: when not habitually menaced they can be gently approached so closely that they have been described as very stupid animals. When alarmed they can remain submerged for as much as a half hour, though normally they surface to breathe about every ten to fifteen minutes. The extent of the territory of individual animals or troops is unknown but is probably extensive.

Three species of manatee are known: *Trichechus senegalensis* inhabits the rivers and coasts of west Africa; *T. manatus* is found in the Caribbean from Florida to the West Indies; and *T. inunguis* ranges the coastal waters and rivers of the Guianas, the Amazon basin, and farther south in Brazil. The female manatee gives birth to a single offspring each year, very rarely to twins, and suckles it at the pectoral mammary glands, sometimes clasping it to the breast with the flipper.

Manatees do not venture into the open sea; in large rivers they are found far into the interior of the continents. Their food is entirely vegetable and consists of aquatic plants and

The sea otter, a member of the weasel family, lives in the coastal waters of the north Pacific and is valued for its fur.

seaweeds. Locally they are valued for their flesh, which resembles pork; for their fat, from which oil is extracted for cooking and lighting; and for their hides.

Dugongs are distinguished from their Atlantic-inhabiting relatives the manatees by, among other anatomical features, their smaller size (7 to 9 feet in the adult), broad crescent-shaped whalelike tail, fewer teeth, tusks in the upper jaw of the male, and absence of nails on the well-developed fore flipper. They frequent the shallow waters of far eastern tropical seas where, in small groups, they may be seen basking on the surface of the water or browsing on submarine pastures of seaweed. When submerged during feeding the dugong surfaces every five to ten minutes for a fresh supply of air. Although it has poor eyesight, its hearing, despite the lack of external ears, is quite good. The female produces a single calf twelve months after mating and is remarkable for its great maternal affection; the young is embraced with one flipper while it nurses on one of the two pectoral teats.

One species, with possibly several races, is known as *Dugong dugong.* It is distributed in the Red Sea, the Indian Ocean, and east in the Pacific as far as the Solomon and

Marshall islands, ranging south along the coast of northern Queensland, Australia, and north into the East China Sea. The islanders frequently hunt it with spears or harpoons, for its flesh is an esteemed delicacy. The oil obtained from its blubber has been of commercial value, and a full-grown dugong may yield from 10 to 12 gallons. In recent years the dugong has been in special danger of extinction.

The sea cow, a gigantic relative (up to 24 feet in length) of the manatee and dugong, formerly inhabited Bering and Copper islands in the Bering Strait near Kamchatka. It was discovered in 1741 and described by the German naturalist Georg Steller, who accompanied the Danish-Russian explorer Vitus Bering on his voyages to North Asia, Alaska, and Bering Island. It was killed in large numbers by Russian sealers and fur hunters, who found the animals easy to hunt; by 1768, less than thirty years after its discovery, the sea cow apparently was exterminated. When discovered, these sirenians were numerous in bays, where they browsed upon the abundant seaweed. Bones of the sea cow are still found from time to time.

Sea Otter

The sea otter, an entirely aquatic member of the subfamily Lutrinae of the weasel family (Mustelidae), is found only in the North Pacific. Like other otters, sea otters have the same general proportions as a weasel—the lithe, slender body, long neck, small ears, and short legs. The head is flattened, and the base of the tail is almost as thick as the body. The sea otter differs from other lutrinids in the structure of the feet. The forefeet digits are short and tightly fused; those of the hind feet are large and paddlelike. The skull, teeth, and other skeletal parts of the sea otter assume a pink to purple coloration as a consequence of the animals having consumed, over some period of time, large numbers of sea urchins in their natural habitat.

Few other animals produce a fur so highly valued by man and so durable. The sea otter has been completely protected in the United States since 1912 and is steadily increasing in numbers.

VI. WEALTH OF THE OCEAN

For as long as there has been recorded history the fish and whales of the ocean have served man as a source of both nutritious, palatable food and raw materials for industry. Since the mid-1800s both the demand for ocean products and the efficiency with which fishermen and whalers can harvest their quarry have increased exponentially.

Although salt has been taken from the sea for centuries it is only within comparatively recent times that men have directed efforts toward the goal of mining the other abundant minerals that are dissolved in seawater or that lie on the ocean floor. The great potential benefits have stimulated the development of a sophisticated oceanic technology that also envisions the drawing of great stores of energy.

Yet, even as man increases his dependence on the resources of the ocean, he is guilty of using these resources prodigally and of polluting the source of this wealth by using the ocean as a vast dump for dangerous substances. Until solutions are found to many grave problems mankind runs a real risk of causing irreversible deterioration in a great reservoir of wealth that until recently seemed to be inexhaustible.

15.
Fishing the World Ocean

When man first ventured to sea he probably was pursuing fish. As fishing developed it prepared the way for sea trade and became a fundamental part of modern civilization. As countries organized large fishing fleets they became sea powers. The Hanseatic League, for example, traced its beginnings to herring fishery. The rise of the Dutch as a sea power in the seventeenth century grew out of their dominance of the fisheries of the North Sea. As early as the days of the Tudors the English were fishing not only in the North Sea and other home waters but also off Iceland and Newfoundland to the west and as far as Vardö, Norway, to the east.

Growth of the Industry

The fishing industry expanded and developed rapidly when improved means for taking fish became available. The introduction of steam vessels enabled fishing crews to travel faster and farther in bigger ships. The development of diesel engines was a further improvement. The use of power equipment aboard ship made it possible to handle bigger nets and to take larger catches. The introduction of methods for icing or freezing the catch aboard ship improved the efficiency of the fishing fleet. The development of man-made fibers made it possible to use more efficient and bigger nets. Construction of factory, or mother, ships on which filleting, freezing, canning, and the manufacture of by-products could be conducted made it possible for large fleets of fishing vessels to operate thousands of miles from home ports. As the improvements were made, fishermen pushed farther and farther from their home ports until they covered most parts of the globe where fish were to be found in large enough quantities to make commercial fishing profitable.

Fish, besides being important as food and one of the world's main sources of protein, came to be a major raw material for several industries, including both the manufacture of fish meal, which is used as a feed for poultry and swine and as a fertilizer, and the production of oils of various kinds, ranging from cod-liver oil to those used in tanning, soapmaking, and the manufacture of margarine. Glue and isinglass are among the by-products of fisheries. Fishskins can be converted into fine leather.

Although it was once thought that the supply of fish in the sea was inexhaustible, since about 1900 it has been recognized that man's activities may jeopardize the stability of the stock. It is important, with the growth of the world's population and the accompanying increase in demand for foods rich in protein, that countries cooperate in managing the world's fish supply in order to take full advantage of this resource.

The oceans and inshore coastal waters of the world provide most of the catch of fish and shellfish totaling about 60 million metric tons annually in the mid-1970s. Inland fisheries in freshwater lakes, streams, farm ponds and rice paddies are estimated to yield more than 9.6 million metric tons of fish and shellfish annually.

Methods

Perhaps the oldest method of catching fish is that of direct attack with a spear. Another ancient method involves the use of a trap, such as the weir, to intercept and capture roving fish. Fishweirs admit fish at high tide and trap them when the tide ebbs. Expansion of the fishweir idea into a trap of wattle hedging and then into fixed nets is a logical evolution. Another form of trap is that into which fish are attracted by food; examples are the traps for catching lobsters, prawns, and crabs.

The baited line was probably first used without a hook, as it still is when eels are caught by "clotting" or "bobbing"—that is, by tying a bunch of worms at the end of a line and, when the bait has been taken by the eel, drawing the line in swiftly before the eel has disengaged its teeth. This method was improved upon by the introduction of a hook, the earliest form of which may have been a thorn. From these methods the more elaborate devices employed in modern commercial fishing were evolved, the most important being the system for bringing the trap, in the form of a net, to the fish instead of trusting to the natural movements of the fish or the lure of the bait to bring the fish to a stationary trap.

In the fisheries of the North Atlantic and North Pacific, which are the most highly developed in the world, the chief methods of fishing are trawling, seining, gill netting (drifting), and lining. In trawling and seining, a net is brought to the fish; in gill netting the fish are driven into the net; and in lining the line may be brought to the fish or the fish to the line.

Trawling

In the case of the trawl, the trawler drags a bag-shaped net whose mouth (also called the wings) is kept open by one of

The otter trawl is most effective for catching bottom-dwelling fish.

three methods: by placing a beam across the head of the net; by towing the net with a pair of ships, one at each side of the net; or by attaching wooden kites, or otter boards, to the sides of the mouth. The beam trawl is used only on a few small fishing craft. Pair trawling is an efficient method for catching hake and herring off the bottom. The otter trawl, which is employed on almost all but the smallest trawlers, is the most effective device for taking demersal (bottom-living) fish. The efficiency of the otter trawl has been improved by several modifications, one of which is the Vigneron-Dahl modification, a French invention in which the otter boards are attached to the wings of the net by wires up to 50 fathoms (300 feet) long.

Seining

In seining, the fish are gradually encircled with a net in the center of which is a bag similar to the one at the end (the "cod-end") of the trawl. Seines are used for catching both pelagic (top-living) and demersal fish.

The types of seine used most frequently in pelagic fisheries are the lampara net, the purse seine, the rather similar ring net, and the Danish seine. When these nets are used, a shoal of fish is first surrounded with a curtain or wall of netting that is buoyed at the surface and weighted at the bottom. The lampara net has a large central bunt and short wings; the school of fish is worked into the bunt and captured. With the purse seine, once the school is surrounded, the bottom of the net is closed by drawing a line through purse rings attached to the lead line; the fish are then concentrated and removed by a brail (a dip net) or are pumped aboard the fishing vessel.

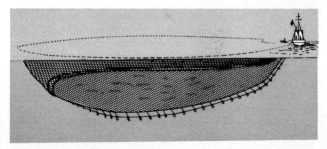

The salmon purse seine is an excellent device for catching fish that stay near the water's surface.

A fishing boat lays out its seine net at Port Day, British Columbia.

The ring net resembles the lampara net in two ways: it has two wings, and the bottom of the central portion is closed with a purse line; it differs, however, in that it does not have a prominent bunt. The Danish seine, so-called because it was invented in Denmark, is a highly efficient means of catching demersal fish. It is widely used in other countries, particularly Scotland and England. With the Danish seine an area of the seabed is first encircled with two ropes of equal length of up to about one mile; to adjacent ends of the ropes is attached a trawl-shaped net. When the ropes and net have been placed in position, the free ends of the ropes are drawn to an anchored ship, gradually reducing the area of seabed surrounded. Fish are driven before the moving ropes to the center of the net, which is drawn up to the ship.

Gill Netting

The drift, or gill, net differs from the trawl and the seine in that it is not actively brought to the fish. It differs from the stationary trap and the many forms of stationary net in that it is attached either to a floating buoy or to a drifting ship and moves with the buoy or ship under the influence of wind and tide. It is lightweight but strong, being made of cotton, linen, or man-made fibers; this net is the principal type used in the European herring fisheries.

Each herring net is from 50 to 60 yards long and about 14

yards deep; fleets of as many as 85 nets may be placed in the water at a time from one vessel so as to form a wall of netting hanging perpendicularly in the water. The net is generally adjusted so that it floats with its top about 3 yards below the surface of the water; it is kept at the desired level by a series of buoys, or "pellets," connected with the headline by strops. This net is devised to catch fish by the gills as they attempt to pass through the netting. Drift nets are also used for catching mackerel, pilchards, sprats, and salmon.

Lining

Fishing with lines and baited hooks was once of much greater commercial importance than it is in modern times. There are three methods of lining: hand-lining, long-lining, and trolling. In hand-lining the line is drawn in by hand as soon as the fish is felt; in long-lining the line is shot out and left unattended until hauled in; and in trolling the lines are towed through the water and hauled in when fish are caught.

Hand lines reached their greatest commercial importance in the Pacific tuna fisheries, but since the early 1960s most of the Pacific tuna catch has been taken with large purse seines. Hand lines are still used in taking such fish as cod, mackerel, and snapper.

The anchor gill net catches fish by the gills as they try to swim through the vertical fiber netting.

A long line is fitted with a great number of hooks (sometimes as many as 5,500) attached to the main line by thin lines of some strong material; the attaching materials vary with the fish sought. Long lines may be set on the sands at low tide but usually are worked from fishing vessels in deep water. When deep-water lines are used to catch demersal fish they are anchored and buoyed at each end and sometimes at intervals along their lengths; when used to catch pelagic fish they are not anchored. Deep-sea long lines are chiefly used on the bottom for cod and halibut and in open-sea fishing for tuna. The baits, which vary according to local custom, include mussels, squid, octopuses, herring, and small pelagic fish.

Troll lines are long, single lines with one or more barbed hooks at the free end. They are baited with a natural or artificial lure and drawn behind a moving boat. The baited hooks are held at the desired depth by the speed of the boat and by weights attached to the line. The lines require constant attention. Troll lines are used principally in the salmon and tuna fisheries.

Harvesting Machines

A relatively new type of fishing gear is the harvesting machine combined with a pump and is used by the Soviets in the northern part of the Caspian Sea for sardinelike fish and by the Americans for squid off the California coast. In both cases the prey is attracted by light. In the Caspian the fish are sucked on board with pumps from depths up to 360 feet (110 meters), but squid fishing can be done near the surface. Once on board the fish or squid are strained from the water. The difficulty in fish pumping is to avoid damage to the catch. Only small fish can be pumped without injury.

Fishing Vessels

Vessels used for fishing in the protected waters of rivers, lakes, and sounds are small and are nearly always open vessels without closed decks. Although subject to many variations in shape and in materials of construction they are essentially the same the world over. While the open boat is still widely used for commercial fishing in many parts of Africa, Asia, and South America, in Europe and the United States most such craft are used by fishermen who fish for sport only.

The *Princess Elizabeth*, a British long-range deep-sea trawler, was built for cod fishing in the north Atlantic.

Short-range boats designed to fish in exposed bays or to make short runs out into the ocean are by far the most numerous of commercial fishing vessels and are used throughout the maritime world. Generally about 20–45 feet in length, they are either partly or totally enclosed; they always have partial decks over the bow and stern and quite often have full decks broken only by fish holds or hatches. There is an infinite variety of craft of this kind. Sails are still used to a limited extent in some areas, but the internal-combustion engine and diesel engine are now practically the universal sources of power.

Intermediate-range boats can go out into the open sea and stay for several days. They range from 45 to 80 feet in length and use various types of fishing gear. With fully enclosed decks, mechanical propulsion, and living accommodations they can fish in relatively exposed waters a considerable distance from the home port. They operate mainly out of ports in the more highly industrialized countries.

Long-range vessels are from 80 to 200 feet in length. Among the various types are the trawlers that operate from both sides of the Atlantic into the Atlantic fishing grounds; the tuna clippers that operate off the western coasts of the Americas; the tuna hand-liners and bait boats operated by the Japanese; and the whale-killer ships operated by Japanese and European interests in the Antarctic. All such craft are highly mechanized and expensive.

Means of preserving a catch of fish is a necessity for inter-mediate-range and long-range fishing vessels. Salt was the first medium, but it was largely replaced in the twentieth century by ice. Modern vessels, particularly the long-range type, use mechanical refrigeration extensively. In such fisheries as the Pacific tuna, fish are held for three or four months before the vessel returns to port.

Mother ships that accompany smaller fishing vessels to distant fishing grounds form a special category. These ships are equipped to supply, feed, and maintain large numbers of men for a long period of time and to process the fish on board. The codfishing schooners of the North Atlantic were proba-bly the first mother ships. They remained at sea for long periods while individual fishermen in dories brought the fish aboard to be salted down. Salmon, tuna, cod, and crab canner-ies and freezer ships of various kinds operate in different parts of the world.

In early times, as distinctive types of vessels were devel-oped in different areas, they generally were named for the area plus an additional name, the derivation of which has often been lost in time. The Yorkshire coble, the Hastings lugger, and Chesapeake sharpie are examples.

As communications developed and fishing spread through-out the world the old names and place designations have been dropped, and vessels are now generally named for the type of fishing gear they use. Ships fishing with nets are called trawlers, seiners, gill netters, draggers, and drifters. Vessels using hooks and lines are called hand-liners, long-liners, trollers, pole boats, and bait boats.

Trends

Since the beginning of the twentieth century the world catch of fish has increased greatly because of increased demands for food and improved methods of capturing, processing, storing, and transporting fish. The progress made in fishing methods since 1930 alone has been greater than that made in the previous three thousand years.

Until the late nineteenth century, methods for taking fish had not changed for centuries. Sails and oars were still used to propel fishing craft, and manpower alone was used to handle the gear. The first great improvement was the adop-tion of steam propulsion in fishing vessels, followed later by gasoline engines and still later by semidiesel and diesel en-gines, which have largely replaced steam power. Of equal and perhaps greater importance was the introduction of power equipment for handling fishing gear. Power winches were adapted to hauling large otter trawls, long lines, troll lines, and gill nets. Mechanically driven turntables and rollers and the introduction of drum reels permitted the handling of large purse seines. Adoption of a hydraulic power block further increased the ability of fishermen to handle this gear rapidly.

The development of electronic fishing aids after World War II also increased fishing efficiency. Use of loran, a system of long range navigation with radio, permitted vessels to return to known fishing areas with greater precision than had previously been possible. Electronic depth sounders enabled fishermen to make a continuous record of water depths and to follow bottom contours. Echo sounders made it possible for fishermen to locate schools of fish that could not be detected by other means. Radar increased safety, and the general adoption of radio communications kept fishermen in touch with shore facilities and other fishing boats.

Use of man-made fibers that can be produced with the characteristics required for fishing gear greatly increased the efficiency of nets and resulted in increased catches. These characteristics included flexibility, resistance to rot and abrasion, high strength, and low visibility in water. Other major improvements included the use of airplanes to locate schools of pelagic fish and the development of powered pumps to transfer fish from purse seines to the fishing boat and to unload the catch at processing plants.

Major Commercial Species

Among the commercially important food fish and the localities in which they are taken are the following: herring, in northern inshore and offshore waters; pilchards, temperate inshore water; menhaden, temperate to subtropical inshore water; anchovies, tropical inshore; shad, temperate; Atlantic and Pacific salmon, northern temperate water of the two oceans; tuna, tropical offshore water; mackerel, temperate offshore; cod, northern water; haddock, northern water; whitings, temperate inshore; croakers, warm to temperate inshore; ocean perch, temperate; and flounder, northern temperate. The principal species used in the manufacture of fish meal and oil are the menhaden and herring in the United States, the herring in Canada and in many northern European countries, anchovies in Peru and Chile, and the pil-

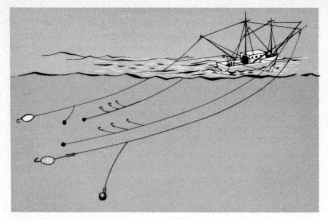

Tuna troll lines are towed through the water and hauled in when enough fish are caught on their many baited hooks.

chards and maasbanker (mossbunker) in southern Africa.

Shellfish

The name *shellfish* embraces the edible species of both crustaceans (such as crabs, lobsters, crayfish, prawns, and shrimps) and mollusks (such as oysters, mussels, cockles, scallops, clams, squid, and whelks). Their economic importance varies from country to country but is usually less than that for fish because of smaller yield, although the average price per pound is usually much higher.

The largest fisheries for shellfish include those for shrimps in the Indian Ocean and Western Pacific; oysters, clams, crabs, and scallops along the Atlantic and Gulf coasts of the United States; northern lobsters in the North Atlantic waters of the United States and Canada; the spiny (rock) lobster of the Republic of South Africa, Australia, and New Zealand; and the king crab of the north Pacific.

Leading Fishing Countries

The fisheries in the cold and temperate waters of the Northern Hemisphere yielded almost 85% of the world catch, which totaled more than 58 million metric tons in 1969. Asia, excluding the U.S.S.R., produced approximately 44% of the world catch; South America 9%; Europe, excluding the

U.S.S.R., 18%; U.S.S.R., 14%; North America, 7%; Africa, 7%; and Oceania, less than 0.5%.

About 27% of the world catch was reduced into meal and oil; nearly 30% was marketed fresh; more than 11% was cured; about 18% was frozen; 10% was canned; and 1.4% was used for miscellaneous purposes. The marketing of frozen fish and the manufacture of fish into meal and oil increased rapidly after 1950.

Japan led all countries in volume of catch, producing one-seventh of the world catch. Other major fish producers were the U.S.S.R., China, Peru, United States, Norway, India, Korea, Spain, Indonesia, the Philippines, Chile, and Canada. These thirteen countries together produced nearly 70% of the world harvest of fish and shellfish.

U.S. Fisheries

Fisheries in the United States are located along the coasts of and in the Atlantic and Pacific oceans, Bering Sea, Gulf of Mexico, Great Lakes, and many rivers. In the Atlantic, U.S. fisheries are conducted from the Grand Banks of Newfoundland to northern South America, and off the coast of Africa.

Many shrimp trawlers operate out of Southport, N. C., where coastal waters offer a wide variety of shellfish.

In the Pacific the range extends from the Bering Sea to the coasts of Peru and Chile.

Although more than two hundred species are taken commercially by U.S. fishermen, the menhaden, used almost entirely in the manufacture of fish meal and oil, accounted for almost 40% of the catch in the mid-1970s. Other leading species were tuna, salmon, shrimps, clams, herring, crabs, and flounder. These fish, together with the menhaden, accounted for 71% of the U.S. catch.

The importance of U.S. fisheries increased considerably in the twentieth century, largely because of an increase in the output of manufactured products, particularly canned and frozen fish, shellfish, and fish meal and oil. The catch reached a peak of 2,429,000 metric tons in 1962 but declined rapidly after that year to about 2.2 million metric tons in 1975. Reduced production of menhaden used in the manufacture of meal and oil accounted for most of the decline.

Fish are taken commercially by U.S. fishermen in 45 states, but almost three-fourths of the catch is normally made by fishermen operating in or out of only seven states: Alaska, California, Louisiana, Massachusetts, Mississippi, North Carolina, and Virginia. About 9% is taken off the coasts of Canada and Central and South America. The major portion of the U.S. catch of ocean perch, one of the principal food fish landed on the Atlantic coast, is taken off Canada; more than 15% of the catch of shrimp taken in the Gulf of Mexico is harvested off Mexico; most of the catch of tuna, the leading species landed on the Pacific coast, is taken in international waters off Mexico and Central and South America.

Purse seines account for more than 60% of the tonnage of the U.S. catch, and otter trawls account for 25%. An important trend in the fisheries of the United States is a decrease in the tonnage used for human food and the rapid increase in the catch used for industrial products and animal food. In four of the years between 1958 and 1972 the catch used for industrial production and animal food exceeded the quantity used for human food.

The U.S. catch failed to keep pace with the rapidly increasing production in most other countries. As the world catch of fish increased from about 14.9 million metric tons (live weight) in 1945 to 70 million metric tons in 1975, the U.S. catch remained static. Production of virtually every other country whose fishermen harvested stocks also fished by U.S. fishermen increased during this period.

Despite the low U.S. catch the use of fishery products in the United States increased steadily over the years until the late 1960s on both a total volume and a per capita basis. In 1950 total utilization of fishery products by the United States amounted to more than 6.5 billion pounds (live weight basis), or 43 pounds per capita. The increased demand was met by a dramatic increase in imports. In 1950 only 13% of the fishery products received in the United States were imported, but in 1975 imports accounted for 52%.

Conservation

As fishing vessels were progressively mechanized, fishing gear was improved, and better methods of preservation developed, a new problem soon appeared. Some of the species in the sea that had been considered inexhaustible began to show signs of being overfished. The taking of fish on older and more readily accessible fishing grounds became more and more difficult, even with increased fishing effort. In some instances the average size of the species decreased below desirable market sizes. This forced the more aggressive fishermen to move to new and more remote fishing grounds, while on the older and nearer fishing banks fewer and smaller fish had to be shared by an increasing number of fishermen from many countries.

The problem of overfishing first attracted attention about 1900 in the northeastern Atlantic (the North Sea and adjacent waters), where fishing fleets were among the first to be mechanized and where intensive fishing had been carried on for many years. It was there that leading biologists of the day first turned their attention to the problems of strictly marine fisheries. There too was organized the International Council for the Exploration of the Sea, the first international scientific organization devoted to the study of the sea and its fisheries. The formation of the council marked the beginning of effective sea fisheries research.

Some authorities estimate that the total world catch should not exceed 61 million tons a year. Others calculate, however, that annual yield of all edible products of the water all over the world could range up to 4 billion tons. Many scientists think that 100 million to 200 million tons is realistic for the 1970s. Yet the increasing pollution of the world's fresh waters and oceans causes uncertainty, not only because entire stocks of fish and other products can be destroyed, but also because an increasing number of living organisms are contaminated at harvest with poisons such as DDT and mercury.

Renewing the Yield

Fish stocks belong to the group of resources that are renewable, in contrast to those resources, such as minerals or fossil fuels, that are irreplaceable within practical limits. To preserve a renewable resource it is not necessary to refrain from using it, but for maximum benefit it must be used in a way that permits the resource to regenerate itself rapidly enough to yield the maximum return on a continuing basis.

Populations of fish and other organisms tend to remain in balance with their environment. The losses in a population must in time be balanced by compensating accessions, otherwise the species will disappear. When losses are increased, accessions increase also, so that the population again tends to come into balance with its environment. It is this natural resiliency or ability to compensate for increased mortality that enables a population to survive an increase in mortality — either from increased predation, which includes fishing by man, or from disease and other natural calamities.

The problem posed to the fisheries scientist is that of determining and recommending the fishing intensity, between zero and the economically practicable maximum, that will meet the two conditions of maximum value to mankind and production in perpetuity. This is often referred to as the maximum sustainable yield. The general objective of maximum sustainable yield is subject to some modification in particular fisheries. For most species, one result of increased fishing is a decrease in the average size and age of individuals in the population. Increased total catch in such instances is often accompanied by a larger proportion of smaller fish. Since smaller fish are usually less desirable in the marketplace, a compromise must be reached between maximum total poundage and the most-desired sizes. In other cases economy of fishing effort may be of at least temporary importance even though total yield is the primary objective of research and conservation measures.

Fisheries Research

In order to develop the minimum information needed for the management of a sea fishery, special biological information is required: data concerning the age of the fish at various sizes and at sexual maturity, the migratory habits of the species, the rate and success of reproduction, the fishery environment, and estimates of population magnitude, particularly of the commercially desirable sizes. Fundamental to all such information are complete records of the amount of the catch and the average size of the fish taken, including information concerning the area in which the catch was made and how much effort was expended.

Fishery research also includes studies that lead to better and fuller use of fishery resources. This branch of research, usually referred to as fisheries technology, involves studies intended to improve fish processing, preservation, and transportation methods; other studies aim at developing useful products from fish wastes. Basic research in this field includes studies of the structure and composition of fish muscle and fish oils, as well as studies in the metabolism of marine bacteria and their role in fish spoilage. Since protein from animal sources is an important component of balanced human nutrition, the full and efficient use of fish and fish products is of first importance.

Most countries with a highly organized fishing industry have made some provision for research study and management. The oldest organized government sea fisheries research units date from just before and soon after the start of the twentieth century.

In the United Kingdom the research station at Plymouth, England, is perhaps the oldest and best known. Special government-supported research stations equipped with seagoing research vessels are located at Lowestoft, England, and Aberdeen, Scotland. Other European fishing countries have similar organizations.

In the United States sea-fishery research is conducted jointly by the federal government and the maritime states. The U.S. Bureau of Commercial Fisheries has special laboratories in Seattle, Wash., and Woods Hole, Mass., as well as in other fishing areas, while some states, such as California, have special sea-fisheries laboratories and research vessels of their own.

In Canada the federal government founded and operates three marine fishery biological stations. Japan and the U.S.S.R. are rapidly expanding their already substantial efforts. Additions of relatively large seagoing fishery research vessels indicate the serious intent of an increasing number of governments to participate in the exploration, research, and harvest of sea fisheries.

The International Council for the Exploration of the Sea, the first organization of its kind, held its inaugural meeting in Copenhagen in 1902. Similar organizations to deal with research in the Mediterranean and North American areas were founded in 1919 and 1920 respectively. In 1943 a council for the Indo-Pacific area was formed by the fisheries division of the Food and Agriculture Organization of the United Nations (UN).

Parallel with these efforts was the development of international agreements in the form of treaties and conventions. Following the success of the international convention for conserving the fur seals of the North Pacific in 1911, Canada and the United States founded the Pacific Halibut Convention of 1924 to deal with halibut in the northeastern Pacific. Similar agreements include the International Pacific Salmon Fisheries Commission (1937), the International Whaling Commission (1946), the Inter-American Tropical Tuna Commission and the International Commission for the Northwest Atlantic Fisheries (both 1950), the International Convention for the High Seas Fisheries of the North Pacific Ocean (1953), and the Convention for the Regulation of the Meshes of Fishing Nets and for Limits of Fish (1954). These and other international conventions and their commissions for carrying out the terms of the conventions have become effective instruments in dealing with regional problems of international fishery conservation and management.

16.
Whaling and Sealing

As Herman Melville put the matter in *Moby Dick*: "The gallant Perseus, a son of Jupiter, was the first whaleman; and to the eternal honor of our calling be it said, that the first whale attacked by our brotherhood was not killed with any sordid intent. Those were the knightly days of our profession, when we only bore arms to succor the distressed, and not to fill men's lamp-feeders." After Melville, the epic qualities of the whaling enterprise of the 1800s hardly need comment. The chase after these greatest of living things was hard and dangerous, and many a Sag Harbor and Nantucket wife was widowed when a fragile whaleboat was broken in the struggle. The dangers were not only from the ocean and the quarry itself: In 1871 alone, thirty-four American whaleships were trapped in the Arctic ice. Although most of the ships were crushed, the crewmen dragged their whaleboats to clear water and made their way to safety without losing a single man. It was a truly heroic conclusion to a great disaster. Yet whaling has now become a technologically efficient industry that exists only to "fill men's lamp-feeders"—and to provide food for animals and human beings and oil for industrial lubrication and for conversion into soaps and fatty acids used in

A watercolor of the 1840s depicts the perils of whaling that existed in the nineteenth century.

cosmetics and detergents. In recent years the whaling industry has rightly become a prime target of the movements dedicated to ecology and the conservation of natural resources. There are sound historic reasons for this concern not only on the part of conservationists but also within the industry itself. The right whale and the great blue whale, the largest creature that has ever lived, have been hunted almost to extinction; the fin whale population has decreased sharply; and the California gray whale has been saved only because it is strictly protected. Popular concern has also been directed against the sealing industry. The focus of this concern, however, is less on the preservation of the populations of commercially important seals and more on the distasteful practices of the trade, in which defenseless and appealing seal pups are clubbed to death on icy killing grounds.

The Beginnings of Whaling

It is likely that Stone Age man hunted the smaller whales and dolphins. Certainly the Eskimos and North American Indians whaled from ancient times with weapons of bone and horn, flint, and slate. One Alaskan whaling settlement dates back to A.D. 100–200. In Europe, the cradle of whaling as it subsequently developed, the earliest records concern Norway and Flanders in the ninth century, but the first important development was the enterprise conducted by French and Spanish Basques from the shores of the Bay of Biscay. Begun in about the tenth century, this hunt for the Biscayan or North Atlantic right whale flourished in late medieval times, was in decline by the mid-seventeenth century, and died out in the eighteenth.

Meanwhile, by 1400, some of the Basques were pioneering the whaling voyage. Leaving the harbors and watchtowers of the shore fishery, they built ships that eventually followed the Biscayan whale to Newfoundland, the Gulf of Saint Lawrence, and, in the sixteenth century, to Iceland, where they found Icelanders and Norwegians already engaged in the business. By 1700, however, the Biscayan whale in the eastern North Atlantic was a much depleted species. But somewhere in their far northern voyages the Basques fell in with the Greenland or Arctic right whale, which was much more massive than the Biscayan whale and had thicker blubber and longer whalebone.

The Greenland whale came to support a new enterprise, the northern whale fishery, which continued for three centuries after 1611 when the Muscovy Company sent English merchant and whaler Thomas Edge with the *Mary Margaret* and the *Elizabeth* of London on the first Spitsbergen whaling voyage. The Basque whalemen were mostly engaged in the north under foreign flags, for they were much sought after as harpooners and expert flensers (blubber-strippers) by the British, German, French, and especially Dutch vessels that came to exploit the Greenland fishery.

At first whales were killed in the Spitsbergen bays and the blubber flensed from them was boiled out in coppers (large kettles) on the beach. The populous Dutch seasonal settlement called Smeerenburg (Blubbertown) belonged to this period. Bay whaling declined after 1635, however, and the ships began to whale along the ice between Spitsbergen and Greenland and in the Davis Strait; they flensed the whales at sea and casked the blubber for "trying-out" (rendering) at home. After 1840 this ice fishery in turn began to decline. The last phase belonged to the Scottish steam and sail whalers, and these sailed as much for the long whalebone (in great demand for use as stays in corsets) as for the oil. The last Dundee whaler came home "clean"—empty—in 1913.

Yankee Whalers

In the Pacific, north of Bering Strait and in the Okhotsk Sea, the Arctic right whale had a last stronghold that was breached by American whalers after 1843. They called this whale the "bowhead." The bowhead fishery was prosecuted so vigorously that it was depleted by 1908.

Turning again to the Atlantic right whale a fishery on the western side of the North Atlantic was started by New England settlers before 1645. This flourished for a time but was dying by 1800. Meanwhile it had given rise to one of the greatest maritime ventures in history, the American sperm-whale fishery, begun in 1712 when a shore whaler, blown off the coast in a storm, fastened a sperm whale and got it safely home. Oil from the sperm whale was found to be a much superior illuminant to that from whalebone whales, while the spermaceti from the head made the finest wax candles. More and more vessels sailed from the ports of New England to "whale out in the deep for sperm whales."

These New Englanders were at the Azores in 1765, on the coast of Brazil in 1774, and in the Indian Ocean by 1789. Although Great Britain first sought sperm whales in the Pacific in 1788, the monopoly of this worldwide industry was

American. In the peak year of 1846 there were 729 Yankee whaleships at sea. The slow decline that followed (although the last sperm-whaling voyage ended as late as 1925) was due to several causes, including the discovery of petroleum in Pennsylvania in 1859. The sperm-whale fishery was the only old-style venture that may not have ended through overfishing.

As a consequence of the sperm whalers' explorations two further species were exploited. The southern right whale, at first taken in great numbers around the southern continents and sub-Antarctic islands, fared like its northern relative and was greatly reduced by 1900. The Pacific gray whale, hugging the California coast on its winter migration, suffered great depredations in the breeding lagoons from the boats of both whaleships and shore stations.

Old-style shore whaling, although extinct or dying on the east and west Atlantic seaboards, was carried on elsewhere during the nineteenth century. Excluding Japan (which had stations for gray, right, and humpback whaling by a netting method evolved independently of the European tradition), there were settlements in California, South Africa, Australia, New Zealand, and Tasmania. By the 1960s these settlements had disappeared except in the Azores, where a shore fishery for sperm whales had existed since 1832, and in Madeira, where the Azores whaling spread in 1941. There the Portuguese islanders hunt in open boats with hand harpoon and lance as did their forebears who learned the trade in Yankee whaleships long ago.

Modern Whaling

In the 1860s, when right and gray whaling were already in decline from overfishing, the industry received a new impetus. The Norwegian sealing captain and whaler Svend Foyn developed a method of hunting the great rorquals, including the blue and finback whales that swim too fast for pursuit in open boats. Foyn fired a heavy grenade harpoon from a cannon mounted in the bow of a steam vessel. His methods revolutionized whaling and have remained unaltered in their essentials.

The new steam whaling, which by 1900 was conducted from many stations in the North Atlantic and Arctic, soon spread to Japan, Korea, British Columbia, and, after about 1908, to the coasts of the southern continents. Its varying fortunes before World War II were usually associated with periods of local overfishing. In Norway, after 1900, a growing scarcity of whales, along with legislation hostile to the steam whalers and designed to protect the Norwegian cod fishermen, caused the industry to look to the Antarctic, where expeditions between 1892 and 1904 had reported abundant rorquals. When in 1904 Norwegian whaling Captain C. A. Larsen established a base at Grytviken in South Georgia the Antarctic industry had begun.

Antarctic Whaling

Whaling from Grytviken and other stations prospered at South Georgia and soon spread to the other Antarctic islands of South Orkney and South Shetland, where the first factory ships operated. Their heyday was the period from 1906 to 1927. They were really mobile shore stations, for they flensed their whales alongside and therefore could not work on the high seas but had to seek the shelter of some island bay or the calm of the ice-locked Ross Sea. Then in 1925 the steamship *Lancing* was fitted with a slipway in the stern so that whales could be hauled on deck. Its great success opened the great era of pelagic (open-sea) whaling.

Factory ships could now operate wherever their whale catchers found whales in the Southern Ocean. They could also operate outside territorial waters where at that time they were free from any controls or regulations. Some tankers were rapidly converted with stern slipways for pelagic whaling, while others were used as transports, bringing fuel oil to factories in the ice and taking home cargoes of whale oil so that the factories could work a protracted season. In the 1930–31 season, within five years of the *Lancing*'s voyage, forty-one factory ships operated to produce 3.5 million barrels of oil. At mid-twentieth century this Antarctic production, and by consequence world production also, remained the highest in the history of whaling.

Technique

Except for the introduction of electronic aids and reconnaissance aircraft, the whaling technique developed by 1931 changed little after 1945. A typical pelagic expedition was made up of a factory ship of about 16,000 gross tons that operated eleven or twelve steam whale catchers, each of about 550 tons, although newer catchers attained 900 tons and had diesel engines. The whale catchers operated within about 100 miles of the factory ship, and helicopters some-

The harpoon, which is fired from a special gun into a whale, has four barbs plus a grenade head that explodes inside the animal.

A whale catcher (foreground), acting as a buoy-boat for dead whales, stands off the stern of a factory ship, where several more inflated blue and finback whales await flensing, processing, and storage.

times helped the search. Experiments with scouting aircraft in the Antarctic were first made in 1929, but it was not until 1950 that, in the form of helicopters, they were used effectively. The search from the catcher is still the job of the lookout at the masthead, but he is often helped by the echowhalefinder, developed from wartime asdic (a sonar device). The whale scarer, another sonar device, frightens whales into flight with ultrasonic vibrations, so that, getting out of breath, they blow more often and are more easily followed. Whales are shot with the grenade harpoon. (Before and after World War II there were experiments with an electric harpoon, but it did not win favor with the industry.)

The dead whale, winched back on the manila whaleline, is inflated to prevent sinking and marked with a flag. At the end of the day the flagged whales are collected and towed back to the factory ship or shore station. Flags are sometimes missed because of fog, heavy seas, or nightfall and, therefore, radio buoys that transmit a continuous signal to the catchers were introduced. Flags with radar reflector cones, which can be detected on the catcher's radar screen, are also used.

A whale delivered to a factory ship is heaved through the stern slipway with a steel claw. On the afterdeck the blubber is removed in three enormous strips. The flensed carcass is then hauled to the foredeck, where it is dismembered and the meat stripped. Blubber, meat, and bone are stuffed into separate cookers, the mouths of which are flush with the deck. Some meat is frozen for human consumption, mainly in Japan. A proportion of the lean meat is usually not pressure-cooked for oil extraction but is fed into the meat meal plant. Little more than 45 minutes is taken to dispose of a blue whale weighing more than 100 tons, and 30 minutes suffice for a finback whale.

Oil is extracted by means of steam pressure cookers, and factory and shore stations may use both vertical pressure cookers and "rotating apparatuses." The latter, introduced after 1925 to speed up oil extraction, are the Hartmann, Kvaener, and Kampden machines: the whale material is cooked in a perforated drum rotating within the horizontal pressure casing of the machine. Rotating apparatuses are more often used for meat and bone than for blubber. The products of cooking are oil, glue water, and the "grax," which is a sludge of bone and protein particles. In most factory ships the grax-and-glue-water mixture, although containing 3 to 13% oil in the glue water, was formerly discharged into the sea, but sludge separators, called superdecanters, were introduced in 1951 both afloat and ashore. In these the grax is removed from the glue water, which then passes through centrifugal separators where most of the oil is recovered. Protein can be concentrated from the separated glue water by space-drying for these processes. Separated grax from the superdecanters is dried to make bone or meat meal. Factory ships usually discard bone grax.

Whale and Sperm Oils

Modern whaling exploits the great rorquals among whalebone whales and the sperm whale among toothed whales. Whalebone whales yield whale oil, which is a mixture of true fats and is edible, whereas the sperm whale yields sperm oil, which is chemically distinct, being a mixture of waxes, and is inedible, having industrial uses only. Most of the oil from whalebone whales and sperm whales comes from the blubber, which yields 50–80% oil by weight, but the bones also yield 10–70%, and the meat yields 2–8% by weight.

Mineral oil, by the late nineteenth century, had replaced whale oil as an illuminant and lubricant—and whale oil was mostly used in soapmaking. The demand for whale oil increased after 1908, however, when the method of hardening fatty oils into solid fats by catalytic hydrogenation was introduced. Whale oil by the mid-twentieth century was mainly hardened to make margarine and high-grade cooking fat.

Sperm oil, although superior to whale oil as an illuminant, was also replaced by mineral oil by the late nineteenth century, and sperm whaling languished until the 1930s, when sperm oil found new industrial uses. The crude oil is used in the quenching and cold rolling of steel, and also in leather dressing. Treated with sulfur it provides extreme pressure lubricants, and it can be hardened to make textile sizes and wax compositions. Saponification yields fatty acids for soaps and fatty alcohols for cosmetics and detergents. Because in modern sperm whaling the great spermaceti organ in the head is usually cooked with the blubber, crude sperm oil contains spermaceti, removed by chilling ("wintering"), which causes the spermaceti to separate as a white waxy solid. Spermaceti is used in textile finishing and for pomades and cosmetics, and it still provides the finest wax candles. After removal of spermaceti the refined sperm oil is used for lubricating high-speed machinery and precision instruments and for textile lubrication.

The by-products of whaling became more important after World War II. The chief by-product, meat meal, is used for cattle cake and poultry food. Other by-products include bone meal and guano for fertilizers, frozen whalemeat for human and animal food, meat extracts and liver meal, liver oil rich in vitamin A, and a certain amount of ductless gland for hormone extracts. Ambergris, still important in perfumery, is occasionally found in sperm whales. Whalebone, the horny plates hanging from the palate of the whalebone whales, is still used, though not widely, for corsets and for bristles on industrial brushes.

The Future of Whaling

The future of whaling and of whales themselves is of great concern to both hunters and conservationists. Because the whale has a gestation period of a year or more, followed by a period of lactation and rest, replenishment of depleted whale herds is slow. The right whale, which supported the Spitsbergen and Davis Strait fisheries, was hunted nearly to extinction and is rarely sighted today. Until the twentieth century, Antarctic waters were a haven for fin and blue whales, which could not be taken by old methods.

Japan alone harvested 2,829 whales valued at $47.4 million in 1975. The result of such intensive fishing has been virtual exhaustion of the Antarctic grounds. Japanese whalers now concentrate on the North Pacific.

Regulation

Modern shore whaling, unlike the old-style whaling, was from its earliest days subject to some kind of regulation in several countries. Norway had legislation for shore stations in 1896. Such regulations took the form of whaling under license and limitation of the numbers of whale catchers employed. Antarctic pelagic whaling was at first unrestricted. After the peak season of 1930–31, however, the whaling companies began (in 1933) certain voluntary agreements designed to protect the whale-oil market, but these were only partially successful in controlling production. Meanwhile it became evident that blue whales (and also humpback whales) were being overfished. Oil production was maintained, but only by shifting the burden from blue whales to the less valuable but populous finback whales. In 1937 and 1938 the governments of Great Britain, Norway, and Germany signed agreements to restrict the pelagic industry, and in

1946 the International Whaling Convention set up the International Whaling Commission.

The governments of most whaling countries joined the commission, and its schedule provides for conservation in most parts of the world. It defines minimum lengths for caught whales, the duration of whaling seasons for separate species, and the areas outside the Antarctic where factory ships may operate; it specifies a sanctuary area in the Antarctic that can be opened or closed at discretion; it protects nursing whales and calves and protects blue, humpback, right whales, and Pacific gray whales entirely; it provides against waste by insisting that meat and bone be processed as well as blubber; and it provides for inspection to see that regulations are carried out.

There is special legislation for Antarctic pelagic whaling, where a limit is set to the actual numbers of whalebone whales that may be killed in any season. The catch limit brought severe competition to Antarctic whaling after World War II. Until 1953 the limit was 16,000 blue whale units (1 blue whale unit equals 1 blue, 2 finback, 2½ humpback, or 6 sei whales). Reductions were made in subsequent years, and whaling for the much depleted humpback and blue whales was completely forbidden in 1963 and 1964. Meanwhile, it was realized that the finback stocks, the main support of the Antarctic industry, were seriously threatened: catches were made up with the smaller and formerly neglected sei whale. In 1965 the commission, in a determined effort to save the whales and the industry, reduced the catch limit to 4,500 blue whale units. New national quotas, subdivided on an area basis, are set annually by the commission. In 1971 the United States ended licensing of whale hunting for the commercial market.

Shore whaling from the west coast of South America is regulated by a separate organization, the Permanent Commission for the Exploitation and Conservation of the Marine Resources of the South Pacific. It was set up by Chile, Peru, and Ecuador in 1952.

Whale conservation measures are assisted by research on the ecology of whales. This work was pioneered in the Antarctic by Great Britain and Norway. The British "Discovery" Committee, founded in 1924, conducted oceanographical surveys and whale marking from the royal research ships *Discovery II* and *William Scoresby* and maintained a laboratory at South Georgia for work on whale carcasses. The "Discovery" investigations became a part of the National Institute of Oceanography in 1949. Whale research continues there, at the Statens Institutt for Hvalforskning in Norway, and in Australia, Canada, Chile, Ecuador, Japan, the Netherlands, Peru, the United States and the U.S.S.R. The Food and Agriculture Organization of the United Nations also advises on whale population dynamics. Since 1953 whale marking has been undertaken on an international basis with the cooperation of whaling companies.

Sealing

Historically, sealing is an offshoot of the North Atlantic whale fishery. The products of sealing are fur, hides, blubber, and oil.

Most commercial sealing is conducted on land or on ice at the breeding grounds, or rookeries, particularly those in the north Pacific and north Atlantic. For many years the taking of seals was accompanied by great waste; the seal herds were threatened by extinction, but sealing in most areas is now regulated by international conventions or other agreements that aim at conserving the breeding stock. Pelagic sealing— the taking of seals in the open sea while the animals are migrating to the breeding grounds—was once practiced indiscriminately in the north Pacific but is now prohibited because it was especially wasteful. As a general rule, regulated sealing is conducted so as to harvest only the superfluous males.

Commercial sealing takes place mainly in the Pribilof Islands of the north Pacific, on pack ice in the northeast and northwest Atlantic, and in rookeries of the south Pacific. The most important seals in the industry are the fur seal in the north Pacific, the harp (Greenland) seal in the north Atlantic, and the elephant seal in the south Pacific. The ringed (jar) seal is also important.

North Atlantic Sealing

Seals were first taken in the sub-Arctic region of the north Atlantic by whalers when whaling began there early in the seventeenth century. Later, in the most prosperous days of north Atlantic whaling, the whalers neglected the seals, but by the latter part of the nineteenth century they included them again in their catch. Sealing as a separate occupation had meanwhile developed in the north Atlantic during the eighteenth century. The chief species taken were the Greenland, harp or saddleback seal, hooded or bladdernose seal, and bearded or square-flipper seal.

The greatest annual kills in the north Atlantic took place off Newfoundland and in the Gulf of Saint Lawrence between 1820 and 1860, when more than 500,000 seals were taken in several individual years. The largest annual kill on record is that of 1831, when 687,000 seals (mostly harp seals) were taken by about 300 ships and 10,000 men. After 1910, between 250,000 and 300,000 seals were taken annually, except during World War II, when most of the sealing ships were inactive.

The ringed or jar seal, the commonest and most widely found seal of the Arctic, is one of the most important animals to the Eskimo. In some places it was, and still is, the backbone of the native economy. In the Canadian Arctic between 30,-000 and 50,000 seals are killed annually, and the skins of about 10,000 of these animals are traded to the Hudson's Bay Company each year. The skin of the one-year-old animal is particularly prized by fur dealers and is called the silver jar. The gray seal and the common or harbor seal are not the subject of organized commercial exploitation. Both the gray seal and the common seal, however, are killed by fishermen, in some places for a government bounty because they are the primary hosts for certain parasites of commercial fish and because they are a nuisance around certain fishing operations.

Sealing in the north Atlantic is done in the spring on floating pack ice from the White Sea to the Gulf of Saint Lawrence. The chief species taken is the harp seal. There are three distinct breeding stocks, all of which are exploited commercially. An eastern stock breeds in the White Sea (now a Soviet fishery exclusively); a central stock, in the region of Jan Mayen Island (U.S.S.R. and Norway); and a third, off Labrador and Newfoundland and in the Gulf of Saint Lawrence (Norway, Canada, U.S.S.R., United States, Denmark, and France). The species is strongly migratory; it occupies the pack ice area during the breeding season in the spring and then moves north to open water in the Arctic in summer and autumn.

The white-coated pups, which are born on the ice, form the basis of the international Atlantic commercial seal fishery. Before World War II almost 90% of the catch was of pups. Sealing in this area is primarily a Newfoundland industry. After 1949 the center of the industry shifted to Nova Scotia.

In another post-World War II development a Norwegian fleet of about sixteen sealing vessels began to fish off Newfoundland and in the Gulf of Saint Lawrence when their Soviet concessions in the White Sea expired. About the same number of Canadian vessels were added to the northwest Atlantic sealing fleet at the same time. After these ships appeared, many older seals were taken and they finally constituted about 30% of the catch.

The pups are taken on the ice beginning early in March. Bedlamers (immature harp seals one year old or older) and adults are shot on the ice while molting during April and May. The pelts with their adherent blubber, called sculps, are removed on the ice and dragged or winched to the sealing ship; there they are stored in ice or refrigerated holds. The annual catch of harp seals in the fifteen years following the end of World War II, including landsmen's net catches in Canada and Greenland, averaged about 225,000 pups and 85,000 immatures and adults—with about 90% of the catch shared equally by Canada and Norway. Sealers in both east and west areas of the north Atlantic used airplanes after World War II to locate herds.

Oil, fur, and leather are the three major commodities produced from seals in the north Atlantic. The pup is the basis of the fur stock, though the short hair of the immature is also used. Neither the pup nor the immature furnishes true fur, and the value of their pelts is less than that of the true fur undercoat of the fur seal. The white coat of the pup consists of fetal hair that is replaced, beginning about ten days after birth, by a short, spotted hair coat that grows in under the white coat.

There were no formal laws in the early 1960s governing the killing of seals in international waters of the western Atlantic, and the herd was being seriously reduced. In 1961 Canada proposed to the International Commission for Northwest Atlantic Fisheries (ICNAF) that the conservation of harp and hooded seals be placed under that organization. This was accepted by the commission and ratified by all member countries. Sealing in the eastern Atlantic was regulated by a Soviet-Norwegian treaty on Arctic marine mammals.

North Pacific Sealing

The fur seals, which, with the sea lions, belong to the family of eared seals (Otariidae), differ from other seals in that they possess a permanent undercoating of short, soft fur that constitutes the sealskin of the costumer. The Pacific fur seal began to be exploited after the Danish-Russian explorer V. J. Bering made his voyage to the north Pacific in 1741. The migration of the fur seal covers the area from the latitude of southern Japan on the west to southern California in the east and the great rookeries on the Komandorski and Pribilof islands on the north. At their heights in the nineteenth century the Pribilof herd included more than 2.5 million seals and the Komandorski group totaled more than 1 million. A herd on Robben (Tyuleniy) Island in the Sea of Okhotsk was of minor importance. These herds were greatly reduced in the last half of the nineteenth century and by 1897 did not exceed a combined total of 600,000 animals. As a result of international treaties and control by the U.S. Bureau of Fisheries the Pribilof herd increased from 125,000 in 1911 to about 1 million by mid-twentieth century.

Pelagic sealing in the north Pacific began in the early nineteenth century. At first the catch averaged 75,000 annually, but after about 1868 it increased rapidly. Beginning in 1879 sailing vessels carrying canoes were employed to attack the migrating seals, which were thus harvested just before the breeding females gave birth to their pups; in some of the catches, half of the animals were pregnant females. At one time pelagic sealing vessels exceeded one hundred in number, and some of them carried as many as twenty-five canoe crews. It has been estimated that by 1902 about 1 million seals had been taken at sea.

The greatest catch, however, was always made on shore. From the Pribilof and Komandorski herds, nearly 2.5 million seals were taken on land between 1868 and 1897.

From a conservation standpoint it is fortunate that the habits of the seals on land permit their taking with the least possible depletion of the breeding stock. The young males, or bachelors, leave the rest of the herd to rest and sleep on beaches that are adjacent to but apart from the breeding grounds. There they are surrounded at night by the sealing crews, rounded up in droves of from 1,000 to 3,000 and driven inland to the killing grounds. The large droves are broken up into groups of from 20 to 50; the males three years of age or in that size class are knocked down with clubs, while those that are too large or too small are allowed to escape. The skins are removed, salted in kenches (bins), and, when cured, exported.

Many laws and treaties have been enacted to protect the north Pacific seals while they are at sea, thereby ensuring a continued sealing industry. In 1911 an international convention was signed by Great Britain (for Canada), Japan, Russia, and the United States to prevent pelagic sealing by their nationals. Land sealing also was regulated. At that time the herd on the Pribilofs numbered about 125,000 animals. The annual take there now runs between 50,000 and 70,000 skins, and the herd numbers well over 1 million animals.

The convention of 1911 was terminated in 1941 by the withdrawal of Japan. A provisional agreement between Canada and the United States ensured continued pelagic protection off North America. Then, in 1957, Canada, Japan, the U.S.S.R., and the United States signed the Interim Convention on Conservation of North Pacific Fur Seals. This pact was to last six years, during which time commercial pelagic sealing continued to be prohibited, and an extensive pelagic and land research program on fur seals was undertaken by the four member countries to form the basis for negotiating a new convention. The North Pacific Fur Seal Commission was set up by the four member countries to coordinate the work. At the end of the six-year-period the time for research was extended.

South Atlantic and Pacific Sealing

The southern fur seal was once taken at the Galápagos Islands, Tierra del Fuego, and Lobos Islands. This or other species also were taken at South Africa, Australia, New Zealand, and many points near the Antarctic circle. It was taken before 1793 and was once abundant in South Georgia and other dependencies of the Falkland Islands.

Great numbers of sea leopard or leopard seal, sea elephants or elephant seals, Weddell seal, and other species were seen by early explorers and voyagers, but at first the skins of the fur seals alone seem to have been taken. One of the earliest recorded landings for seals is that of the Argentine ship *Juan Nepomucena*, which brought in 13,000 skins in 1820. In that and the two following years more than ninety vessels, divided about equally between Great Britain and the United States, worked the southern grounds. In the first season, catches of 18,000 were not unusual for individual ships, and five British ships took a combined total of 95,000 seals. Seal oil and blubber, particularly from the elephant seals, began to be taken. The British explorer and sealer

James Weddell estimated that in the two seasons of 1820–21 and 1821–22, about 1.2 million fur seals were taken from South Georgia and 320,000 from the South Shetlands, along with 940 tons of elephant seal oil.

By 1892, because of the diminution of the herds, sealing vessels returned to their home ports from South America with mixed cargoes. Though in the early 1890s a Scottish whaling expedition to the Ross Sea took 20,000 sealskins with four ships, by the end of the nineteenth century the fur seal had almost completely disappeared from the Falkland Island dependencies, and other seals, sea elephants in particular, had been greatly diminished in number.

From 1881 sealing in these territories had been regulated; closed seasons were introduced, and sealing is now permitted only by licenses, which may specify both the kind and number of seals taken. The capture of fur seals is prohibited.

Most sealing in the southern region is conducted in pursuit of the elephant seal; this sealing has responded satisfactorily to regulations. The elephant seal is taken by whalers, but pups may not be taken, nor, as far as practicable, are female seals to be harvested. There is also a closed season, and areas along certain stretches of coast are closed. The absence of segregation of young males on the rookeries is a hindrance to the observance of the regulations. Elephant seals are of great size, the females reaching 11½ feet and the males sometimes 22 feet in length. Mating takes place within the harem immediately after the young are born early in October, and the young, which are born singly, are usually weaned in November; these circumstances have determined the closed season. Shortly after mid-twentieth century the number of seals taken at South Georgia was about 6,000 per annum.

17.
The Ocean as a Natural Resource

The ocean is the place where life began, and without the ocean, human life as we know it today would not exist. The sea acts as a great heat reservoir, leveling the temperature extremes that would otherwise prevail over the Earth and expand the desert areas. The oceans provide the least expensive form of transportation known to man; their margins serve as one of his major sites of recreation. The sea is a primary source of food and a dumping ground for wastes. And the ocean is a major potential source of protein, minerals, and power—all of which are required in ever-increasing quantities by all industrialized societies.

A Source of Food

Man extracts about 60 million tons of food from the ocean annually by fishing. The food-producing potential of the sea, however, is many times the present rate of production—some authorities believe it can be increased several hundreds of times. The methods by which man takes food from the sea are inefficient, and the fact that he takes only certain choice species of fish makes fishing in the ocean doubly inefficient.

Estimates of the productivity of the ocean as a source of human food range from highly optimistic to quite pessimistic. Optimistically, it has been estimated that the daily protein requirements for a human being can be produced as a concentrate from fish for less than a penny. It has also been estimated that by efficient harvesting of all the fish of the sea the ocean could produce a sustained yield of about 2 billion tons of food annually, but it must be noted that such utilization requires, in many instances, a change in human attitudes toward their food.

The Japanese have instituted a substantial program of continental-shelf studies to develop the eventual farming of adequate supplies of fish and edible plants. Though Japan has farmed oysters in its oceanic bays for many years its fishermen were active around the world's oceans. With that activity seemingly at a point of diminishing return, Japan has turned to home waters.

Fish need not be fenced in to be farmed. They will stay where the food supply is. By creating an artificial food supply in a given location, fish can be kept where they are wanted. Creating a food supply for the fish need not mean the adding of fish nutrients to the sea but the development of some means of mixing the nutrient-rich bottom layers of water in the ocean with the life-rich upper layers of water.

Wherever a natural upwelling of the bottom layers of water occurs, such as off Peru, a tremendous fish population is also found. By encouraging such an upwelling artificially, the fish population can be greatly increased at some more convenient point than at the location nature provided. Developing this technique could probably increase the potential yield of the ocean by many times over the present potential productive capacity of the ocean. The energy for sustaining this upwelling in the ocean can be produced by several sources; for example, by nuclear reactors on the bottom of the ocean. The development of this or any other means of producing upwelling, however, will probably await economic necessity, if not actual crisis. In any case, reactors on the seafloor do not appear likely in the immediate future.

Marine biologists are not by any means agreed as to the level of productivity that can be expected from the ocean. The more pessimistically inclined biologists point out that early estimates of marine production were misleadingly high and generated a premature hope that the sea represented a vast untapped food resource that could be used to feed an expanding human population for a long time to come. In fact, they argue, the food resources of the sea are quite limited.

Marine organisms are small and have a very active metabolism; thus, a large part of marine production is consumed by the producing organisms themselves. Because many generations per year contribute to the modest production of the sea, there is never a large harvestable crop available for convenient gathering. Even the zooplankton, which consists of larger organisms with a longer life cycle, is not a feasible food source because the energy needed to collect the zooplankton is equal to the food energy it yields.

The best hope for a sustained food supply from the sea seems to be the whales and clupeid fishes, such as herring, anchovies, and sardines. Whales are currently being harvested faster than they can replenish their populations, and it is suspected that most of the clupeid and other pelagic fish stocks of the world have become overfished as well. At the same time, pollution and general disturbance of estuarine breeding grounds threaten shellfish and game fish of the inshore waters; these make a negligible contribution to man's caloric intake but an important one to the quality of life.

A Source of Fresh Water

Although springs of fresh water issuing on the ocean floor are known to occur in water depths as great as 3,500 feet (about 1,000 meters), they will never prove to be a major source of fresh water for the world. Of greater interest is the prospect of desalting salt water itself. Throughout the world, hundreds of desalination units, producing from a few thousand to 10 million or more gallons a day, are already in operation. In 1967 Key West, Fla., became the first U.S. city to be supplied solely by water from the sea, drawing its supplies from a plant that produces more than 2 million gallons of refined water daily.

In general, the desalination plants in production are in areas where the population has outstripped the onshore water supply and where high-cost desalinated water can be afforded. This situation tends to arise in coastal-desert areas or on densely populated islands, because the costs of pumping water through pipelines to interior areas would add prohibitively to the basic costs at the sites of desalination.

A population usually can afford to pay about ten times as much for water for domestic purposes as it does for agricultural water. Proposals for large-scale nuclear desalination facilities, when constructed, promise to lower the cost of desalinated water to the range of ten cents to thirty cents per 1,000 gallons at the desalination sites—a price that all domestic users, most industries, and a few agricultural enterprises can afford.

The bulk of water produced from seawater is produced by some form of evaporation and condensation. Although the principle of this technique is quite simple, the mechanics of achieving high efficiencies can become quite complicated. Superheated water and multiple evaporation and condensation units, operating at varying temperatures and pressures, are employed in a number of these facilities. The choice of construction materials is quite important because the brines produced in extracting pure water can be corrosive. Other processes under consideration as potential economic methods of desalting seawater are freezing, reverse osmosis, ionic processes, electrodialysis, and techniques that change the physical or chemical properties of water itself so that it can be separated from the salts in seawater. In the future, it can be expected that the ocean will become an increasingly important source of fresh water. If production and transportation costs can be lowered sufficiently, it may be possible to produce fresh water to irrigate large areas that border the oceans in many parts of the world.

An Energy Resource

There are a number of recognized techniques by which energy can be extracted from the sea. The major problem in taking energy resources from the sea is that they tend to be diffused over a large area. A point-concentrated energy source is necessary if it is to be exploited economically.

Although energy is presently extracted from the ocean tides, it is unlikely that man will develop a technique for extracting large amounts of energy efficiently from such sources as the waves. Another potential power source in the ocean, however, is the temperature differential between the surface layers and the lower layers of the water; this differential can be as large as 50° over vertical distances of as little as 300 feet (90 meters) in some areas of the ocean.

For many years the French have experimented with techniques of using this temperature differential to generate electricity. The processes they used were a technical success, but they were not economic, mainly because the plant was located on land, and most of the energy obtained from this system was used in pumping the seawater into and out of the plant.

A group in the United States has developed a system whereby the energy can be extracted by a floating power plant that eliminates the pumping problem. Propane or some similar fluid that will boil at the temperature of the surface layer of water is used, the gaseous phase then being released to a subgenerator to manufacture the power.

After the gas is condensed to a liquid in the cooler, lower layers of water, it is pumped to a surface boiler to be recycled. To be economically practical, the temperature differential should be several tens of degrees, and major markets for the energy created should not be more than a few hundred miles from the power plant. The areas of the ocean in which it would be most efficient to operate such a plant, normally in the tropics, are not near major markets.

Some techniques have been developed in the 1970s for handling liquid hydrogen and liquid oxygen on a large scale.

If power generated in remote areas of the ocean were used to reduce seawater to hydrogen and oxygen, these gases might be utilized economically in shoreside thermal power plants. This procedure is, however, hypothetical at present. Followed to its logical though futuristic conclusion, it suggests that oceanic thermal power plants may someday be used to power artificial upwellings on the ocean floor to encourage greater fish populations.

Because the thermal differential required in the processes described is generated by the sun, it is renewing itself about a hundred times as fast as it could be used to provide the whole world with its present total energy consumption. Man could take from the sea about 200 million megawatt hours of energy each day. The United States presently consumes about 1 million megawatt hours of power each day. Thus, the sea can produce power at a rate of about two hundred times the present consumption rate of the United States. There are, of course, no fuel costs involved in generating power in the sea, and the estimated plant operational and capital costs indicate an overall power-production cost substantially lower than that of power generated from conventional sources.

Petroleum from under the Ocean

In the mid-1950s the production of oil and gas from oceanic areas was negligible. By the 1970s about 6 million barrels per day, or about 16% of the world's production, came from ocean wells; it is presumed that by 1980 the offshore areas will yield about 23 million barrels per day or about 35% of the 1980 world production.

About three hundred offshore drilling and production rigs were at work in the early 1970s at more than sixty offshore locations throughout the world—drilling, completing, and maintaining offshore oil wells. Estimates have placed the potential offshore oil resources at about 2 trillion barrels, or about half of the presently known onshore potential oil sources.

It was once thought that only the continental-shelf areas contained potential petroleum resources, but discoveries of oil deposits in deeper waters of the Gulf of Mexico (about 10,000–13,000 feet, or 3,000–4,000 meters) have led to a revision of this idea. It is now believed that the continental slopes and neighboring ocean-floor areas will contain large oil deposits, thus enhancing potential petroleum reserves of the ocean bottom.

An oil drilling rig in the harbor of Long Beach, Calif., has its derricks disguised as luxury apartment buildings surrounded by palm trees.

A Source of Minerals

The rivers of the world dump billions of tons of material into the sea each year. Seafloor springs and volcanic eruptions also add many millions of tons of elements. Even the winds contribute solid materials to the sea in appreciable quantities. Most of these sediments rapidly settle to the seafloor in near-shore areas, in some cases forming potentially valuable placer mineral deposits. The dissolved load of the rivers, however, mixes with seawater and is gradually dispersed over the total oceanic envelope of the Earth.

Because of the nature of the minerals and their mode of formation, it is convenient to consider the occurrence of sea deposits in several environments, namely marine beaches, seawater, continental shelves, sub-seafloor consolidated rocks, and the marine sediments of the deep-sea floor. Minerals are mined from all of these environments except for the deep-seafloor area, which was only in the 1970s recognized as a repository for mineral deposits of unbelievable extent and significant economic value.

Minerals that resist the chemical and mechanical processes of erosion in nature and that possess a density greater than that of the Earth's common minerals have a tendency to concentrate in gravity deposits known as placers. During the ice ages (about 10,000 to 2.5 million years ago), sea level was appreciably lowered as the ocean water was transferred to the continental glaciers. Because of the cyclical nature of the ice ages and the intervening warm periods, series of beaches were formed in nearshore areas both above and below present sea level. Furthermore, when sea level was lowered in past ages, the streams that now flow into the sea coursed much further seaward, carrying placer minerals to be deposited in channels that are now submerged. With geophysical-exploration techniques these channels and beaches can be easily delineated, even though these features are totally covered by Recent or Holocene sediments—that is, those deposited during the past 10,000 years.

Sand and gravel mined from a number of offshore locations around the world, generally with hydraulic dredges, are used mainly for construction purposes or for beach replenishment or nearshore fills. Sulfur, which is taken from salt domes in the Gulf of Mexico, is mined by a process in which pressurized hot water is pumped into the sulfur-containing cap of the dome, melting the sulfur and forcing it to the surface. Compressed air is also used to pump sulfur to the surface; the still-molten sulfur is then pumped ashore through insulated pipelines.

Of considerable interest are the seafloor phosphorite deposits on the coastal shelves of many countries. The phosphorite off California occurs as nodules that vary in shape from flat slabs, several feet across, to small spherical forms called *oolites*. The nodules commonly are found as a single layer at the surface of coarse-grained sediments. Phosphorite composition from the California offshore area is surprisingly uniform and contains potentially economically attractive amounts of phosphorus.

Another type of phosphate deposit has been found off the west coast of Mexico, namely, a fine-grained, unconsolidated deposit in about 160 feet (50 meters) of water. It contains as much as 40% apatite (a common phosphate mineral), and it is speculated that there is as much as 20 trillion tons of recoverable phosphate rock in this deposit.

Manganese Nodules

From an economic standpoint the most interesting oceanic sediments are manganese nodules—small, black to brown, friable (crumbly) lumps found during the nineteenth-century expeditions of the *Challenger* and *Albatross* to be widely distributed throughout the three major oceans. Many theories have been proposed to account for the formation of manganese nodules, the best probably being that the ocean is saturated at its present state of acidity-alkalinity in iron and manganese. For this reason, these elements precipitate as colloidal particles that gradually increase in size and filter down to the seafloor. Colloids of manganese and iron oxides collect many metals and bear an electrical charge; they tend to agglomerate as nodules at the seafloor rather than settle as particles in the general sediments.

An estimated 1.5 trillion tons of manganese nodules are on the Pacific ocean floor alone, and they are estimated to be forming at an annual rate of about 10 million tons. Averaging slightly less than two inches (about four centimeters) in diameter and found in concentrations as high as 100,000 tons per square mile, these manganese nodules contain as much as 2.5% copper, 2% nickel, 0.2% cobalt, and 35% manganese.

Manganese nodules recovered from the seafloor by a wire dredge basket are unloaded for analysis on board a research ship.

In some deposits the content of cobalt and manganese is as high as 2.5% and 50%, respectively. Such concentrations would be considered high-ore if found on land, and, because of the large horizontal extent of the deposit, they are a potential source of many important industrial metals.

Relatively simple mechanical cable bucket or hydraulic dredges with submerged motors and pumps can mine the nodules at rates as high as 10,000–15,000 tons per day, from depths as great as 20,000 feet (6,000 meters). The estimated costs to mine and process the nodules indicate that copper, nickel, cobalt, and other metals can be economically produced from this source.

Oozes and Hot Brines

Mineral deposits of monumental size and potential economic significance are found in the deep-sea areas of the ocean. Minerals formed in the deep sea are frequently found in high concentrations because there is relatively little clastic (detachable) material generated in these areas to dilute the chemical precipitates.

An estimated 10^{16} tons of calcareous oozes, formed by the deposition of calcareous shells and skeletons of planktonic organisms, cover about 50 million square miles (130,000,000 square kilometers) of the ocean floor. In a few instances these oozes, which occur within a few hundred miles of most countries bordering on the sea, are almost pure calcium carbonate, but they often show a composition similar to that of the limestones used in the manufacture of portland cement.

Covering about 15 million square miles (39 million square kilometers) of the ocean floor in great bands across the northern and southern ends of the Indian and Atlantic oceans are other oozes, consisting of the siliceous shells and skeletons of plankton animals and plants. Normally these oozes could serve in most of the applications for which diatomaceous earth is used, for fire and sound insulation, for lightweight concrete formulations, as filters, and as soil conditioners.

An estimated 10^{16} tons of red clay covers about 40 million square miles (104 million square kilometers) of the ocean floor. Although compositional analyses are not particularly exciting, red clay may possess some value as a raw material in the clay-products industries, or it may serve as a source of metals in the future. The average assay for alumina is 15%, but red clays from specific locations have assayed as high as

25% alumina; copper contents as high as 0.20% also have been found. A few hundredths of a percent of such metals as nickel and cobalt and a percent or so of manganese also are generally present in a micronodular fraction of the clays and probably can be separated and concentrated from the other materials by screening or by some other physical method.

Underlying the hot brines in the Red Sea are basins containing metal-rich sediments that potentially may prove to be one of the great metal-deposit discoveries of all time. It has been estimated that the largest of several such pools, the Atlantis II Deep, contains more than $2 billion worth of copper, zinc, silver, and gold in relatively high grades. These pools lie in about 6,500 feet (2,000 meters) of water, midway between the Sudan and the Arabian peninsulas. Because of their gellike nature, pumping these sediments to the surface should prove to be relatively uncomplicated. These deposits are forming today under present geochemical conditions, and they are similar in character to certain major ore deposits on land.

18.
The Future of the Ocean

For millennia man has assumed that the vastness of the ocean rendered it proof against his most determined incursions. Who indeed could have believed otherwise? Yet, during the twentieth century, man has at last performed the impossible and must now count the ocean among the potential

Though today's ocean looks much the same as it has for centuries, man has disturbed the steady state of its chemical balance, leaving its future, along with his own, in jeopardy.

victims of a technology that appears to expand without limits. Since World War II particularly the coastal and island countries—the United States preeminent among them—have used the ocean as a dump for the most dangerous industrial and military garbage—nerve gases, radioactive wastes, and noxious chemicals among them. Locally, the disposal of human wastes from such great metropolises as New York City has created substantial environmental problems. Other issues besides pollution arise from man's increasing exploitation of the ocean's resources. Overfishing and overwhaling have driven some species close to extinction and threaten to cut off forever rich sources of nourishment. The future exploitation of the mineral resources of the deep-sea bed present many problems, both technical and political, to which no generally accepted solutions have yet been forthcoming. The best that can be said is that the level of concern is rising, not only among environmentally aroused individuals and public-interest groups, but also in the form of purposeful action in the international arena.

Pollution of the Ocean

The ocean is the great sump, or drain, of the hydrosphere (the water that is found on the surface of the globe and in the atmosphere). The dissolved and suspended loads of rivers are the chief contributors of new material to the ocean. Before the advent of modern industrialized society the ocean appears to have been in a steady state, chemically speaking, with no measurable changes in its constitution from year to year or from century to century. From the viewpoint of the chemist the main buffer in the system consists of reactions between seawater and solid compounds, such as silicates. This, for example, is the mechanism that buffers the ocean in the face of a continual input of acidic gases from volcanoes. Short-term and local buffering is dominated by reactions with carbonates and bicarbonates.

The steady state has been disturbed, however, by a massive input of man's industrial, municipal, and agricultural wastes. Some persistent synthetic chemicals, such as the chlorinated hydrocarbon insecticide DDT, for example, are carried into the sea, where they accumulate in the fatty tissues of organisms and become concentrated as they are transferred up the food chain, particularly in the tissues of some birds and fish. (Because of these effects, severe restrictions were imposed on the use of DDT in the United States in 1972.)

Oil spills and leaks from oil wells, which formerly had disastrous effects only locally, now appear to be polluting the surface water on a worldwide scale. The lead content of surface seawater also appears to be increasing rapidly. The ecological effects of these chemical changes, though they are not likely to have such devastating and immediate results as some alarmists have claimed, are nevertheless cause for serious concern.

If man continues the present regrettable practice of using the ocean as a dumping ground, it is quite possible that the deep parts of the entire ocean will become profoundly modified. Because of the slowness of the deep circulation, serious and irreversible harm to the ocean ecosystem could be inflicted before the effects become noticeable.

Who Owns the Ocean?

Political considerations are among the first on which agreement must be found if the ocean is to be managed rationally for the welfare of future generations. Even after eight thousand years or more of seafaring, agreements have yet to be reached on what constitutes national and international waters.

The traditional three-mile territorial limit was loosely agreed upon by coastal nations for military reasons; it evolved in the days when that distance was beyond the range of shells fired from guns aboard naval vessels lying offshore. Today, however, this limit has become useless for defense and is not widely recognized for any other purpose.

Disputes over fishing rights have led to a more general acceptance of a 12-mile (19-kilometer) limit to the seaward boundaries of national territories, but even this is not acceptable to all. Many Latin American countries now insist on jurisdiction over waters to a distance of 200 miles (300 kilometers) from their shores. The United States joined these countries when, in the spring of 1976, U.S. President Gerald R. Ford signed a bill extending the territorial waters of the United States for fishing purposes to 200 miles. Although welcomed by the fishing industry, this action came under fire from some observers who regretted its unilateral nature while the United States was engaged in international negotiations in the United Nations Law of the Sea Conference. The Soviet Union followed suit, announcing a 200-mile limit later in 1976.

In 1970 it was proposed at the United Nations that resources lying on or beneath the floor of the continental shelf (the zone of shallow ocean floor that gradually slopes from the seashore to an abrupt drop-off) be under national jurisdiction out to a point at which the mean water depth is 650 feet (200 meters). Beyond that depth, which generally marks the limit of the continental shelf, the resources of the continental slope down to the floor of the ocean would be internationally owned but under the management and control of the coastal state involved.

The Law of the Sea Conference

Beginning in 1973, the third United Nations Law of the Sea Conference convened at intervals with a charge as important as any that has confronted an international body—to bring into being a comprehensive treaty to govern the management of more than 70% of the Earth's surface. It considered not only territorial jurisdiction but also such matters as the management and conservation of ocean life, the control of pollution, the management of oceanographic research, and, most notably, the creation of a future international structure to govern the exploitation of deep-sea mineral resources.

By May 1975, at the conclusion of an eight-week session in Geneva, Switzerland, the Law of the Sea Conference had produced a draft treaty, called the "informal single negotiating text," a document that reflected consensus on a number of important issues but a clear lack of agreement on other issues. Among issues on which agreement was reached were:

Territoriality. The territorial waters of all coastal countries would be extended from 3 miles to 12 miles offshore. In addition, coastal countries would control an "economic zone" extending 200 miles out to sea.

Transit Rights. The extension of territorial waters to 12 miles from shore would have the effect of closing off 116 straits formerly open to ship traffic. The draft treaty ensures that international traffic will continue to pass freely through these straits.

Pollution. The draft treaty provides that an international body will set the standards governing the dumping of waste materials in the ocean and other activities that pollute the ocean.

Research. A distinction is made in the "informal single negotiating text" between "fundamental" research and research into the resources of the economic zone of the continental shelf. The first type of research can be conducted freely, but the permission of the coastal state must be obtained for the second type—and scientists or other observers from the coastal state must be given the opportunity to take part.

Transfer of Technology. The draft treaty also included provisions encouraging the transfer of scientific and technological knowledge and skills from advanced to developing countries, or those with no or limited access to the sea.

The single great stumbling block that was responsible for the slow progress of the Law of the Sea Conference was the difficulty in resolving the extremely difficult questions raised by the possibilities of profitable deep-sea mining. The virtual deadlock reached with regard to this issue found inland and developing countries ranged against those coastal countries, such as the United States and Japan, which have already invested much energy and money in developing the technology of undersea mining. Their opponents—which represent a large majority of the countries taking part in the conference —argue that any mining of the deep-sea benthos must be carried out under an International Seabed Authority that will ensure that the world as a whole will benefit from the resources of the oceanic abyss—and not just those countries actively engaged in the mining operations. The issues involved are most difficult ones, with grave economic and political repercussions.

The Perilous Future

Mankind's relation to the world ocean has clearly changed in a most critical way since the first seafarer ventured from shore. For almost the entire millennia during which human beings have been, in a sense, aquatic animals, the dominant theme of the relationship has been man's helplessness in the face of the awesome power of the sea. During the past fifty years the roles have become reversed. It is now the ocean that is at the mercy of man's seemingly inexhaustible talent for destruction.

Nobody has put the matter more directly, and more dramatically, than French ocean explorer Jacques-Yves Cousteau did when he declared in 1976, "The ocean is sick, very sick. Marine life in the Mediterranean is getting scarcer and scarcer. Whales now number less than 7% of what they did at the turn of the century. Coral is dying. The marine environment everywhere is raped and torn up. If the ocean dies, mankind will die soon after."

Bibliography

The New Encyclopaedia Britannica (15th Edition)

Propaedia: This one-volume Outline of Knowledge is organized as a ten-part Circle of Learning, enabling the reader to carry out an orderly plan of study in any field. Its Table of Contents—consisting of 10 parts, 42 divisions, and 189 sections—is an easy topical guide to the *Macropaedia*.

Micropaedia: If interested in a particular subject, the reader can locate it in this ten-volume, alphabetically arranged Ready Reference of brief entries and Index to the *Macropaedia*, where subjects are treated at greater length or in broader contexts.

Macropaedia: These nineteen volumes of Knowledge in Depth contain extended treatments of all the fields of human learning. For information on *The Ocean: Mankind's Last Frontier*, for example, consult: Air-Cushion Machines; Alluvial Fans; Aquatic Ecosystem; Atmosphere; Atmosphere, Development of; Beaches; Bioluminescence; Bird; Canyons, Submarine; Climate; Coastal Features; Continental Drift; Continental Shelf and Slope; Coral Islands, Coral Reefs, and Atolls; Density Currents; Earth, Heat Flow in; Earth, Physiography of; Earth, Structure and Composition of; Ecology; Estuaries; Fish; Fish and Marine Products; Fishing, Commercial; Fishing, Sport; Geography; Gulfs and Bays; Harbours and Sea Works; Hydrographic Charting; Hydrologic Cycle; Hydrologic Sciences; Icebergs and Pack Ice; Island Arcs; Lagoons; Life-Support Systems; Lighthouse; Mammalia; Maps and Mapping; Marine Sediments; Mountain-Building Processes; Mountain Ranges and Mountain Belts; Natural Gas; Naval Ships and Craft; Navigation; Ocean Basins; Ocean Currents; Oceanic Ridges; Oceans, Development of; Oceans and Seas; Petroleum; Plankton; Plateaus and Basins; Reptilia; Riff Valleys; River Deltas; Rock Magnetism; Sails and Sailing Ships; Sea-Floor Spreading; Ship; Ship Design and Construction; Swamps, Marshes, and Bogs; Tides; Transportation, Water; Undersea Exploration; Water Waves; Wave Motion; Weather Forecasting; Whale; Winds and Storms. For biographical, biological, and geographic entries, check individual names.

Other Publications

Atlas of the Oceans. New York: Rand McNally and Company, 1977.

Fairbridge, Rhodes Whitmore, ed. *The Encyclopedia of Oceanography*. Encyclopedia of Earth Sciences Series, Vol. 1. New York: Reinhold Publishing Company, 1966.

Firth, Frank E., ed. *The Encyclopedia of Marine Resources*. New York: Van Nostrand Reinhold Company, 1969.

Food and Agriculture Organization of the United Nations. Dept. of Fisheries. *Atlas of the Living Resources of the Seas*. (English, French, and Spanish parallel texts) 3d ed. Rome: FAO, 1972.

Hill, Maurice N., ed. *The Sea: Ideas and Observations on Progress in the Study of the Seas*. 3 vols. New York: Wiley-Interscience, 1962–63.

McConnaughey, Bayard H. *Introduction to Marine Biology*. 2d ed. St. Louis, Mo.: C. V. Mosby Company, 1974.

Munro-Smith, R. *Merchant Ships and Shipping*. South Brunswick, N.J.: A. S. Barnes, 1968.

Sverdrup, Harald U.; Johnson, Martin W.; and Fleming, Richard H. *The Oceans: Their Physics, Chemistry and General Biology*. New York: Prentice-Hall, 1942.

Picture Credits

Index

a

abyssal hills, 63
abyssal plains, 63
aircraft carriers, 135
ambergris, 186
anadromous fish, 172
Arabs
  dhow development, 103
  early explorations, 32
Arctic Ocean
  climate influence, 89, 90
Atlantic Ocean
  currents and eddies, il. 76
  early commerce, 117
  early explorations, 32
  Mid-Atlantic Ridge, 61
Atlantis, 21
atmosphere
  interaction with ocean, 88

b

Baffin, William, 37
Balboa, Vasco Nuñez de, 34, il. 35
baleen, 184
ballistic missiles, 135
Barents, Willem, 37
barnacles, il. 142
barramundi, il. 169
bathymetry, 59
bathythermograph, 49
battleships, 132
beluga, il. 181
benthic division, 141
Bible
  ocean in Old Testament, 22
biological oceanography, 52
bivalves, 159
  metabolism, 147
  mussels, il. 152
  predation by sea stars, 158
blubber, 185
bore, tidal, 71

bottle post, 77
Breaking Wave off Kanagawa, The (Hokusai Katsushika), 29
brittle stars, il. 147, 149

c

Cabot, John, 34
calcareous oozes, 64, 241
Carpenter, William B., 44
carrack (ship), 104
Carthage
  war with Rome, 127
Cartier, Jacques, 36
catadromous fish, 173
cetaceans, 178
Challenger Deep, 61
Challenger Expedition, 44
Chancellor, Richard, 36
Chaucer, Geoffrey
  ocean in literature, 25
chemical oceanography, 51
China
  early explorations, 39
  junk design development, 102
  merchant fleet, 124
Civil War, U.S.
  warship development, 131
clams, 159
  metabolism, 147
  predation by sea stars, 158
Clermont (steamboat), 106
climate, 87
clipper ships, 105
cog (ship), 103
Coleridge, Samuel Taylor
  ocean in literature, 26
Columbus, Christopher, 34
Commonwealth of Nations
  merchant fleet, 123
compass, 33, 39, 104
Conrad, Joseph
  ocean in literature, 27
conservation of fish stocks, 213
Constantinople
  early ocean commerce, 115